ecodesign

Instructions for the dust jacket
To create the two lanterns (back and front) and the two bookmarks (flaps), slip the dust jacket off the book and cut it along the black lines on the front and back, including the flaps, using scissors or a paper-cutter. Then proceed as follows:

Bookmarks: separate the two flaps from the rest by cutting along the vertical lines. The bookmark is thus ready and can be placedalong the bend of the page of the book that you are reading.
Lanterns: cut the two lanterns along the external lines, including the triangular flaps on the spine, and cut the three vertical lines that correspond to the flaps on the opposite side of the sheet. Roll up the sheet to create a cylinder and fit the three triangles into the three slits obtained. Insert a candle into a glass container that is of a suitable size, light it and stand the paper cylinder around it.

Re-adjust the remaining part of the dust jacket onto the book.

NOTA BENE The publisher has taken due care to seek the required information for the preparation of lanterns. Nevertheless, the publisher assumes no responsibility for the use of the dust jacket as a lantern. Please remember that candles must be used with the utmost caution.

Anleitung für den Buchumschlag
Für die Herstellung der beiden Windlichter (Vorder- und Rückseite des Umschlags) und der beiden Lesezeichen (Umschlagklappen) zuerst den Umschlag vom Buch entfernen und die Vorder- und Rückseite mit einer Schere oder einem Cutter den schwarzen Linien entlang ausschneiden, einschließlich der beiden Umschlagsklappen. Danach wie folgt vorgehen:

Lesezeichen: die beiden Umschlagklappen den senkrechten Linien entlang schneiden und vom Rest des Papiers trennen. Das Lesezeichen ist somit bereits fertig und kann in einem beliebigen Buch, auf der gewünschten Seite eingefügt werden.
Windlichter: die beiden Windlichter den äußeren Linien entlang schneiden, einschließlich der dreieckigen Laschen auf dem Umschlagsrücken. Danach die drei den Laschen gegenüber liegenden senkrechten Linien einschneiden. Das Blatt dann zu einem Zylinder aufrollen und die pfeilförmigen Laschen in die Einschnitte einfügen. Zum Schluss ein Teelicht in ein angemessen großes Glas stellen, anzünden und darüber den Papierzylinder aufstellen.

Den restlichen Buchumschlag wieder um das Buch legen.

NOTA BENE Der Verlag hat die Anleitung zum Basteln eines Windlichtes aus dem transparenten Schutzumschlag mit der nötigen Sorgfalt recherchiert. Dennoch ist eine Haftung des Verlages im Hinblick auf die Verwendung des Schutzumschlags als Windlicht ausgeschlossen. Wir weisen ausdrücklich darauf hin, dass die bei einem Umgang mit offenem Feuer erforderliche Sorgfalt zu beachten ist.

Instructions pour la couverture
Pour créer les deux lampions (recto et verso) et les deux marque-pages (rabats), retirer la couverture du livre et couper à l'aide d'une paire de ciseaux ou d'un coupe-papier le recto et le verso de la couverture ainsi que les rabats, le long des lignes noires. Procéder ensuite comme ceci :

Marque-pages: séparer les deux rabats du reste en coupant le long des lignes verticales. Le marque-page est ainsi prêt et peut être inséré sur la page du livre en cours de lecture.
Lampions: redécouper les lampions sur les lignes extérieures, y compris les languettes en triangle situées à l'arrière. Inciser les trois lignes verticales correspondant aux languettes sur le côté opposé de la feuille. Enrouler la feuille de manière à obtenir un cylindre et glisser les triangles dans les fentes obtenues. Allumer une bougie chauffe-plat dans un photophore de taille adaptée et les entourer du cylindre décoratif.

Recouvrir le livre du restant de couverture.

NOTA BENE L'éditeur a soigneusement recueilli les informations nécessaires à la réalisation des lampions. Toutefois, l'éditeur décline toute responsabilité quant à l'utilisation de la couverture sous forme de lampion. Nous tenons de plus à rappeler qu'une attention maximale est requise lors de l'utilisation de bougies.

© 2009 Tandem Verlag GmbH
h.f.ullmann is an imprint of Tandem Verlag GmbH

Original title: *ecodesign*
ISBN of the original edition: 978-3-8331-5461-4

Editorial project: LiberLab, Italy (www.liberlab.it)
Consulting editor: Paolo Tamborrini
Book and cover design: Maya Kulta
Layout: gi.mac grafica, Italy (www.gimacgrafica.it)
Jacket concept: www.glyphisabox.net

Project coordination: Dania D'Eramo

© 2009 for this edition: Tandem Verlag GmbH
h.f.ullmann is an imprint of Tandem Verlag GmbH

Coordination of the translations: Textcase, Utrecht
Translation into English: Michelle Tarnopolsky (for Textcase)
Translation into German: Alessandra Rossi
Translation into French: Aurélie Blain (for Textcase)

Printed in China

ISBN 978-3-8331-5278-8

10 9 8 7 6 5 4 3 2 1
X IX VIII VII VI V IV III II I

If you like to be informed about forthcoming h.f.ullmann titles, you can request our newsletter by visiting our website **www.ullmannpublishing.com** or by emailing us at: newsletter@ullmann-publishing.com
h.f.ullmann, Im Mühlenbruch 1, 53639 Königswinter, Germany
Fax: +49(0)2223-2780-708

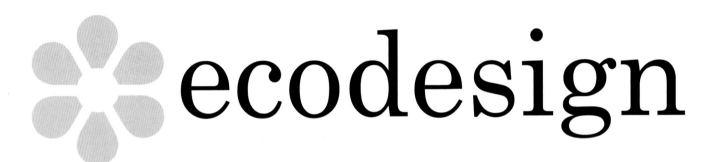

ecodesign

Silvia Barbero
Brunella Cozzo

h.f.ullmann

8 What is ecodesign?
Was ist ökologisches Design?
Comprendre l'écodesign

16 Ecodesign approaches
Herangehensweisen ökologischen Designs
Approches de l'écodesign

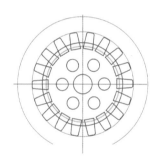

Transportation
Transport
Transports

Clothing & accessories
Bekleidung & Accessoires
Habillement & accessoires

Toys
Spielzeug
Jouets

Packaging
Verpackung
Packaging

288

Graphic design
Grafikdesign
Design graphique

312

Appendix
Anhang
Annexes

342

What is ecodesign?

Was ist ökologisches Design?
Comprendre l'écodesign

The economic system we live in has progressively modified the relationships that exist between material energy and human resources. At the same time, the impact of industrial production on the planet's ecosystem continues to increase exponentially. It has therefore been necessary to reassess our concepts of growth and development in the light of the environmental problems they cause. Although this reassessment began in the early 1960s and took on a global perspective, particularly with *The Limits to Growth* by D. H. Meadows, D. L. Meadows, J. Randers and W. W. Behrens published in 1972, it has only been since the 1990s that close ties have been established between environmental themes and industrial production, following the political and regulatory discussions of the 1980s.

Experience has since taught us that considering the environmental impact of a product once it is placed on the market is absolutely unavoidable when it comes to sustainable ideation and design. This means incorporating production processes, the products themselves and the behaviors they trigger within the limits of ecological sustainability. The performance required of the products, in particular, cannot remain limited to functionality and aesthetics.

Since ecodesign means thinking about objects in their functional entirety, the designer is able not only to develop the form but also to change production processes and behavioral habits in the name of greater environmental sustainability. Savings in energy, materials, packaging and transport, in addition to problems tied to disposal, are all issues that make up the fundamental structure of sustainable design. In fact, ecodesign is characterized by a vibrant creative ability to search for alternative

Das Wirtschaftssystem, in dem wir leben, hat nach und nach den Zusammenhang zwischen materiellen, energetischen und menschlichen Ressourcen verändert. Gleichzeitig nahmen die Auswirkungen der Industrieproduktion auf das Ökosystem exponentiell zu. Wachstum und Entwicklung müssen angesichts der Umweltprobleme, die sie verursacht haben, neu durchdacht werden. Die Auseinandersetzung mit diesen Konzepten begann bereits Anfang der 1960er Jahre und wurde fortgeführt in dem Werk *Die Grenzen des Wachstums* von D.H. Meadows, D.L. Meadows, J. Randers und W.W. Behrens von 1972. Auf die politischen und gesetzlichen Diskussionen der 1980er Jahre folgte in den 1990er Jahren die Erkenntnis, dass eine enge Verbindung zwischen Umweltthemen und industrieller Produktion besteht.

In dieser Zeitspanne hat uns die Erfahrung gezeigt, dass für eine nachhaltige Planung

und Gestaltung der Umwelteinfluss der jeweiligen Produkte, wenn sie einmal auf dem Markt eingeführt werden, unbedingt zu berücksichtigen ist. Dies bedeutet, dass die Produktionsprozesse, die Produkte selbst und das Konsumverhalten innerhalb der Grenzen der ökologischen Nachhaltigkeit gehalten werden müssen. Die an die Produkte gerichteten Erwartungen sollen sich nicht allein auf Funktionalität und Ästhetik beschränken. Was die Gestaltung betrifft, bietet ökologisches Design die Möglichkeit, nicht nur die Form zu bestimmen, sondern gleichzeitig auch die Produktionsprozesse zu erneuern und die Gewohnheiten in Richtung einer größeren Umweltverträglichkeit zu verändern. Einsparungen bei Energie und Material, Verpackung und Transport sowie die mit der Entsorgung verbundenen Probleme sind die Eckpfeiler einer nachhaltigen Gestaltung. Beim ökologischen Design ist eine lebendige Vorstellungskraft für die

Le système économique dans lequel nous vivons a progressivement modifié les relations entre les ressources naturelles, énergétiques et humaines. Dans le même temps, l'impact de la production industrielle sur l'écosystème a augmenté de manière exponentielle. Il s'est donc avéré nécessaire de revoir les concepts de croissance et de développement, à la lumière des problématiques environnementales qui en découlent. Cette révision a déjà vu le jour au début des années 1960 : elle visait un objectif mondial, exposé plus particulièrement dans *Les limites du développement* de D.H. Meadows, D.L. Meadows, J. Randers et W.W. Behrens en 1972. Ce n'est cependant qu'à partir des années 1990 qu'un lien étroit s'est véritablement instauré entre la thématique écologique et la production industrielle, faisant suite aux discussions politiques et législatives entamées dans les années 1980.

Dans ce laps de temps, les créateurs de projets éco-durables ont systématisé la réflexion sur l'impact environnemental engendré par les produits une fois sur le marché. Celle-ci requiert d'inscrire les processus de production, les produits mêmes et les comportements que ceux-ci provoquent, dans les limites du développement durable. Dans cette optique, les prestations demandées aux produits ne peuvent rester limitées à la fonctionnalité et à l'esthétique.

En tant que projetation d'objets dans leur complexité fonctionnelle, l'écodesign a la possibilité non seulement d'en créer la forme, mais aussi de renouveler les processus de production et les comportements des consommateurs pour une plus grande durabilité : les questions d'économie des énergies et des matériaux, de l'emballage et du transport, ainsi que les problèmes liés au désassemblage constituent la structure portante du design

systems, technologies and production strategies. Compared to conventional industrial production, ecodesign, like design in general, goes to the source to assess the desired result in all its aspects and for the entire duration of the product: how it will be used, the need it will serve, its intended market, its costs and its feasibility. The object's form is therefore linked with such considerations and is optimized according to its functionality and sustainability. In this sense, ecodesign too subscribes to the principle of "form follows function." Products designed this way are flexible and durable, modular or multifunctional and adaptable or recyclable.

A survey of such products and their various types is presented in this book. They are subdivided by category into separate chapters. Within each category, the products are grouped according to theme, sometimes indicated in the

chapter's introduction. The basic characteristics of each product are described clearly and concisely. To better understand their eco-compatible features, the descriptions are accompanied by icons that refer to the main ecodesign approaches discussed in the first chapter of the book. The reader can thus use this information to study such approaches in greater depth and discover the instruments designers have at their disposal when they begin developing an eco-compatible product. The book therefore promotes a dynamic, cross-referential reading, following either the categories or a thread of the reader's choice to reconstruct different ecodesign approaches. These two types of reading reveal various relationships between the different products.

A brief glossary closes the book to provide background knowledge and a starting point from which to read and

Suche nach alternativen Systemen, Technologien und Produktionsstrategien von entscheidender Bedeutung. Im Gegensatz zur industriellen Produktion bewertet ökologisches Design, wie auch Design im Allgemeinen, bereits vorab das gewünschte Resultat in allen seinen Aspekten und für die ganze Lebensdauer des Produktes: die für das Produkt voraussichtliche Verwendung, das Bedürfnis, aus dem sich die Idee heraus bildete, der Markt, an den sich das Produkt richtet, die Kosten und die Umsetzbarkeit. Die äußere Form des Objektes wird an diese Überlegungen geknüpft und im Sinne der Funktionalität und der Nachhaltigkeit optimiert. Dabei befolgt auch ökologisches Design den Gestaltungsleitsatz *Form follows function* (Die Form folgt der Funktion). Die so entwickelten Produkte sind flexibel, beständig, modulierbar oder multifunktionell, anpassungsfähig oder recycelbar.

Das vorliegende Buch gibt einen Überblick dieser Produkte und ihrer verschiedenen Typologien. Die Objekte wurden in acht Kategorien unterteilt, die jeweils ein eigenständiges Kapitel bilden. In jedem Kapitel werden die einzelnen Gegenstände in Themenbereiche zusammengefasst, die auch in der Kapiteleinleitung aufgeführt sind. Jedes Produkt wird in seinen grundlegenden Eigenschaften auf klare und kurz gefasste Weise beschrieben. Symbole, die sich auf die im ersten Kapitel erläuterten wichtigsten Ökodesign-Grundsätze beziehen, veranschaulichen die umweltfreundlichen Eigenschaften der Produkte. Durch diese zusätzlichen Informationen bekommt der Leser einen Einblick in die komplexen Ansätze von Ökodesign. Gleichzeitig lernt er die Hilfsmittel des Designers kennen, der sich mit der Gestaltung eines umweltverträglichen Produktes befasst. Auf diese Weise ermöglicht das Buch eine

éco-durable. Ce qui caractérise l'écodesign est en réalité une vive capacité d'imagination, appliquée à la recherche de systèmes, de technologies et de stratégies de production alternatives. Comparé à la production industrielle conventionnelle, l'écodesign, tout comme le design en général, évalue en amont le résultat désiré dans tous ses aspects et pour toute la durée de vie du produit : usage qu'il en sera fait et besoin à l'origine du projet, marché auquel il s'adressera, coûts et faisabilité. La forme externe de l'objet est ainsi liée à ces considérations et optimisée pour la fonctionnalité et la durabilité. En ce sens, l'écodesign obéit lui aussi au principe *form follows function*, où la forme est au service de la fonction. Les produits ainsi créés s'avèrent flexibles et durables, modulaires et multifonctions, adaptables ou recyclables.

Cet ouvrage présente une vue d'ensemble de ces produits et de leurs diverses

typologies. Ils sont subdivisés en huit catégories, chacune explorée par un chapitre. A l'intérieur de chaque catégorie, les produits sont regroupés selon des aires thématiques, qui vous seront mentionnées dans l'introduction du chapitre. Chaque produit est décrit dans ses caractéristiques fondamentales, de manière claire et concise. Pour comprendre au mieux les caractéristiques de l'éco-compatibilité, chaque produit est accompagné d'icones renvoyant aux principales approches de l'écodesign, abordées dans le premier chapitre du livre. Grâce à ces informations, les différentes approches de la projetation en matière d'écodesign prennent un sens global et le lecteur peut ainsi découvrir les instruments dont le designer dispose au moment de la création d'un produit éco-compatible. L'ouvrage offre ainsi la possibilité d'une lecture dynamique et transversale par catégories ou de reconstruire les différentes approches de

understand our increasingly global, continuously transforming world.

Given the vast, heterogeneous nature of the products on the market and in development, we believe the choices clearly represent the principles of ecodesign. They also show how ethics and aesthetics, i.e. environmental awareness on the one hand and appealing, trendy forms on the other can easily coexist in products that are functional and not necessarily expensive.

dynamische und transversale Lektüre. Der Leser kann die verschiedenen Kategorien nacheinander betrachten oder die grundlegenden Ansätze miteinander verknüpfen. Beide Lesarten ermöglichen die Herstellung von Bezügen zwischen den unterschiedlichen Produkten.

Im abschließenden Teil dieses Buches befindet sich ein kurzes Glossar, das hoffentlich die Entstehung eines Background-Wissens fördert und Anregungen liefert, um die immer globalere und sich fortlaufend verändernde Welt von heute zu verstehen.

Angesichts der Vielzahl und Verschieden-
artigkeit der Produkte, die auf dem Markt
erhältlich sind oder sich in der Entwicklungsphase befinden, wurde eine
Auswahl getroffen, die unserer Ansicht
nach auf klare Weise die Grundsätze des
Ökodesigns präsentiert. Sie zeigt
ebenfalls, dass Ethik und Ästhetik bzw.
Umweltschutz und ansprechende Formen
und Tendenzen neben einem funktionalen Produkt mit einer ästhetischen
Wertigkeit, und das nicht kostspielig sein
muss, bestehen können.

l'écodesign en suivant un fil conducteur
déterminé. Quel que soit votre choix, tous
les objets seront mis en relation.

Un glossaire vous est proposé en fin
d'ouvrage ; il pourra favoriser
l'élaboration d'un fond de connaissances
et offrir une première impulsion pour lire
et comprendre le monde d'aujourd'hui,
en transformation continue et toujours
plus global.

Étant donnée la vaste gamme et
l'hétérogénéité des produits présents
sur le marché ou en phase de
développement, nous avons fait un choix
qui à notre avis représente simplement
les principes de l'éco-design. Il démontre
comment éthique et esthétique, par
l'attention à l'environnement ou la
création de formes attractives et
tendance, peuvent facilement coexister
dans des produits fonctionnels,
possédant une valeur esthétique et
pas nécessairement coûteux.

Ecodesign approaches

Herangehensweisen ökologischen Designs
Approches de l'écodesign

The strength of parts
Die Kraft der Bauteile
La force des parties

Design for components
Komponentendesign
Design de composants

The goal of *designing for components* is to identify and optimize the external form of an object, starting with its size and the arrangement of its parts, or components. Each of these is considered as a finished product with an autonomous life cycle, though still in relation to the other parts. The design starts with the analysis of disassembled objects of the same type, taking into account the relationships between components, the physical-mechanical laws that distinguish them and technologies of manufacturing. Once the single parts are defined, the key elements that make the object work are identified, and the creative phase begins, at which point the designer works according the following guidelines:

• combining components of the same material and avoiding the use of different materials;
• marking the materials permanently (with stamps or labels);
• minimizing waste production;
• pre-determining any breakage points to facilitate rapid removal of parts;
• avoiding forms and systems that could complicate disassembly.

Designing for components also means taking into account the accessibility of the product in terms of making it easy to use and maintain.

Komponentendesign hat zum Ziel, die äußere Form eines Produktes anhand seiner Maße, dem Aufbau und der Anordnung seiner Komponenten zu ermitteln und zu optimieren. Die Komponenten werden als Endprodukt mit einem eigenen Lebenszyklus betrachtet, aber auch in Beziehung zu den anderen Bestandteilen. Bei der Analyse der zerlegten Objekte, die einer gleichen Typologie angehören, werden die physisch-mechanischen Gesetze und die Produktionstechnologien untersucht.

Nachdem die einzelnen Teile bestimmt worden sind, werden die Schlüssel-elemente zum Betrieb des Gegenstands identifiziert. Darauf folgt die kreative Phase, in der der Designer unter Beachtung der folgenden Grundsätze arbeitet:

• Komponenten aus dem gleichen Material (monomateriell) einsetzen und die Verwendung von verschiedenen Materialien vermeiden;
• Materialien unauslöschlich markieren (mit Aufdruck oder Etikett)
• Menge der Produktionsabfälle auf ein Minimum reduzieren
• Mögliche Bruchstellen bestimmen, um einen schnellen Austausch bzw. Entfernung der Einzelteile zu erleichtern;
• Formen und Systeme vermeiden, die übermäßig lange Zerlegungsprozesse erfordern.

Ein weiteres wichtiges Ziel ist die einfache Benutzung und Wartung des Produktes, um eine einfache Handhabung zu gewährleisten.

Le *design de composants* a pour but de déterminer et d'optimiser la forme globale de l'objet à partir de la dimension et de la disposition des parties qui le composent, c'est-à-dire les composants. Chacun d'entre eux est considéré comme un produit fini, dont le cycle de vie, autonome, est aussi lié aux autres. Le projet commence alors par l'analyse d'objets démontés appartenant à la même catégorie : les relations entre les composants, les lois physico-mécaniques qui les caractérisent et leurs techniques de production sont les différents aspects pris en compte.

Une fois ces parties définies, on identifie les éléments clés de fonctionnement de cet objet et l'on passe à la phase créative.

Ici, le créateur travaille en suivant les lignes directrices suivantes :
• intégrer des composants de même matériau (objet monomatériau) et éviter de recourir à des matériaux différents;
• marquer les matériaux de manière indélébile (par impression ou étiquette);
• minimiser la production de déchets;
• prédéterminer les éventuels points de rupture pour faciliter le démontage rapide des parties;
• éviter les formes et systèmes pouvant causer des procédures de désassemblage trop longues.

Lancer un projet visant des composants signifie aussi tenir compte de l'accessibilité du produit en termes d'utilisation et de manutention, pour en faciliter l'usage.

The sustainable lightness of the material
Die nachhaltige Leichtigkeit der Materie
La légèreté durable du matériau

Reduction of materials and design for disassembly
Materialreduktion und Produktzerlegung
Réduction de la matière et design pour le désassemblage

An analysis of the products on the market shows that there is a general tendency towards redundancy in the use of materials. Designing according to a logic of *reducing materials* means optimizing the amount of both materials and energy in the development of a product. Such reductions have a double advantage, helping to both protect resources and decrease harmful emissions.

In taking this approach, the designer should also avoid using different materials, since this complicates the recycling and disposal processes. Products created this way also satisfy the principle of *design for disassembly*, since an object needs to be taken apart before it can be recycled. Correspondingly, it is important to make the materials easy to recognize, since each component can either be reused or recycled even when made of different materials. For this reason, many countries have launched regulations that require the marking of objects and components for fast identification.

Die Analyse der auf dem Markt vorhandenen Produkte zeigt die allgemeine Tendenz zu einer redundanten Verwendung der Materialien. Design im Sinne der *Materialreduktion* bedeutet die Entwicklung eines Produktes mit einer effizienten Verwendung von Material und Energie. Die *Materialreduktion* bietet somit gleich zwei Vorteile: zum einen führt die größere Sorgfalt in der Materialverarbeitung zu einem geringeren Verbrauch an Rohstoffen und zum anderen zu einer Senkung der Umweltemissionen.

Eine weitere Aufgabe des Designers ist es, die Verwendung von verschiedenen Materialien zu vermeiden, so dass ein

schnelle und einfache Wiederverwertung und Entsorgung gewährleistet ist. Die auf diese Weise hergestellten Produkte erfüllen auch den Grundsatz der *Produktzerlegung*. Ihm zufolge wird bei der Produktplanung berücksichtigt, dass vor der Wiederverwertung eine Zerlegung erfolgen muss. Daher ist es besonders wichtig, die Materialerkennung zu vereinfachen, damit alle Bestandteile, auch wenn sie aus verschiedenen Materialien bestehen, wieder verwendet oder recycelt werden können. Aus diesem Grund ist in vielen Ländern die Kennzeichnung der Produkte und ihrer Bestandteile gesetzlich vorgeschrieben, um eine schnellere Identifizierung zu ermöglichen.

Une analyse des produits présents sur le marché met en évidence une tendance générale à la sur-utilisation de matériaux. Projeter selon une logique de *réduction de la matière* signifie réaliser un produit en optimisant les quantités de matériau et d'énergie. La réduction de matière présente ainsi un double avantage : elle consent la protection des ressources, grâce à l'utilisation attentive des matériaux travaillés et réduit les émissions nocives pour l'environnement.
S'il suit cette approche, le designer a aussi pour mission d'éviter la multiplication des matériaux, qui compliqueraient le

processus de recyclage et de démontage. Les produits réalisés dans cette optique satisfont ainsi également le *design pour le désassemblage*. Ce dernier prévoit qu'en amont de leur construction, les objets soient pensés pour être démontés et ainsi recyclés. Dans cette optique, il est important de faciliter l'identification du matériau, afin que tous les composants puissent être réutilisés ou recyclés, même s'ils sont remplacés par des matériaux différents. De nombreux pays ont ainsi initié des réglementations prévoyant le marquage des objets et des composants pour une identification rapide.

Material discretion
Die Bescheidenheit der Materie
La discrétion de la matière

The use of mono-materials and bio-based materials
Monomaterial und „Bio"-Materialien
Monomatériau et matériaux « bio »

Despite how easy it is to apply, the ecodesign principle of using just one material is often neglected. Unfortunately, the request for product appeal often prevails over environmental issues, resulting in the increased spread of high-impact products. Designing in a sustainable way, however, means using the most suitable resources for an object and its function, not just satisfying the laws of the market.

There are many advantages to using only one material, since designing this way means simplifying both the initial manufacturing and the final recycling processes. This approach generally applies to relatively simple products, disposable objects and the single components of more articulated products.

Considering the environmental costs of extraction, transformation and disposal of resources, ecodesign also generally involves the use of *"bio-based" materials*. These include both organic materials and the derivatives of natural products, such as biodegradable non-oil plastics, produced for example with cornstarch or potato starch (PLA).

Obwohl das Prinzip des *Monomaterials*, d.h. der Verwendung eines einzigen Materials, einfach umzusetzen wäre, ist dies ein Grundsatz des Ökodesigns, der häufig vernachlässigt wird. Dem „Appeal" – dem Kaufanreiz – eines Produktes wird eine größere Bedeutung beigemessen als den damit verbundenen Umweltaspekten. Dies führt zu einer immer größeren Verbreitung von Produkten, die die Umwelt stark belasten. Produktentwicklung im Sinne der Nachhaltigkeit erfordert den Einsatz von angemessenen und wirkungsvollen Ressourcen.

Die Planung mit einem einzigen Material bietet zahlreiche Vorteile, wie z. B. einen optimierten Produktions- und Recyclingprozess. Dieser Ansatz ist üblicherweise auf einfache Produkte, Wegwerfprodukte und auf Einzelteile von komplexeren Gütern anwendbar.

Angesichts der Umweltkosten für die Rohstoffgewinnung, -verarbeitung und -entsorgung werden beim Ökodesign „Bio"-Materialien bevorzugt. Dazu zählen sowohl natürliche Materialien wie auch aus Naturprodukten gewonnene Stoffe, wie z. B. biologisch abbaubare „No-Oil"-Kunststoffe, die mit Maisstärke oder Kartoffelstärke (PLA) hergestellt werden.

Pourtant simple à appliquer, l'idée de *monomatériau* (ou utilisation d'un seul matériau) est un principe de l'écodesign souvent négligé. Malheureusement, la nécessité d'offrir un produit attractif prévaut souvent sur les questions environnementales ; le résultat en est une diffusion de plus en plus forte de produits dont l'impact environnemental est lourd. Projeter dans un esprit durable signifie au contraire employer des ressources plus adaptées à un objet et à sa fonction, et non pas à la satisfaction des lois du marché.

Les avantages du monomatériau sont nombreux, étant donné que projeter avec un seul matériau signifie simplifier autant le processus de production que le recyclage en fin de vie. Cette approche s'applique généralement à des produits peu complexes, à des objets jetables et aux composants primaires de produits plus élaborés.

Étant donné les coûts environnementaux d'extraction, de transformation et de désassemblage des ressources, l'écodesign s'oriente généralement vers l'emploi de *matériaux « bio »* parmi lesquels des matériaux naturels dérivés de produits bruts, comme les plastiques sans pétrole biodégradables, issus de l'amidon de maïs ou de pomme-de-terre (PLA).

Multi-use materials
Mehrzweck-Materialien
Trans-matériau

Recycling and reuse
Recycling und Wiederverwendung
Recyclage et réemploi

Though similar, the concepts of *recycling* and *reuse* differentiate themselves in the products they generate. Whilst recycling involves the transformation and reuse of the material or materials of the object being recycled, reuse puts the object itself back to work, involving purely formal and structural, rather than chemical or physical, changes. When it comes to life-span, whereas in the first case the materials outlast the product, whereas in the second case it is the object itself that endures.

Recycling includes numerous subcategories, the best known of which are cascade, post-consumer and preconsumer recycling. The first involves the recovery of materials for increasingly simplified uses with respect to their original one; this is due to the loss in structural and chemical quality involved in their transformation. Post-consumer recycling, the most well-known, involves the transformation of materials or parts of a product at the end of its life, following separated waste collection. More theoretical and less well-known is preconsumer recycling. Here the actual need to put the product on the market is checked at the start. If the results are unsatisfactory, pre-recycling takes place, that is, production is suspended, thereby avoiding the waste of resources beforehand.

Trotz der großen Ähnlichkeit unterscheiden sich *Recycling* und *Wiederverwendung* nur in ihrem Endprodukt. Recycling ist die Gewinnung von Rohstoffen aus Abfällen, ihre Rückführung in den Wirtschaftskreislauf und die Verarbeitung zu neuen Produkten. Bei der Wiederverwendung wird das Produkt mehrfach verwendet, ohne dass es physikalisch oder chemisch verändert oder aufbereitet werden muss, wie beispielsweise beim Mehrwegsystem. Beim Recycling wird das Produkt einem neuen Verwendungszweck zugeführt, während bei der Wiederverwendung die Nutzungsdauer des Gegenstandes verlängert wird.

Recycling schließt weitere Unterkategorien ein: „Down-Recycling", „Post-Consumer-Recycling" und „Pre-Consumer-Recycling". Die erste Kategorie bezeichnet die Wiederverwendung von

Materialien für immer einfachere Nutzungsweisen im Gegensatz zum Originalprodukt. Dies ist auf den Verlust von strukturellen und chemischen Eigenschaften während der Umwandlung zurückzuführen. „Post-Consumer-Recycling" ist die bekannteste Variante und besteht in der Umwandlung der Materialien oder der Einzelteile eines Produktes nachdem eine getrennte Sammlung erfolgt ist. Theoretischer und auch weniger bekannt ist hingegen das „Pre-Consumer-Recycling": hier wird bereits in der Gestaltungsphase die tatsächliche Notwendigkeit eines Gegenstandes geprüft, den man auf dem Markt einzuführen gedenkt. Falls die Ergebnisse nicht zufrieden stellend ausfallen, wird das so genannte Pre-Recycling angewandt, d.h. die Realisierung wird gestoppt und die Verschwendung von kostbaren Rohstoffen verhindert.

Pourtant similaires, les concepts de *recyclage* et de *réemploi* se différencient par la nature des produits qu'ils génèrent. Tandis que le recyclage prévoit la transformation et la réutilisation du ou des matériaux de l'objet recyclé, le réemploi utilise à nouveau l'objet même, en lui apportant des modifications structurelles ou formelles, sans pour autant opérer de transformations chimiques ou physiques. En termes de durée, dans le premier cas ce sont les matériaux qui durent dans le temps et dépassent la durée de vie du produit, tandis que dans le second, c'est l'objet lui-même.

Le recyclage comprend de nombreuses sous-catégories, dont les plus connues sont le recyclage en cascade, le recyclage post-consommation et le recyclage pré-consommation. Le premier consiste en la récupération de matériaux pour des usages chaque fois plus simplifiés par rapport à la matière originale; ceci étant dû à la perte des qualités structurelles et chimiques entrainée par la transformation. Le recyclage post-consommation, le plus connu, prévoit la transformation des matériaux ou de parties du produit en fin de vie, après un tri sélectif. Le recyclage pré-consommation est plus théorique et moins connu : on vérifie à priori la nécessité réelle du produit à mettre sur le marché. Si les résultats ne sont pas satisfaisants, le pré-recyclage est mis en œuvre : la réalisation de l'objet est bloquée et évite ainsi, en amont, la perte de ressources.

Decreasing the volume
Verminderung des Volumens
Volume diminué

Size reduction
Reduzierung der Maße
Réduction des dimensions

Compressing, reducing, limiting consumption during transport: these are the requirements an eco-designer must keep in mind when developing an idea for a new object. Saving materials is only part of it; the intelligent design of a product's dimensions also means preventing excessive consumption by the vehicles used for its transportation. The more products carried on a single trip, the less aggravating are the CO_2 emissions on the environment. Immediate benefits are also felt in terms of fuel savings.

Size reduction follows two main guidelines:
• designing both product and packaging at the same time;
• providing for assembly following purchase.

There is a close relationship between these two guidelines during the design phase. An acknowledgement of their needs and characteristics produces a highly functional result, which is essential when it comes to the size and use of materials. Space during the transport phase is thereby optimized and the packaging, in its turn, has to comply with the object as much as possible, both protecting it and avoiding unnecessary empty spaces. This does not however lessen the communicative strength of the packaging, whose role is also to present the product on the market in the best way.

In addition to the size and weight of the merchandise, the means of transport itself is also important. A more widespread use of alternative-energy vehicles, ones that use natural fuels or renewable sources instead of fossil fuels, would contribute to a drastic reduction of a product's environmental footprint.

Bei der Entwicklung eines Objekts muss ein Designer bestimmte Vorgaben beachten: das Produkt so kompakt wie möglich zu halten und den Energieverbrauch während des Transports zu vermindern. Es geht aber nicht nur um die Einsparung von Material. Das Ziel einer intelligenten Planung der Abmessungen besteht auch in der Vorbeugung von übermäßigem Energieverbrauch während des Transports. Je mehr Produkte beim Transport aufgeladen werden, desto weniger belasten die CO_2–Emissionen die Umwelt. Nicht zu vergessen die Einsparungen beim Kraftstoffverbrauch.

Die *Reduzierung der Maße* folgt zwei Prinzipien:
• Produkt und Verpackung gleichzeitig planen;
• Montage nach dem Kauf vorsehen.

In der Gestaltungsphase besteht eine enge Verbindung zwischen diesen beiden

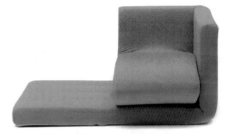

Richtlinien. Der Vergleich von Anforderungen und Eigenschaften liefert gute Ergebnisse in Bezug auf effiziente Abmessungen und Materialverbrauch. Durch die Produktgestaltung kann in der Transportphase der Laderaum in optimaler Weise genutzt werden. Die Verpackung ihrerseits sollte so eng wie möglich am Produkt liegen, um es zu schützen und gleichzeitig unnötige Leerräume zu verhindern. Die kommunikative Kraft der Verpackung soll dabei aber nicht verloren gehen, denn sie präsentiert das Produkt auf bestmögliche Weise auf dem Markt.

Die mit dem Transport verbundenen Probleme liegen nicht nur beim Gewicht und bei den Maßen der Ware. Ebenso entscheidend ist die Wahl eines umweltfreundlichen Transportmittels. Der Einsatz von Verkehrsmitteln, die natürliche Kraftstoffe oder erneuerbare Energien statt fossiler Brennstoffe nutzen, könnte zu einer deutlicheren Verringerung der Emissionen führen.

Le designer s'attelant à la projetation d'un nouvel objet travaille selon des pré-requis : compacter, réduire ou limiter la consommation engendrée par le transport. Certainement pour économiser des ressources, mais aussi pour prévenir des consommations excessives durant le transport, une projetation intelligente des dimensions reste inévitable. Plus on peut stocker de produits en un seul voyage, moins les émissions de CO_2 aggravent la situation écologique ; ce qui implique aussi une économie directe de carburant.

La *réduction des dimensions* suit deux lignes directrices principales :
• projeter produit et emballage simultanément;
• prévoir l'assemblage après l'achat.

Dans la phase de projetation, il existe une étroite relation entre ces deux idées clés; la confrontation de leurs nécessités et de leurs caractéristiques permet d'obtenir un résultat hautement fonctionnel, essentiel dans les dimensions et dans l'emploi des matériaux. La forme du produit permettra ainsi une véritable exploitation de l'espace durant le transport. L'emballage, quant à lui, devra adhérer le plus possible à l'objet, en le protégeant et en évitant de créer des zones de vide inutiles. Cette étape ne fait aucunement perdre de force communicative à l'emballage, dont la fonction est aussi celle de présenter au mieux le produit sur le marché.

La problématique du transport ne se limite pas au poids et aux dimensions des marchandises; la question du moyen de transport est tout aussi importante. La diffusion des moyens alternatifs, qu'ils utilisent des carburants naturels ou des sources d'énergies renouvelables au lieu de combustibles fossiles, amènerait à une réduction encore plus drastique des émissions de CO_2.

0% products
0% Produkte
0% produits

Service design
Dienstleistungsdesign
Le design de services

Can an object be replaced with a service? The sphere of *service design* aims to provide an affirmative answer to this question by studying systems that offer alternatives to the individual use of an object. The response to this kind of service is generally very positive, since the use of a product is generally born out of the need to facilitate an action rather than the desire to possess the object in itself. In this approach, the offering becomes a mix of products and services, with a single owner who supplies a service to several users. The owner profits financially by minimizing resource consumption, emissions and waste, and therefore aims to look after the product for its duration.

This is the case with car-sharing. A service like this, which puts a car owner in touch with someone who needs a ride, satisfies the needs of a group with a single vehicle, reducing the costs of both owning a car, on the one hand and traveling, on the other. It also stimulates users to develop conscious and sustainable habits, since car trips are reduced to strict necessity, and it fosters new relationships between people, places and objects.

Kann ein Gegenstand durch eine Dienstleistung ersetzt werden? Bei der Beantwortung dieser Frage setzt das *Dienstleistungsdesign* an, das sich mit Alternativen zur individuellen Benutzung eines Gegenstandes beschäftigt. Die Akzeptanz von diesen Dienstleistungen ist im Allgemeinen sehr gut, da die Verwendung eines Konsumguts vor allem aus dem Bedürfnis entsteht, eine bestimmte Handlung zu erleichtern, und nicht aus dem Wunsch, einen bestimmten Gegenstand zu besitzen. Beim Dienstleistungsdesign bietet ein einziger Besitzer mehreren Benutzern eine Dienstleistung an. Der Besitzer erwirtschaftet damit einen Ertrag, in dem er den Rohstoffverbrauch, die Emissionen und die Abfälle minimiert. Um diesen

Ertrag zu sichern, wird der Besitzer das Produkt während seiner gesamten Nutzzeit mit besonderer Sorgfalt pflegen. Ein Beispiel von Dienstleistungsdesign ist *Car Sharing*. Der Besitz eines Autos ist die Folge des Bedürfnisses, sich schnell und flexibel fortbewegen zu können. Eine solche Dienstleistung, die zwischen denen, die ein Auto besitzen und denen, die eine Reise unternehmen müssen, einen Kontakt herstellt, ermöglicht die Befriedigung der Bedürfnisse einer ganzen Gruppe mit einem einzigen Mittel. Dadurch können Besitz-, Unterhalts- und Reisekosten vermindert werden. Eine solche Dienstleistung trägt außerdem zur Sensibilisierung für ein bewusstes und nachhaltiges Handeln bei.

Est-il possible de substituer un service à un objet ? Répondre à cette question signifie entrer dans le contexte du *design de services*. Cette approche étudie les systèmes alternatifs à l'utilisation individuelle des objets. La réponse à ce type de services est généralement très positive, puisque l'utilisation d'un bien naît avant tout du besoin de faciliter une action, et non du désir de posséder l'objet en soi. Il en résulte une forme hybride de produit et service, où un propriétaire unique fournit un service à plusieurs utilisateurs. Il tire un bénéfice économique de la diminution de sa consommation des ressources, des émissions et des déchets, et gagne ainsi personnellement à prendre soin du produit jusqu'à sa fin de vie.

C'est le cas du *covoiturage* : si posséder une voiture est la conséquence du besoin de se déplacer plus rapidement, ce type de service (mettant en relation le propriétaire de la voiture et qui a besoin de se déplacer) permet de satisfaire les besoins d'un groupe à l'aide d'un seul moyen. Les coûts engendrés d'une part par la possession et de l'autre par le voyage, sont ainsi diminués. Un service de ce genre sensibilise également les utilisateurs à des comportements conscients et durables (les déplacements en voiture se réduisant au strict nécessaire) et favorise les nouvelles relations entre les personnes, les lieux et les objets.

Techno/ecologically
Techno/ökologisch
Techno/écologique

Technology for sustainability
Technologie im Dienste der Nachhaltigkeit
Technologie pour le développement durable

An object can be made eco-compatible through the use of the appropriate *technology*. We might think, for instance, of the technological opportunities for improving the efficiency of products, promoting energy savings and combining several functions in one object, not to mention nanotechnology and biotechnology. While industrial production remains strongly tied to the exploitation of materials and resources, despite well-founded accusations of excessive use and consequent pollution, sustainable technological development operates increasingly towards saving materials, which also boosts the spread of the services. Moreover, technologies with a low environmental impact are becoming increasingly widespread.

Unlike conventional design, ecodesign moves within a rich imagination of qualities and values, in which communication between products and systems is open and reciprocal. Creative solutions thus take shape at the technological avant-garde, with ecological sustainability as their goal.

Durch die Anwendung von entsprechenden *Technologien* kann ein Produkt umweltverträglich gemacht werden, wie z. B. bei den technischen Möglichkeiten zur Verbesserung der Produktwirksamkeit, bei der Entwicklung von Energiesparmaßnahmen, bei der Hinzufügung mehrerer Funktionen, oder aber auch bei Nano- und Biotechnologien. Während die industrielle Produktion stark mit einer Ausnutzung der Materialien und Rohstoffe verbunden ist, steht bei einer umweltfreundlichen Technologie die Materialeinsparung im Vordergrund. So

wird einerseits eine Verbreitung von Dienstleistungen gefördert und andererseits finden Technologien mit niedriger Umweltbelastung immer mehr Anklang.

Im Gegensatz zur klassischen Produktgestaltung umfasst Ökodesign ein breites Feld aus Qualität und Werten, in dem die Kommunikation zwischen den Mitteln und Systemen offen und auch bereichsübergreifend ist. Es entstehen phantasievolle Lösungen, die aus technologischer Sicht als Vorreiter gelten und gleichzeitig auf Nachhaltigkeit bedacht sind.

À travers l'emploi d'une *technologie* adaptée, il est possible de rendre un objet éco-compatible : pensons par exemple aux possibilités technologiques capables d'améliorer l'efficacité des produits, de favoriser les économies d'énergie ou d'intégrer de nouvelles fonctions à un objet, et considérons aussi les nano-technologies et biotechnologies. Malgré les accusations fondées d'un emploi excessif et la pollution qui en résulte, la production industrielle reste fortement liée à l'exploitation de matériaux et ressources naturels. Les avancées technologiques dans le cadre du développement durable œuvrent de plus

en plus dans le sens des économies de matériaux, en encourageant la diffusion des services, tandis que les technologies à faible impact environnemental vivent un véritable essor.

À la différence de la projetation traditionnelle, l'écodesign évolue au cœur d'un large éventail de qualités et de valeurs, où la communication entre moyens et systèmes est ouverte et transversale. C'est ainsi que prennent forme des solutions originales, avant-gardistes du point de vue technologique et ayant pour but un développement durable.

Saying, doing, sustaining
Sagen, Machen, Erhalten
Dire, faire, durer

Eco-advertising
Ökologische Werbung
Écopublicité

While the usual means of communication are used to express and spread environmental sustainability, *eco-advertising* exists on several levels and takes various forms. In fact, messages about environmental issues reach the public through more than just the media and focused promotional campaigns, which use graphics and slogans as their immediate tools of expression; there is always a new product on the market that declares its sustainability in one way or another, making it the strength of the company. Sometimes these products convey the message directly by integrating it as part of their design. Others carry environmental certifications born of meticulous and complex procedures, though these are often difficult for the consumer to read. Others call for eco-friendly behavior or propose educational games that spur kids to adopt a new point of view on the world in which we live. Sustainability can therefore be both the direct subject of the message and a tool for validating and publicizing a product on the market.

Im Gegensatz zur Darstellung von Nachhaltigkeit mit klassischen Kommunikationsmitteln, werden bei der *ökologischen Werbung* verschiedene Ebenen und Formen eingesetzt. Botschaften zum Umweltschutz erreichen den Konsumenten vor allem durch die Medien und gezielte Werbekampagnen. Auf dem Markt gibt es allerdings immer mehr Produkte, die auf die eine oder andere Weise ihre Nachhaltigkeit selbst verkünden. Diese Produkte vermitteln ihre Botschaft auf direktem Weg, indem sie Teil ihres Designs wird.

In anderen Fällen führen sie Umwelt-
zertifikate an, die aus komplexen
Prozessen hervorgehen und für die
Verbraucher oft schwer zu entziffern sind.
Oder sie fordern zu nachhaltigem
Verhalten auf oder schlagen Lehrspiele
vor, die auch Kinder dazu anspornen
sollen, die Welt, in der wir leben, aus
einem anderen Blickwinkel zu betrachten.
Nachhaltigkeit kann also entweder direkt
der Inhalt der Botschaft sein oder ein
geeignetes Instrument, um ein Produkt
auf dem Markt aufzuwerten oder dafür
zu werben.

Pour exprimer et diffuser le concept de
développement durable, la communication peut s'effectuer par les moyens
habituels ; mais *l'écopublicité* existe à bien
d'autres niveaux et sous diverses formes.
En réalité, les messages relatifs aux
questions environnementales
n'atteignent plus leur public uniquement
grâce aux *médias* et aux campagnes
de communication employées, faisant de
l'affichage et du pay-off leurs instruments
d'expression les plus immédiats; il existe
sur le marché de plus en plus de produits
qui, d'une manière ou d'une autre,
déclarent leur durabilité et en font leur
point fort. Ces produits communiquent

parfois un message très direct en
l'intégrant à leur propre design; dans
d'autres cas, ils mentionnent leurs
certifications environnementales, les-
quelles naissent pourtant de procédures
méticuleuses et complexes, souvent
difficiles à comprendre par l'acheteur de
l'objet; dans d'autres cas encore, ils
invitent à des comportements durables
ou proposent des jeux éducatifs, qui
stimulent aussi les enfants à adopter un
regard neuf sur le monde dans lequel
nous vivons. La durabilité peut ainsi être
soit le sujet direct de la communication,
soit un instrument pour valoriser et faire
la publicité d'un produit sur le marché.

Zero emissions
Null Emissionen
Zéro émissions

Systemic design
Systemisches Design
Le design systémique

The secret of good design is not just about showing off a product and enhancing its aesthetics. Operating within a set of social, cultural and ethical values, ecodesign must also take into account the systems and relationships within which the products are generated. It is therefore important to sketch out and plan the flow of materials from one system to another, since the impressive economic cycle thus generated gradually reduces the ecological footprint of products. This is the purpose behind *systemic design*: to carefully study all secondary and waste products created by the use of resources, both to obtain information and to make a genuine assessment. Production waste, for example, remains unused and is therefore a cost. Systemic design is about devising a new production model in which industrial cycles are open and connected to one another. This way, flows of material resources (secondary products) and energy resources could be generated that both ensure all waste products are used and stabilize single systems over the long-term.

Das Geheimnis von gutem Design liegt nicht nur in der Inszenierung eines Produktes, um seine ästhetische Seite hervorzuheben. Da Ökodesign in einem Umfeld von verschiedenen sozialen, kulturellen und ethischen Werten handelt, muss es die Systeme und die Zusammenhänge, in denen die Produkte entwickelt werden, berücksichtigen. Der Materialfluss, der von einem System in ein anderes übergeht, muss bestimmt und geplant werden, da der daraus entstehende Wirtschaftszyklus die ökologischen Merkmale der Produkte vermindert. Dieser Prozess wird *systemisches Design* genannt. Auf dieser

 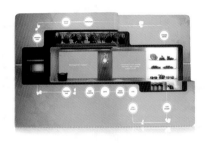

Grundlage werden alle Sekundär- und Abfallprodukte, die aus der Verwendung von Rohstoffen entstehen, sorgfältig untersucht, um daraus die größtmögliche Menge an Informationen und eine realistische Bewertung zu gewinnen. Denken wir z. B. an Abfälle aus Produktionsprozessen, die noch immer ungenutzt bleiben und einen Kostenpunkt darstellen. Systemisches Design zielt auf die Entwicklung eines neuen Produktionsmodells ab, in dem die Industriezyklen offen und miteinander verbunden sind. So können Ressourcen (Sekundärprodukte) und Energien hin und her fließen, ohne dass Rückstände unbenutzt bleiben.

Le secret d'un bon design ne réside pas seulement dans la mise en scène d'un produit pour en valoriser la composante esthétique. En opérant dans un ensemble de valeurs sociales, culturelles et éthiques, l'écodesign doit tenir compte des systèmes au sein desquels les produits sont réalisés. Il est de ce fait important de visualiser et gérer le flux de matériau passant d'un système à l'autre, afin que le cycle économique visible ainsi généré réduise au fur et à mesure l'empreinte écologique des produits. Celui-ci s'appelle *design systémique* : selon ce principe, les produits secondaires et déchets dérivant de l'usage des

ressources sont attentivement étudiés afin de recueillir un maximum d'informations et d'en faire une évaluation réelle. Nous pensons par exemple aux déchets des processus de production, qui pour le moment demeurent en grande partie inutilisés et représentent ainsi un coût. Le design systémique vise à la conception d'un nouveau modèle productif, où les cycles industriels sont ouverts et interconnectés : il se génère ainsi des flux de matériaux (les produits secondaires) et d'énergies, au cours desquels aucun déchet ne reste inutilisé et qui rendent chaque système plus stable à long terme.

Legend
Legende
Légende

Design for components

Komponentendesign
Design de composants

Recycling and reuse

Recycling und Wiederverwendung
Recyclage et réemploi

Technology
for sustainability

Technologie im Dienste
der Nachhaltigkeit
Technologie pour le
développement durable

Reduction of materials and design for disassembly

Materialreduktion und
Produktzerlegung
Réduction de la matière
et design pour le désassemblage

The use of mono-materials and bio-based materials

Monomaterial und
„Bio"-Materialen
Monomatériau et matériaux « bio »

Size reduction

Reduzierung der Maße
Réduction des dimensions

Service design

Dienstleistungsdesign
Le design de services

Eco-advertising

Ökologische Werbung
Écopublicité

Systemic design

Systemisches Design
Design systémique

Household appliances

Haushaltsgeräte
Applications domestiques

Introduction

Einleitung
Introduction

Household appliances belong to the spheres of production that emerged primarily after the Second World War. Conceived to facilitate domestic activities, they are still chiefly linked to the formal and aesthetic needs of home furnishings. However, thanks to the new strides made in scientific and applied research, this production approach is becoming obsolete. The designs of new-generation washing machines and dishwashers tend to be determined by the function of the product, independent of current fashions. Moreover, environmental issues are forcing manufacturers to be increasingly aware and sensitive, since the emissions and consumption figures of this industry can make up to 60-70% of the totals.

These are the aspects that ecodesign takes into consideration and puts into practice through production approaches such as sustainable technology, systemic design and component design. The household appliances and domestic products presented in this section were born out of these new sustainable trends. They show that it is possible to rethink old functions in a new light and discover other seemingly unusual ones that can nevertheless improve our lifestyles, and not just in terms of savings. The products have been divided into three thematic areas: Water, Air and Food.

Die Produktion von Haushaltsgeräten erfuhr nach dem Zweiten Weltkrieg einen Aufschwung und hatte zum Ziel, die Tätigkeiten im Haushalt zu erleichtern. Bis heute sind Haushaltsgeräte an die formellen und ästhetischen Eigenschaften der Küchen- und Wohnungseinrichtung gebunden. Angesichts neuer wissenschaftlicher Untersuchungen ist dieser Ansatz veraltet. In der Entwicklungs- und Gestaltungsphase steht nunmehr zur Bestimmung der modernen Geräteform die Funktion im Mittelpunkt, unabhängig von gegenwärtigen Trends. Die Reduzierung der Emissionen und des Energieverbrauchs, die zusammen einen Anteil von 60-70% darstellen, werden auch in dieser Branche angesichts aktueller Umweltprobleme immer wichtiger.

Diese Aspekte werden beim ökologischen Design berücksichtigt und durch neue Produktionsansätze wie nachhaltige Technologie, systemisches Design und Bauteiledesign ersetzt. Die in diesem Kapitel vorgestellten Haushaltsgeräte und Wohngegenstände gehen auf diese Strömungen zurück. Sie zeigen, dass es möglich ist, alte Funktionen auf neue Weise einzusetzen oder auch neue, bislang ungewöhnliche Funktionen zu etablieren, die eine Verbesserung des Lebensstils bedeuten, und zwar nicht nur durch Einsparungen. Die gewählten Themenbereiche sind: Wasser, Luft, Ernährung.

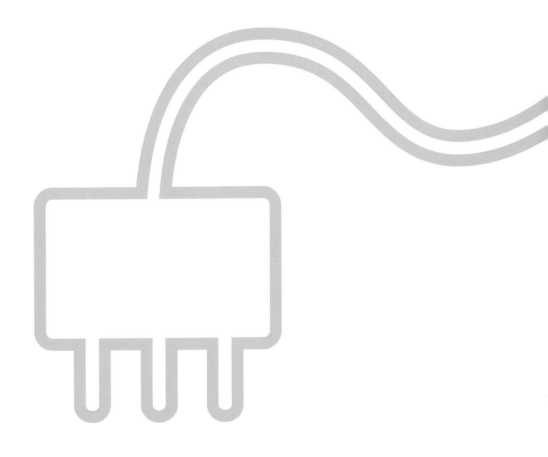

L'électroménager est né de la réalité de la production, principalement après la Seconde Guerre mondiale. Pensé pour faciliter les activités domestiques, les appareils électroménagers sont restés jusqu'à aujourd'hui cantonnés aux nécessités formelles et esthétiques de l'ameublement. Grâce aussi à de nouvelles impulsions de la recherche scientifique et appliquée, cette approche productive tombe actuellement en désuétude. La projetation propose des formes nouvelles de machines à laver, de lave-vaisselle, qui sont déterminées par la fonction du produit, indépendamment des modes du moment. Les problématiques environnementales, en outre, imposent à ce secteur une attention toujours plus grande et une sensibilité à réduire les émissions et la consommation qui peuvent atteindre jusqu'à 60-70% du total. Voici les aspects dont l'écodesign tient compte et qu'il met en pratique à travers des approches productives comme les technologies durables, le design systémique et le design de composants. L'électroménager et les produits domestiques présentés dans ce chapitre naissent de ces nouvelles tendances durables et montrent qu'il est possible de repenser les anciennes fonctions sous un nouveau jour ou d'en découvrir d'autres, en apparence insolites, mais qui pourraient améliorer nos styles de vie, pas uniquement en termes d'économies. Les produits sont classés par domaine : Eau, Air et Alimentation.

Greenkitchen

Continuous-cycle kitchen
Küche der Zukunft
Cuisine en circuit fermé

www.whirlpool.co.uk

GCD, Whirlpool Europe
2008
prototype

Whirlpool Global Consumer Design brings us the kitchen of the future. It may look just like its traditional counterpart, but Greenkitchen is actually based on an intelligent continuous cycle of water and heat. Clean tap water is identified by sensors placed in the sink's drain, channeled into a special tank and reused for watering plants or running in the dishwasher; the latter, in turn, uses the heat generated by the fridge's motor to heat the water. Everything that is expelled from one unit therefore gets filtered and sanitized so it can be used by another unit, which translates into energy savings of up to 70%. This amount can even be increased by 10% when Greenkitchen is used with particular knowledge and care.

Greenkitchen ist ein innovatives Projekt für den nachhaltigen Umgang mit Ressourcen, entwickelt von Whirlpool Global Consumer Design. Auf den ersten Blick gleicht Greenkitchen herkömmlichen Modellen. Der Unterschied liegt allerdings in einem zusätzlich eingebauten intelligenten Wasser- und Wärmezyklus. Das saubere Wasser, das aus dem Hahn in die Spüle fließt, wird von Sensoren erkannt und in einen speziellen Tank zur Wiederverwendung, beispielsweise für den Geschirrspüler, geleitet. Der Geschirrspüler wiederum nutzt die Wärme, die vom Kühlschrankmotor produziert wird, um das Wasser zu erhitzen. So wird die Energie, die innerhalb eines Gerätes erzeugt wird, an einer anderen Stelle wieder verwendet. Dadurch kann der Energieverbrauch um bis zu 70% reduziert werden. Bei umweltbewusster und effizienter Benutzung von Greenkitchen können noch weitere 10% eingespart werden.

La cuisine du futur a été pensée chez Whirlpool par l'équipe de Global Consumer Design. Apparemment semblable aux cuisines traditionnelles, Greenkitchen fonctionne sur un judicieux cycle continu de l'eau et de la chaleur : l'eau qui sort du robinet est dirigée, grâce à des capteurs situés dans le tuyau d'évacuation, vers un filtre spécial et réutilisée pour l'arrosage ou le lave-vaisselle, qui à son tour utilise l'énergie générée par le moteur du réfrigérateur pour chauffer l'eau. Ainsi, tout ce qui est perdu d'un côté est filtré ou désinfecté pour être réutilisé de l'autre, permettant une économie d'énergie d'environ 70%, auxquels s'ajoutent 10% si Greenkitchen est exploitée consciemment et attentivement.

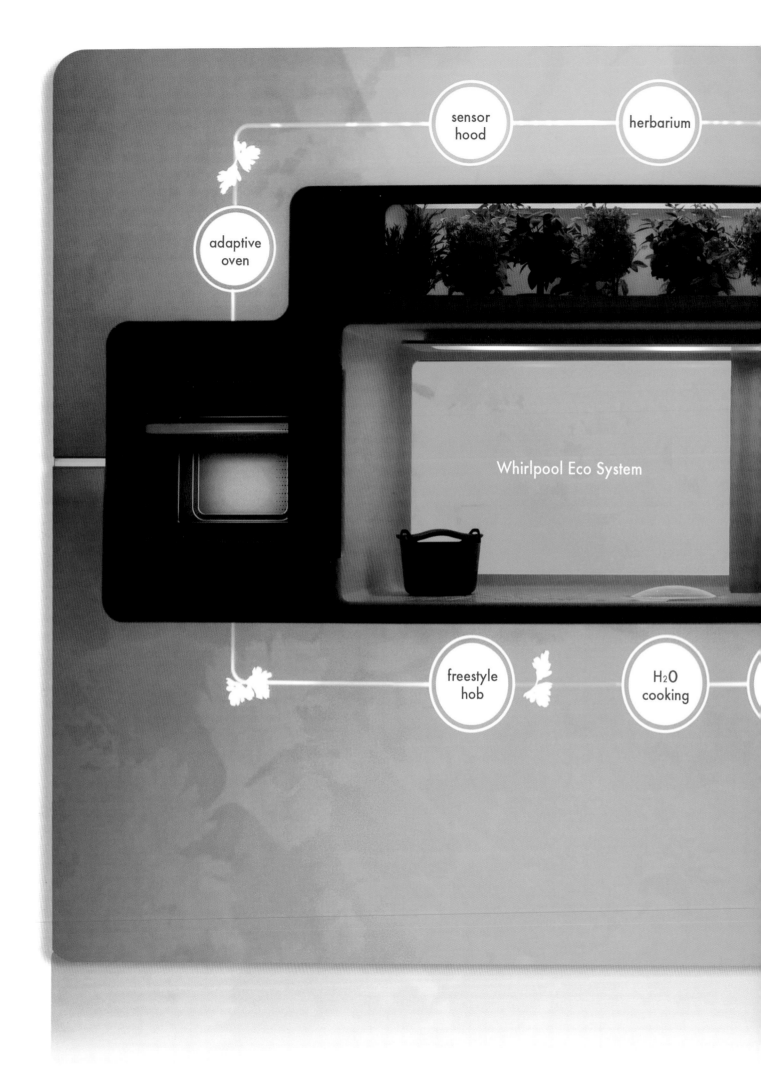

sensor
hood

herbarium

adaptive
oven

Whirlpool Eco System

freestyle
hob

H₂O
cooking

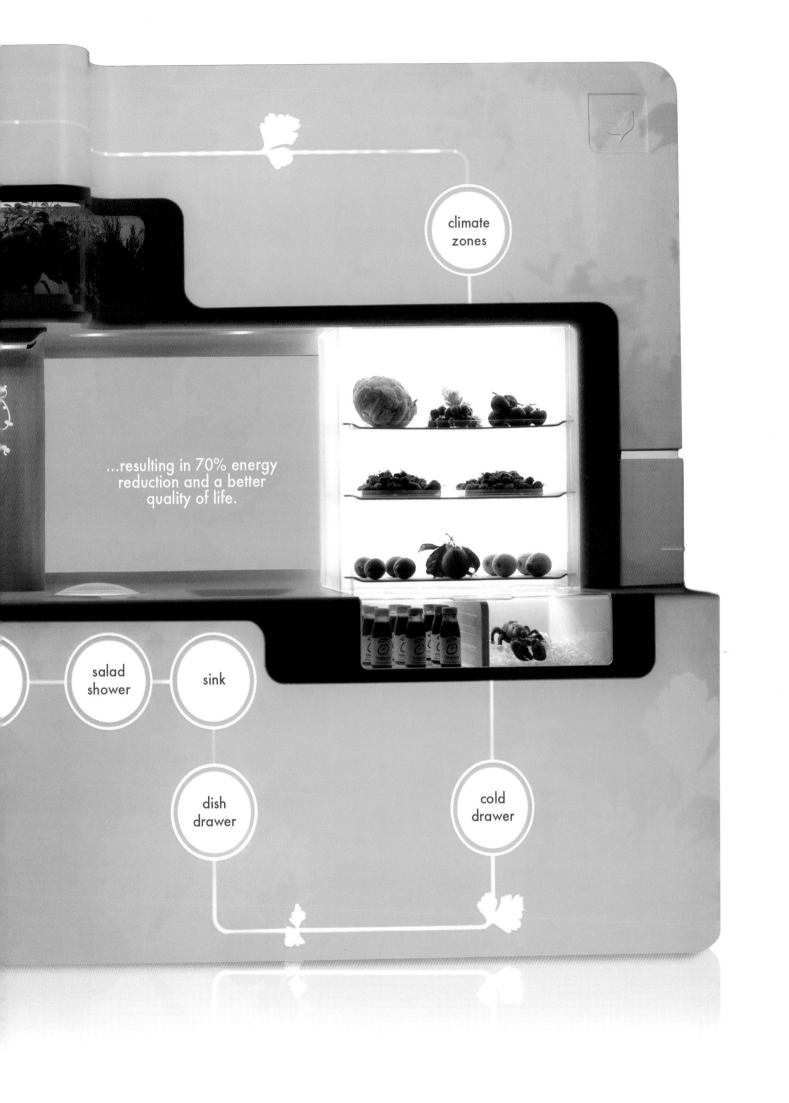

...resulting in 70% energy reduction and a better quality of life.

climate zones

salad shower

sink

dish drawer

cold drawer

Handpresso

Manual espresso maker
Manuelle Espressomaschine
Machine manuelle à expresso

design by NIELSEN INNOVATION

design by NIELSEN INNOVATION

Handpresso is a dream come true for coffeeholics. This portable, manual espresso machine makes it possible to prepare a real espresso anywhere. Because of its linear design and the lack of certain components of traditional machines, the product is compact (8.5 x 4 x 2.8"), and lightweight (16.8 oz) and easy to use. The water is boiled separately and kept hot inside a thermos. When it is poured into the machine it reaches the same pressure as conventional machines (16 bars) thanks to the use of a hand pump, and it flows into a cup through an E.S.E. paper coffee pod, which is widely available on the market. With its lack of electrical components and simple design, Handpresso is not only unique for its convenience but also for the energy it saves.

Für alle Kaffeesüchtigen ist Handpresso ein Traum, der wahr geworden ist. Mit dieser tragbaren Kaffeemaschine ist die Espressozubereitung jederzeit und überall möglich. Das lineare Design und der Verzicht auf bestimmte Komponenten herkömmlicher Kaffeemaschinen ermöglichen die geringen Maße von 22 x 10 x 7 cm und das leichte Gewicht von 476 g. Die Handhabung bleibt dennoch einfach. Mit einer manuellen Pumpe wird das separat erhitzte Wasser auf den für Kaffeemaschinen üblichen Druck von 16 Bar gebracht. Es fließt dann durch ein E.S.E.-Pad in die Tasse. Handpresso besitzt keine elektrischen Bauteile und wechselt somit von der Kategorie der elektrischen Haushaltsgeräte zu den „Handhaltgeräten".

www.handpresso.com

Pour tous les accros au café, Handpresso est un rêve devenu réalité :
avec cette version portable et manuelle de la machine à café, se
préparer un véritable expresso n'importe où devient possible.
Grâce à un design linéaire et à l'élimination de certains composants
présents dans les machines traditionnelles, ce produit est petit
(22 x 10 x 7 cm) et léger (476 g), sans être pour autant difficile à
utiliser. Par l'intermédiaire d'une pompe manuelle, l'eau,
chauffée à part et maintenue à température dans un thermos,
atteint la même pression que les machines conventionnelles
(16 bars) et s'écoule dans la tasse à travers un filtre de type E.S.E.,
disponible sur le marché. Sans aucun composant électrique,
Handpresso abandonne la catégorie de l'électroménager pour
entrer parmi les « mano-ménagers ».

**Patrick Château and David Petitdemange
(Nielsen Innovation) for Handpresso (France)
2007**

47

Local River

In-home food-production system
Private Lebensmittelproduktion
Système d'auto-alimentation

In its conception of Local River, Artist Space was inspired by the "locavore" movement that was started in California to invite to the consumption of food that is exclusively local and thus always fresh. Rather than just decoration, as one might expect, this sophisticated and provocative aquarium of hothouse plants is primarily intended for the breeding of plants and fish destined for household consumption. Just as in nature, Local River needs no external intervention in order to work. In fact, the relationship that is established between the floral and ichthyic systems creates a self-sufficient biotope: the nitrates in the fish excrement fertilize the plants, which in turn act as filters to re-clean the water. Both the attractive design and the savings tied to in-home food-production could even cause one to forget the unusual way this aquarium is used.

Dieses Aquarium erhielt seinen Namen in Anlehnung an die kalifornische Bewegung „Locavores". Anhänger dieser Bewegung konsumieren nur Lebensmittel, die in einem kleinen Umkreis von ihrem Wohnort produziert werden und die Umwelt nur wenig belasten. Das raffinierte und gleichzeitig provozierende Projekt Local River wurde von Artist Space vorgestellt. Es dient nicht der Dekoration wie man annehmen könnte, sondern vielmehr der Pflanzen- und Fischhaltung für den privaten Verbrauch. Local River erfordert keine äußeren Eingriffe. Die Pflanzen in den Glasbehältern über dem Aquarium und die Fische bilden ein eigenständiges Biotop, genau wie in der Natur: die nitratreichen Ausscheidungen der Fische dienen als Dünger für die Pflanzen, die wiederum mit ihren Wurzeln das Wasser filtern und säubern. Sowohl das attraktive Design wie auch die mit der häuslichen Pflanzen- und Fischhaltung verbundenen Einsparungen lassen vielleicht den ungewöhnlichen Zweck dieses Aquariums vergessen.

En s'inspirant des Locavores, un mouvement californien invitant à la consommation d'alimentation exclusivement locale et ainsi toujours fraîche, Artist Space propose avec Local River un aquarium-serre aussi sophistiqué que provocateur. Il n'est pas réellement destiné à la décoration comme on pourrait s'y attendre, mais à l'élevage de plantes et poissons, destinés à la consommation quotidienne. Le fonctionnement de Local River ne requiert aucune intervention extérieure, comme à l'état naturel. Le rapport qui s'instaure entre les plantes et les poissons crée en réalité un biotope autosuffisant : le nitrate présent dans les déjections des poissons sert d'engrais aux plantes, qui à leur tour agissent comme un filtre purifiant l'eau. Le design attrayant, d'une part, et les économies liées à l'élevage domestique, de l'autre, feront peut-être oublier l'utilisation insolite de cet aquarium.

www.mathieulehanneur.com

Mathieu Lehanneur in collaboration with Anthony Van Den Bossche for Artists Space (USA)
2008
prototype

BioLogic

Washing machine with plants
Waschmaschine mit Pflanzen
Lave-linge avec plantes

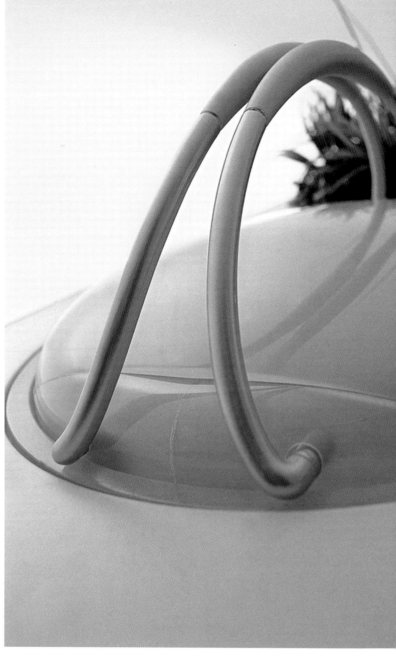

The name says it all. In this intelligent and sustainable washing machine, nature in fact works in the service of logic through a system of macrophyte purification. The hydroponic plants placed between the six laundry pods filter the water of the substances released by detergents so they are prevented from polluting the waste water. The six pods allow the laundry to be distributed according to type so that several cycles can run at once. BioLogic sprouted from an analysis of the interrelationships between product, environment and functioning times, based on the simple, logical principle that results are improved and guaranteed when operations are carried out with patience and care. In this sense, washing speed takes a back seat to sustainable functionality.

Im Namen steckt bereits das Konzept: Bei dieser intelligenten und umweltschonenden Waschmaschine arbeitet nämlich die Natur im Dienste der Logik. Zwischen den sechs Wäschebehältern befinden sich Zuchtpflanzen, die das Wasser nach dem Waschvorgang von den im Waschmittel enthaltenen Schadstoffen reinigen. In den Behältern kann die Wäsche nach Bedarf verteilt werden. Dadurch können gleichzeitig mehrere Waschzyklen durchgeführt werden. Das Projekt entstand durch die Untersuchung der Wechselwirkungen zwischen Produkt, Umwelt und Betriebsdauer. BioLogic basiert auf dem einfachen aber auch logischen Prinzip, dass Ruhe und Konzentration bei der Ausführung einer Tätigkeit ein bestimmtes Ergebnis gewährleisten und sogar verbessern können. In diesem Sinne wird der nachhaltigen Funktionalität eine wichtigere Rolle zugesprochen als der Schnelligkeit des Waschvorgangs.

Le nom est en soi tout un programme : dans ce lave-linge intelligent et respectueux de l'environnement, la nature travaille au service de la logique. Les plantes hydroponiques, placées entre les cellules destinées au linge, servent à filtrer l'eau de lavage (par phytodépuration) et débarrassent les eaux usées des substances polluantes des lessives. La présence de six cellules permet de répartir le linge par catégorie et de réaliser plusieurs cycles de lavage en même temps. Issue de l'analyse des corrélations entre produit, environnement et temps de fonctionnement, BioLogic se base sur un principe aussi simple que logique : réaliser une action avec calme et attention garantit un meilleur résultat. En ce sens, la rapidité de lavage passe au second plan face à la fonctionnalité durable.

www.project-f.whirlpool.co.uk

Ruben Castano, Patrizio Cionfoli and Giuseppe Netti for GCD, Whirlpool Europe
2002
prototype

iSave

Consumption indicator
Wasserverbrauchsanzeige
Indicateur de consommation

While there is increasing talk of reducing the consumption of raw materials, it is not easy to change attitudes, especially when there is no clear or direct idea of how much is being consumed. To make up for this problem when it comes to water, Chinese designer Yu Guoqun developed iSave, a consumption indicator that is installed on faucets and shows immediately how much water comes through each time it is used. As it runs through the turbines that help calculate the amount consumed, the water also feeds the LED display where the numbers appear. So even if it does not reduce consumption directly, quantifying the water flow draws attention to the consequences that daily actions have on the environment.

Oft spricht man von der Notwendigkeit, kostbare Rohstoffe wie z. B. Wasser nicht zu verschwenden. Gleichzeitig aber ist es nicht leicht, die eigenen Gewohnheiten zu ändern, vor allem wenn der Verbrauch nicht exakt messbar oder sofort erkennbar ist. Um dieses Problem beim Wasserverbrauch zu lösen, hat der chinesische Designer Yu Guoqun die Verbrauchsanzeige iSave entwickelt. Diese wird auf dem Wasserhahn angebracht und zeigt bei jeder Benutzung die verbrauchte Wassermenge an. iSave verbraucht keine zusätzliche Energie, sondern wird von einer Mini-Turbine angetrieben, die durch den Wasserdruck aktiviert wird. Zwar wird der Wasserverbrauch durch diese Neuheit nicht unmittelbar verringert, aber die Quantifizierung sorgt dafür, dass sich der Verbraucher der täglichen Umweltbelastung bewusst wird.

Si d'un côté la réduction de la consommation des matières premières telles que l'eau est un sujet récurrent, de l'autre, changer ses habitudes reste difficile, surtout lorsque l'on ne connaît pas précisément les quantités consommées. Pour remédier à ce problème, le designer chinois Yu Guoqun a développé iSave, un indicateur de consommation à installer sur le robinet. Il permet de visualiser immédiatement la quantité d'eau consommée à chaque utilisation. De plus, l'eau coulant dans les turbines servant au calcul des consommations alimente les DEL de l'écran où apparaissent les chiffres. Ainsi, bien que ne réduisant pas la consommation en soi, la quantification du flux d'eau permet de prendre conscience des conséquences de nos gestes quotidiens sur l'environnement.

www.beingobject.com

Yu Guoqun for Being Object Design (China)
2006
prototype

Bel-Air

Air purifier
Luftreiniger
Purificateur d'air

www.mathieulehanneur.com

Mathieu Lehanneur in collaboration
with David Edwards, Harvard University
for Le Laboratoire Paris (France)
2007

Considering all the harmful substances in the air, home environments are not always as protected as is commonly believed—suffice it to think of the formaldehyde found in some disinfectants. As a solution, French designer Mathieu Lehanneur offers Bel-Air, an air-purifier for interiors that uses the filtering capabilities of certain plants. In the research conducted by NASA in the 1980s on how to improve the air quality on board space shuttles, the leaves and roots of plants like gerbera, philodendron and spathiphyllum were found to be particularly suitable for this purpose. The plants are placed inside this futuristic apartment purifier that works like a living filter and therefore needs no electrical replacement parts. Bel-Air's designer calls it the "tutelary deity" of the house.

Betrachtet man die vielen verschiedenen Schadstoffe in der Luft genauer, ist auch das häusliche Umfeld bei weitem nicht so geschützt wie man meinen könnte – man denke z. B. an den Schadstoff Formaldehyd in einigen Pflege- und Reinigungsmitteln. Mit Bel-Air entwickelte der französische Designer Mathieu Lehanneur eine Lösung zur Luftreinigung der Innenräume, die auf der Filterfähigkeit bestimmter Pflanzen beruht. In den 1980er Jahren forschte die NASA nach einem System zur Verbesserung der Luftqualität auf Raumschiffen. Dabei entdeckte man, dass Blätter und Wurzeln von bestimmten Pflanzen wie Gerbera, *Philodendron* und *Spathiphyllum* besonders geeignet sind. Die Pflanzen werden in dieser futuristischen Kapsel eingesetzt und verwandeln sie in einen „lebenden" Filter. Für Bel-Air werden keine Austauschfilter benötigt.

Si l'on considère les substances nocives présentes dans l'air, l'environnement domestique n'est pas aussi protégé que l'on croit (il suffit de penser aux formaldéhydes présents dans certains désinfectants). Bel-Air est la solution proposée par le designer français Matthieu Lehanneur pour purifier l'air de notre intérieur grâce à la capacité filtrante de certaines plantes. Selon les recherches conduites par la NASA dans les années 1980 pour améliorer la qualité de l'air dans les navettes spatiales, les feuilles et racines de plantes comme le *gerbera*, le *philodendron* et le *spathiphyllum* se sont avérées particulièrement adaptées. Les plantes sont placées à l'intérieur de ce dépurateur d'appartement aux allures futuristes, qui fonctionne comme un filtre vivant et n'a besoin d'aucune pièce électrique de rechange. Bel-Air est défini par ses créateurs comme le « dieu tutélaire » de nos maisons.

Furniture

Möbel
Ameublement

Introduction

Einleitung
Introduction

Indoor furniture tends to be made in such a way that it satisfies needs like organization, space-optimization and the storing of goods. However, in the continuous modernization of society, these principles are often superseded by the must-have consumer status symbol. Original function is therefore increasingly determined by appearance, thereby becoming a distinguishing mark of a certain social class.

Parallel to this development in the furniture industry, with its all-too-often negative consequences for the environment, trends in sustainable development that show how protecting our natural resources does not have to mean forgoing aesthetics. In our society, which has gotten so used to the politics of consumerism and needs productive, social and economic change, this tendency is asserting itself more all the time. As a result, the products selected here are just a sample of the many functional, aesthetic and environmental solutions available on the market or in the experimental phase. They all, however, take principles of ecodesign into account, including reducing and compressing (Ori.Tami), designing for components (EVA), mono-materials (Loco), bio-based materials (especially unusual ones for the industry, like cornstarch for the Starch Chair) and recycled materials (Cabbage Chair).

The six types presented here are: kitchens, tables, chairs, lamps, various furnishing elements and containers.

Inneneinrichtung entsteht aus dem Bedürfnis nach Ordnung, Platzoptimierung und Aufbewahrungsmöglichkeiten. Die Modernisierung der Gesellschaft hatte zur Folge, dass diese Idee von dem Wunsch nach Konsum und Statussymbolen verdrängt wurde. Die ursprüngliche Funktion wird immer mehr durch das Design bestimmt und als Ausdruck einer bestimmten Gesellschaftsschicht verstanden.

Neben dieser Entwicklung, die häufig negative Folgen für die Umwelt mit sich bringt, zeigt sich ein neuer Trend zu nachhaltigen Lösungen, die vor allem die natürlichen Ressourcen schonen und gleichzeitig die Ästhetik wahren. In unserer Gesellschaft, die sich inzwischen der Konsumpolitik ergeben hat und einen produktiven, sozialen und wirtschaftlichen Wechsel benötigt, hat sich dieser Trend noch verstärkt. Die hier vorgestellten Möbel zeigen die Bandbreite an funktionellen, ästhetischen und umweltfreundlichen Lösungen, die bereits auf dem Markt bestehen oder sich in der Entwurfsphase befinden. Sie alle stehen für bestimmte Grundsätze des Ökodesigns. Ori.Tami steht für eine kompakte Gestaltung, EVA für Bauteiledesign, Loco für die Verwendung nicht sichtbarer Materialien oder der Starch Chair für die Verwendung ungewöhnlicher Materialien wie Maisstärke.

Die hier vorgestellten Typologien sind: Küchen, Tische, Sitzmöbel, Lampen, verschiedene Ausstattungselemente und Behälter.

Les produits entrant dans la catégorie ameublement naissent d'une nécessité : satisfaire les besoins de rangement, d'optimisation de l'espace et de conservation des biens. Dans notre société en constante modernisation, le must du consumérisme qu'est le signe extérieur de richesse est venu se superposer à ces besoins. La fonction originelle de l'objet est de plus en plus déterminée par son apparence et devient un élément distinctif d'une classe sociale donnée.

Parallèlement à cette évolution, dont les conséquences sur l'environnement sont trop souvent négatives, le secteur de l'ameublement a aussi vu l'apparition de niches tournées vers le développement durable. Celles-ci prouvent qu'il est possible de sauvegarder les ressources naturelles tout en maintenant un certain niveau d'esthétique. Les produits sélectionnés ici ne représentent qu'une petite part des nombreuses solutions fonctionnelles, esthétiques et environnementales aujourd'hui présentes sur le marché ou en phase d'expérimentation. Tous, cependant, respectent les principes de l'écodesign, parmi lesquels la réduction des dimensions (Ori.Tami), le design de composants (EVA), les matériaux invisibles (Loco), les matériaux visibles (surtout dans l'utilisation des matériaux inhabituels pour le secteur, comme l'amidon de maïs pour le fauteuil Starch Chair) et matériaux recyclés (Cabbage Chair).

Les types d'objets présentés ici sont des cuisines, des tables, des chaises, des lampes, des éléments d'ameublement divers et des récipients.

EVA

Convertible kitchen
Modulare Küche
Cuisine modulable

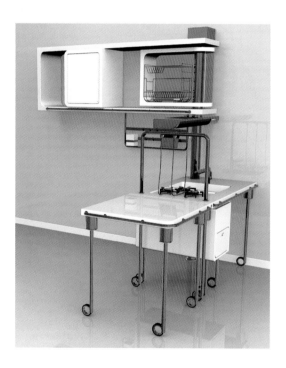

While functionality and practicality are the cornerstones of a good kitchen, the EVA kitchen console has turned these two principles into a philosophy. Its various modules have many different functions. The drying rack can also be used as a cupboard, the counter converts into a kitchen table when needed and the drawers are in a mobile trolley for greater flexibility. The design's purpose is to improve the comfort of the living environment where most housework takes place, particularly in small apartments that require flexible structures. This dynamic, simple and complete kitchen is reduced to functional and material essentials and thus reconciles well with the principles of good ecodesign.

Funktionell und praktisch sollen Küchen sein, das ist ein allgemeiner Leitsatz. Diese zwei Prinzipien wurden bei der Küchenkonsole EVA angewandt. Die verschiedenen Küchenmodule haben mehrere Funktionen: Der Abtropfständer ist gleichzeitig auch Küchenschrank, die Arbeitsfläche kann jederzeit in einen Esstisch verwandelt werden und der Küchenwagen ist beweglich, so dass ein hoher Grad an Flexibilität gewährleistet ist. Ziel des Projektes ist es, den Komfort des Wohnbereichs, in dem die meisten häuslichen Tätigkeiten ausgeführt werden, zu erhöhen. Dieser Aspekt ist besonders in kleinen Wohnungen sehr wichtig, weil dort aus Platzgründen flexible Strukturen benötigt werden. Diese dynamische, einfache und vollständige Küche wird jedoch nicht von funktioneller und materieller Redundanz bestimmt, die schlecht mit den Grundsätzen des Ökodesigns vereinbar wäre.

Si fonctionnalité et praticité sont les atouts d'une bonne cuisine, la console de cuisine EVA a fait de ces deux principes une philosophie. Les différents modules qui la composent ont plusieurs fonctions : l'égouttoir sert aussi de placard, le plan de travail se transforme en table et le chariot est mobile, afin de garantir une plus grande flexibilité. Le projet vise à améliorer le confort de l'environnement intérieur où se concentrent les principales activités du foyer, notamment des petits appartements nécessitant des structures flexibles. Cette cuisine dynamique, simple et complète ne tombe pas dans la redondance fonctionnelle qui concilie mal les principes d'un bon écodesign.

www.adrianodesign.it

adriano design for Scavolini (Italy)
2006
prototype

Kitchenette
Functional kitchen
Funktionale Küche
Cuisine fonctionnelle

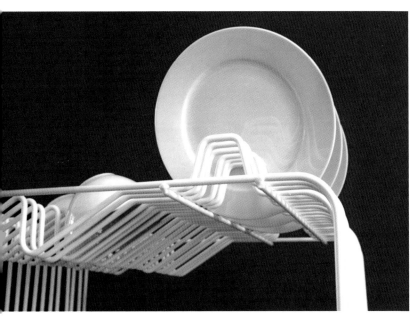

"Bare essentials" is the basic concept here, as demonstrated by the limited use of materials and the extreme functionality. Kitchenette is a modular kitchen made exclusively of plastic-coated metal wire. Fully synthesizing separate functions in one minimalist structure that has no use for aesthetic charms, this kitchen includes four elements that can be freely positioned according to space and need. With an extremely spare but consistent design, Kitchenette provocatively redefines the idea of the kitchen as being synonymous with large convivial spaces, partly in accordance with the real needs of reducing space. What it lacks in practicality during cleaning, it makes up for in the extreme conservation of the materials used to create it.

Das zugrundeliegende Konzept ist hier Essentialität, davon zeugen der minimale Materialverbrauch und die besondere Funktionalität. Die vier Elemente der Kitchenette bestehen ausschließlich aus Metalldraht, der mit Kunststoff überzogen wurde. Sie können je nach Platz und Bedarf aufgestellt werden. Die minimalistische Struktur hebt die Funktionen der Küche besonders hervor, wobei kein Raum für ästhetische Reize bleibt. Mit extrem reduziertem aber trotzdem kohärentem Design definiert Kitchenette die Idee der Küche als Ort der Geselligkeit neu. Zudem berücksichtigt dieses Projekt das aktuelle Bedürfnis nach Platzeinsparungen. Die Tatsache, dass viel weniger Material verwendet wurde, trägt vielleicht dazu bei, dass der unpraktischen Reinigung nicht so viel Beachtung geschenkt wird.

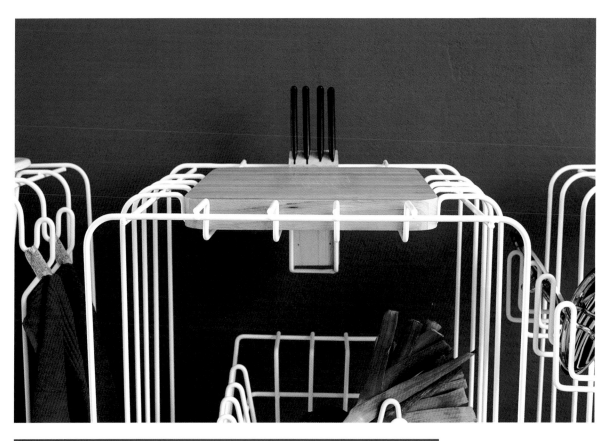

www.janjannes.com

L'essentialité est ici le concept de base, comme le montrent l'utilisation limitée de matériaux et la fonctionnalité extrême du produit. Kitchenette est une cuisine modulaire réalisée exclusivement à partir d'un fil métallique recouvert de plastique. En synthétisant au maximum chaque fonction dans une structure minimaliste qui ne laisse pas de place au chichi esthétique, les quatre éléments qui composent la cuisine peuvent être librement positionnés, selon les espaces et les exigences. Avec ce design réduit à l'extrême mais cohérent, Kitchenette redéfinit de manière provocatrice l'idée de cuisine synonyme de grand espace convivial, partiellement en accord avec la nécessité actuelle de réduire les espaces. L'extrême économie des matériaux fera peut-être oublier les difficultés de nettoyage.

Jan Dijkstra for Studio JanJannes
(The Netherlands)
2005
prototype

Tile Kitchen

Ceramic-tile modular Kitchen
Modulare Küche aus Keramikfliesen
Cuisine en carreaux de céramique

This product returns the kitchen to its basics and, by re-conceiving the aesthetic, makes it a pure sum of its essential functions: cooking, washing, preparing, hanging, preserving, cleaning and time-management. Tile Kitchen is produced entirely of white ceramic tiles and thereby offers the maximum formal intelligence with a minimum of materials and sizes. The design includes twelve basic tiles. Four are structural, including three with different angles and one to hold water. The remaining eight are functional: herb container, magnet, mortar, utensil holder, book stand, dish rack, alarm clock and towel holder. Each of these functions are thus in full view. The kitchen is also equipped with five steel burners, each connected separately to the cooking surface and therefore easy to re-position. The whole kitchen measures 158.5 x 78 x 65". However, being a "free-choice kitchen," as the company proclaims, it could also be enlarged according to need.

Die Küche kehrt zu ihren Wurzeln zurück und bildet die Summe ihrer essentielen Funktionen: kochen, spülen, vorbereiten, aufhängen, aufbewahren, reinigen und optimales Timing. Tile Kitchen besteht ausschließlich aus Fliesen und bietet so maximale formale Intelligenz bei minimalem Material- und Platzverbrauch. Das Projekt besteht aus zwölf Fliesentypen: vier strukturgebende Fliesen, drei davon mit unterschiedlichen Winkeln und eine, in der Wasser fließen kann. Acht Fliesen sind hingegen rein funktional und dienen verschiedenen Zwecken: zur Kräuteraufbewahrung, als Magnet, Mörser, Werkzeughalter, Buchstütze, Abtropfständer, Wecker oder Handtuchhalter. Die Küche ist mit fünf Stahlkochern ausgestattet. Jeder Kocher ist separat mit dem Herd verbunden und kann an jedem beliebigen Ort in der Küche eingesetzt werden. Die Küche, die sich noch in der Experimentierphase befindet, misst 403 x 198 x 165 cm, kann aber nach Bedarf vergrößert werden.

www.droog.com

La cuisine fait un retour aux sources et, en concevant son esthétique de manière nouvelle, devient la somme pure et simple de ses fonctions essentielles : cuisiner, laver, préparer, suspendre, conserver, nettoyer et gérer le temps. Tile Kitchen se présente sous forme de carreaux de céramique et combine ainsi intelligence formelle et dépense minimale en espace et matériaux. Le projet prévoit douze éléments de base : quatre forment la structure principale, dont un peut contenir de l'eau et trois proposent des inclinaisons ; les huit autres sont à l'inverse purement fonctionnels : aimants, mortier, porte-ustensiles, porte-livre, égouttoir... La cuisine est de plus équipée de cinq brûleurs en acier, reliés séparément au plan de cuisson et ainsi librement positionnables. Cette cuisine, encore en phase expérimentale, mesure 403 x 198 x 165 cm, mais reste une cuisine du « libre choix », car elle pourra être agrandie selon les exigences.

Arnout Visser, Erik Jan Kwakkel and Peter van der Jagt for Droog (The Netherlands)
2001
prototype

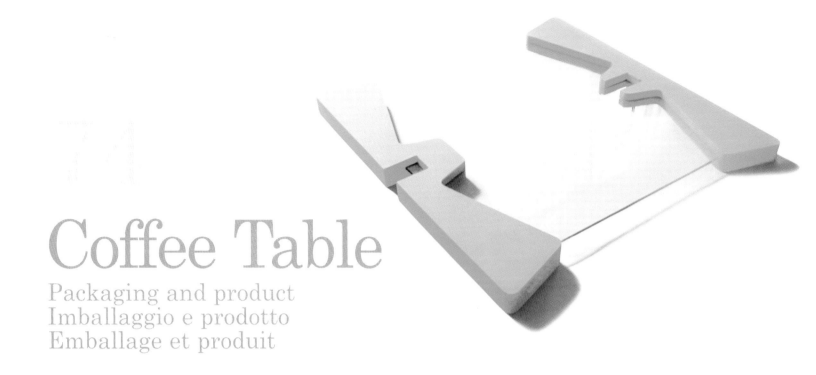

Coffee Table

Packaging and product
Imballaggio e prodotto
Emballage et produit

Packaging is traditionally conceived mainly for "single use," to be discarded as soon as the purchased object has reached its destination. Coffee Table shows how it can become instead an integral part of the object itself, thereby avoiding useless waste. The two colored parts that make up this unusual packaging are made of EPP (expanded polypropylene) and have thin slits into which the glass surface is inserted for transport and storage. Once they have served their protective function, the pieces can be easily assembled at home to create a support for the sheet of glass that, with its weight, stabilizes this amusingly-designed little table.

Die Verpackung wird mehrheitlich als „Einweg-Gegenstand" betrachtet, den man, sobald die Ware ihr Bestimmungsziel erreicht hat oder ausgepackt wurde, wegwirft. Beim Coffee Table ist es anders: die Verpackung wird zum Bestandteil des Möbelstücks selbst und unnötige Abfälle werden vermieden. Die beiden farbigen Elemente dieses ungewöhnlichen Packagings bestehen aus EPP (expandiertes Polypropylen). Schmale Kerben an den Seiten schützen die Ablagefläche aus Glas während des Transports und der Zwischenlagerung. Diese einzelnen Bestandteile werden dann zu Hause auf einfache Weise zusammengebaut. Sie bilden den stützenden Teil für die Glasplatte. Stabilität erhält der Tisch zudem durch das Gewicht der Glasplatte.

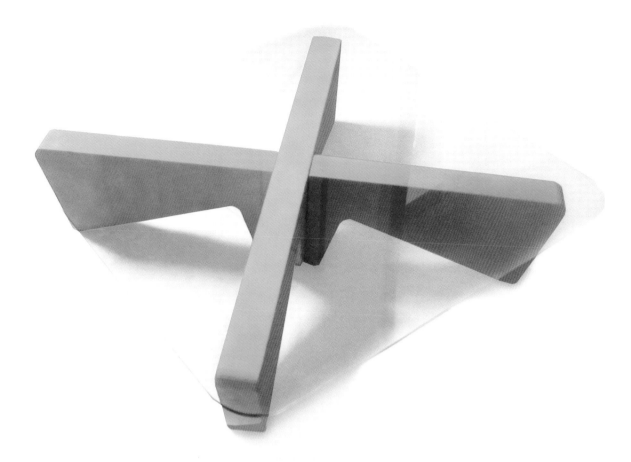

Un packaging est la plupart du temps conçu à « usage unique » : l'emballage est jeté dès son contenu arrivé à destination. Coffee Table montre que l'emballage peut au contraire devenir partie intégrante de l'objet lui-même et ainsi prévenir des déchets inutiles. Les deux éléments colorés qui constituent cet emballage insolite sont en EPP (polypropylène expansé) et présentent une mince fente dans laquelle vient s'encastrer la plaque de verre, le temps du transport et du stockage. Une fois leur fonction protectrice terminée, ils peuvent être facilement assemblés chez soi et constituent la base de la table : en posant la plaque de verre dessus, son poids stabilise cette table basse au design amusant.

www.studioboca.it

Studio BoCa (Italy)
2007
prototype

Tavolo Infinito
Extendable table
Ausziehbarer Tisch
Table Infinie

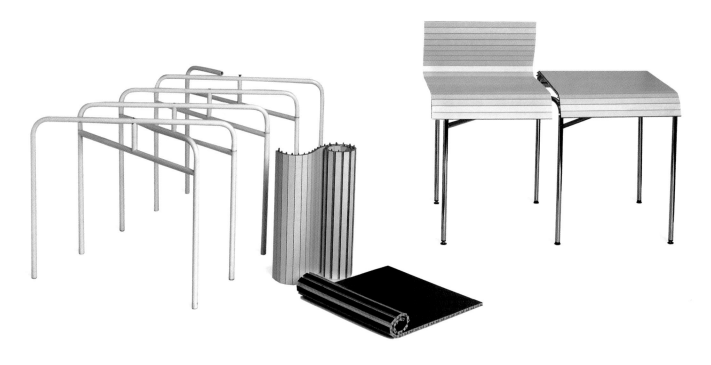

In 2004, working under her professional name Missdesign, Laurence Humier presented an aluminum table that can be extended—not infinitely as the name suggests, but according to the needs of the user. The design is intended for those who live in a restricted space but still want to host dinner parties. The folding structure is made of aluminum, an infinitely recyclable material: thus the true origin of the name. Meanwhile, the surface looks like an extendable blind that takes up very little space when the table is dismantled. The product is also indestructible: with no permanent joints, each element can be replaced in case of malfunction, so one damaged part does not compromise the whole table.

2004 stellte die belgische Designerin Laurence Humier unter ihrem Künstlernamen Missdesign einen ausziehbaren Aluminiumtisch vor. Auch wenn er nicht bis ins Unendliche reicht, wie es der Name suggeriert, kann er den unterschiedlichen Bedürfnissen angepasst werden. Das Projekt richtet sich vor allem an jene, die trotz eines begrenzten Wohnraums, nicht auf gesellige Mahlzeiten verzichten wollen. Die biegsame Struktur besteht aus Aluminium, einem unendlich oft wieder verwertbaren Material. Darauf ist auch der Name des Tisches tatsächlich zurückzuführen. Die Auflagefläche sieht wie ein Rollladen aus und nimmt wenig Platz ein, wenn der Tisch nicht aufgestellt ist. Ein weiterer interessanter Aspekt liegt in der Unzerstörbarkeit: der Tisch besitzt keine festen Verbindungs-stellen. Jedes Element kann ersetzt werden, falls es nicht mehr funktionieren sollte, so dass die Verwendung des ganzen Gegenstandes nicht beeinträchtigt wird.

www.missdesign.it

Missdesign, nom de scène de Laurence Humier, a présenté en 2004 une table en aluminium capable comme son nom l'indique de s'allonger, si ce n'est à l'infini, au moins selon les besoins. Le projet s'adresse à ceux qui, bien qu'habitant un espace restreint, ne veulent pas pour autant renoncer à recevoir leurs amis. La structure pliable est en aluminium, matériau indéfiniment recyclable (d'où le nom de la table) tandis que le plan horizontal ressemble à un rideau de fer extensible qui occupe peu de place lorsque la table est démontée. Un autre aspect intéressant de ce produit réside dans son indestructibilité : sans connexions permanentes, chaque élément peut être remplacé en cas de mauvais fonctionnement ; le mauvais état d'une partie ne porte ainsi pas préjudice au produit dans son ensemble.

Laurence Humier (Italy)
2004

Cabbage Chair

Paper armchair
Papiersessel
Fauteuil en papier

The possibilities offered by paper recycling are often unusual. This armchair was made for an exhibition with scraps of pleated paper, which is used in large quantities by the company of Japanese designer Issey Miyake. Initially, the sheets were rolled up, creating a cylinder that was then cut vertically along one side to mid-height. Falling backward, the sheets of paper created an armchair—a light and animated design that recalls the leaves of a cabbage. At the end of the process, a thin layer of resin was added to make the structure compact and prevent its deformation with use. The pleating of the paper makes it especially elastic, resulting in a chair that is comfortable, fun to look at and inspiring in its creative recycling of materials that would otherwise be discarded.

Die Wiederverwertung von Papier bietet ungeahnte Möglichkeiten. Der Sessel wurde 2008 bei einer vom japanischen Designer Issey Miyake initierten Ausstellung in Tokyo vorgestellt. Im Mittelpunkt der Ausstellung standen Objekte aus Plisseepapier, einem Material das bei bestimmten Verarbeitungsprozessen in großen Mengen entsteht und danach entsorgt wird. Die aussortierten Bögen werden zunächst aufgerollt. Der so entstandene Zylinder wird senkrecht auf einer Seite bis zur Hälfte eingeschnitten. Die einzelnen Papierbögen fallen nach hinten herab und bilden einen Sessel, der mit seinem schwungvollen und luftigen Aussehen an die Blätter eines Kohls erinnert. Eine dünne Schicht aus Harz verleiht der Struktur Festigkeit und verhindert Verformungen, die bei der Benutzung entstehen können. Gleichzeitig gewährleisten die Falten im Papier eine gute Elastizität. Das Ergebnis ist ein gemütlicher und witziger Sessel, der die Fantasie leidenschaftlicher Bastler beim Experimentieren und Herstellen neuer Gegenstände aus einem Material, das sonst für den Abfall bestimmt wäre, anregen wird.

Le recyclage du papier offre des possibilités parfois étonnantes. Ce fauteuil a été créé à l'occasion d'une exposition avec des rebuts de papier plissé, utilisé en grande quantité par la société du styliste japonais Issey Miyake. Ces feuilles ont été au départ roulées; le cylindre obtenu a été fendu verticalement d'un seul côté et jusqu'à mi-hauteur. En retombant vers l'extérieur, les feuilles créent un fauteuil au design dynamique et léger, rappelant les feuilles de chou. Une fine couche de résine a été ajoutée en fin de processus pour rendre la structure compacte et empêcher la déformation à l'usage. Les plis du papier garantissent une bonne élasticité, et ainsi le confort et l'attirance. Il invite ainsi au recyclage créatif de matériaux autrement destinés à la décharge.

www.nendo.jp

nendo for XXIst Century Man (Japan)
2008
prototype

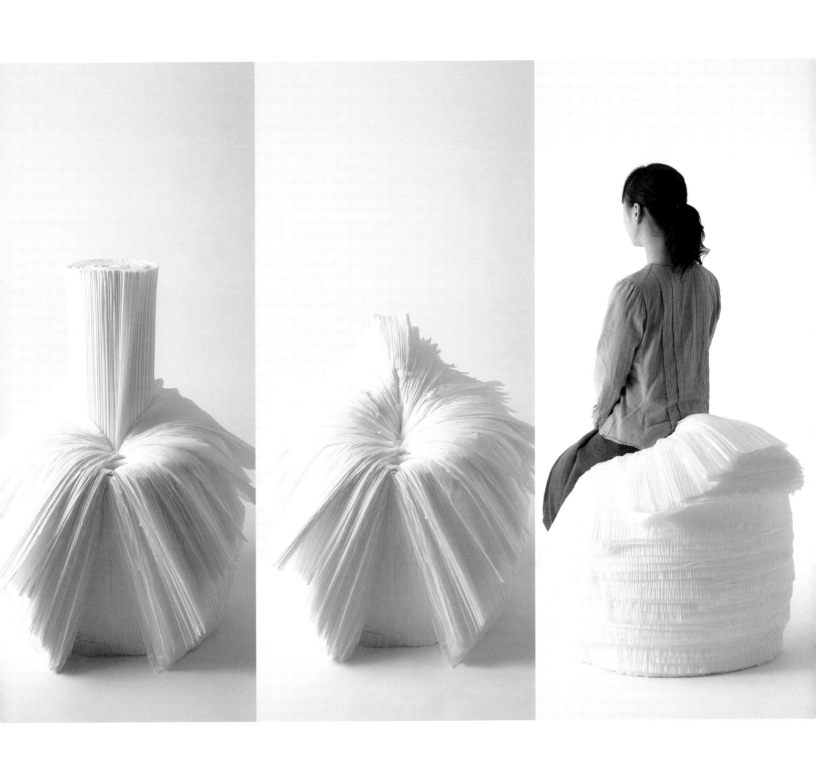

Catifa
Trestle chair
Stuhl mit Drehfußgestell
Chaise à pied

With colored polypropylene bodywork and recycled-steel trestles, the chairs in the Catifa 46 and Catifa 53 collections by Italian company Arper may look like other chairs, but in fact they are quite unique. An evaluation of their environmental impact has been carefully analyzed for every phase of their life cycle, from the choice and treatment of the raw materials to the packaging and recycling of the final product. The analysis led to the development of a complex calculation procedure that was assigned an EPD (Environmental Product Declaration) in accordance with ISO 14025, which attests to the product's sustainability at the international level. Its simple, essential form hides the precise work that went into improving Catifa's performance, ergonomic and otherwise.

Auf den ersten Blick ähnelt dieses Modell anderen Stühlen mit Sitzschale aus farbigem Polypropylen und Drehfußgestell aus Recycling-Stahl. Die Catifa-Modelle 46 und 53 der italienischen Firma Arper weisen jedoch einen bemerkenswerten Unterschied auf. Während ihrer Produktion wurde für jede Lebensphase die Umweltbelastung untersucht, von der Auswahl der Materialien über die Materialbehandlung und Verpackung bis hin zur Gebrauchsphase und Entsorgung. Diese Analyse führte zur Entwicklung einer komplexen Berechnung, die mit der international anerkannten Norm EPD (Enviromental Product Declaration), auch bekannt als ISO 14025, ausgezeichnet wurde. Dieses Zertifikat gibt Auskunft über die Umweltverträglichkeit und Nachhaltigkeit von Produkten.

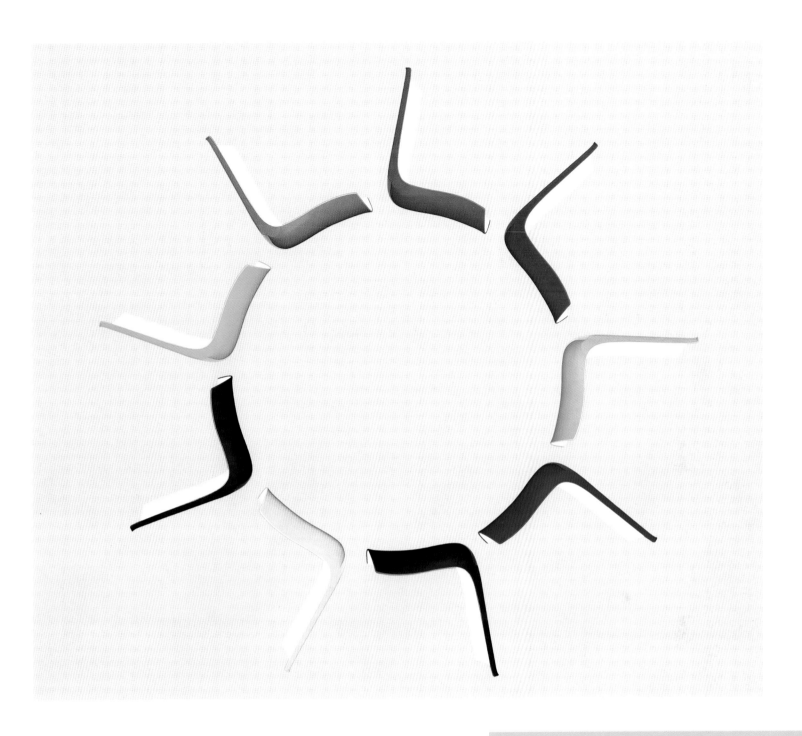

Apparemment similaire à d'autres chaises grâce à sa coque colorée en polypropylène et à son pied en acier recyclé, les modèles Catifa 46 et 53 de la marque italienne Arper ont une particularité substantielle : une évaluation de leur impact sur l'environnement a été attentivement menée à chaque phase de leur cycle de vie, depuis le choix des matières premières jusqu'au traitement des matériaux, en passant par l'emballage et le recyclage final. Cette analyse a conduit au développement d'une procédure de calcul complexe ayant obtenu la reconnaissance de l'EPD (Environmental Product Declaration). Connue aussi sous le sigle ISO 14025, elle atteste au niveau international de la durabilité d'une production. Sa forme simple et essentielle cache en réalité un travail poussé visant à l'amélioration du modèle Catifa, entre autre au niveau ergonomique.

www.arperitalia.it

Alberto Lievore, Jeannette Altherr and Manel Molina for arper (Italy)
2004

Kada
Multi-functional stool
Multifunktionaler Hocker
Tabouret multifonction

For this multi-functional piece of furniture, designer Yves Béhar took inspiration from the low table on which coffee is served on the Turkish island of Büyükada. With its changing surfaces, Kada can be reinvented daily to become either a padded stool or a little table with a painted metallic top, which can also be used as a tray. The structure is laminated with a neoprene zipper. It is sold unassembled in a flat package, but once put together, it demonstrates its capacity (19.5 x 23.5 x 30.5"). Kada was the winner of the Red Dot Design Award in 2007.

Für dieses Multifunktionsmöbel hat der Designer Yves Béhar sich von den charakteristischen Tischchen, die auf der türkischen Insel Büyükada zum Kaffeetrinken benutzt werden, inspirieren lassen. Kada hat trotz der schlichten Form vielfältige Funktionen und kann etwa als gepolsterter Hocker oder als Beistelltisch mit einem Aufsatz/Servierbrett aus Metall benutzt werden. Die Struktur ist aus Laminat, mit Scharnieren aus Neopren. Nach dem Aufbau hat er ein Fassungsvermögen von 50 x 59,5 x 78 cm. Kada erhielt 2007 den Red Dot Design Award.

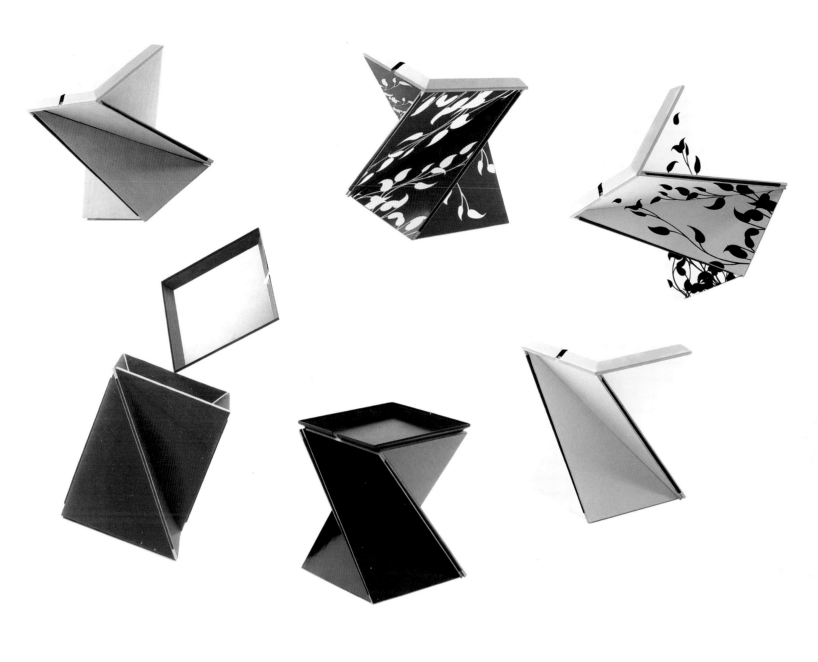

Pour cet objet déco multifonction, le designer Yves Béhar s'est inspiré de la table basse sur laquelle on sert le café dans l'île Turque de Büyükada. Avec son plateau interchangeable, Kada peut être réinventé chaque jour et passer du tabouret rembourré à la table basse avec plateau en métal indépendant. La structure en mélaminé est surmontée d'une fermeture en néoprène. Le tabouret est vendu en kit dans un emballage plat, mais mesurera 50 x 59,5 x 78 cm une fois monté. Kada a remporté le Red Dot Design Award en 2007.

www.danesemilano.com

Yves Béhar for Danese (Italy)
2006

Net Chair

Wire mesh armchair
Sessel aus Metallnetz
Fauteuil en maille métallique

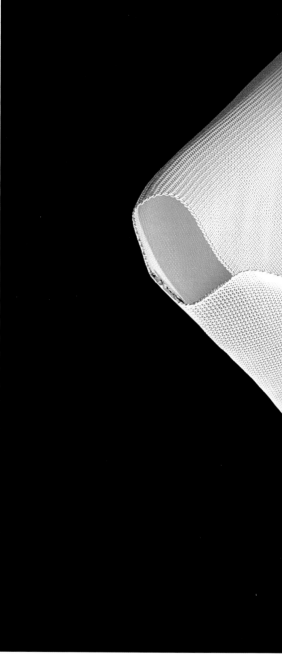

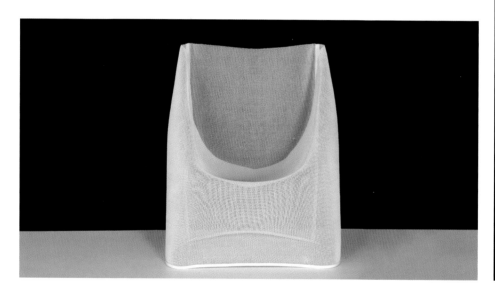

The Little Wild Garden of Love: this was the name of the visionary showroom by Italian company Moroso presented at the Milan International Furniture Salon in 2008. With its light effects and materials, the garden formed the ideal backdrop for the company's fantastical outdoor furniture, which included the Net Chair. The design for this modern armchair, which can also be used indoors, was the result of an experiment with the concept of comfort and the use of unusual materials. The semi-transparent chair measures 23.5 x 21.5 x 39" and is made entirely of wire mesh without any internal structure. The sinuous forms created by the bending sheets of reticular steel ensure its sturdiness, which sets off the ethereal lightness of its design. The points of conjunction and contact with the floor are reinforced to ensure stability. Through the use of a single material, the design is both modern and sustainable.

The Little Wild Garden of Love: So hieß der beim Salone Internazionale del Mobile 2008 in Mailand vorgestellte visionäre Showroom des italienischen Herstellers Moroso. Der mit Licht- und Materialeffekten gestaltete Garten war die ideale Bühne für die phantasievollen Outdoormöbel der Firma, darunter auch der Net Chair. Die Idee für diesen modernen Sessel, der auch für Innenräume geeignet ist, entstand durch den Versuch Sitzkomfort auch mit ungewöhnlichen Materialien zu erreichen. Der Sessel (60 x 55 x 100 cm) ist semitransparent, vollständig aus Metallnetz hergestellt und besitzt keine innere Struktur. Die nötige Stabilität, die in Kontrast zur immateriellen Leichtigkeit des Designs steht, wird durch zwei gebogene Stahlgitterplatten und durch verstärkte Verbindungs- und Bodenkontaktstellen erzielt. Auf Grund der Verwendung eines einzigen Materials erscheint das Projekt auf moderne Weise nachhaltig.

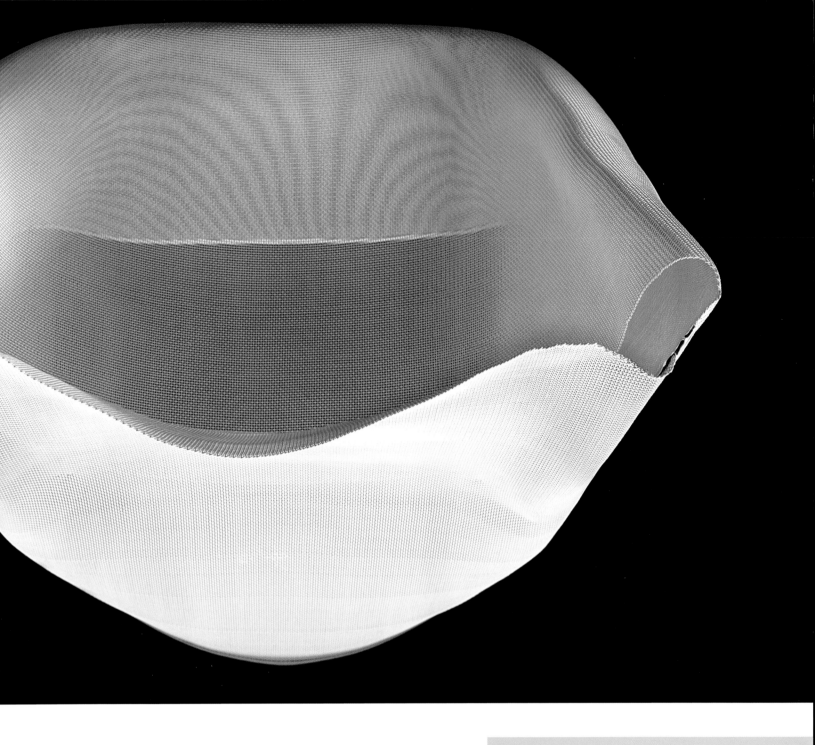

The Little Wild Garden of Love : c'est ainsi que l'on nomme le show-room visionnaire de l'entreprise italienne Moroso, présenté au Salon international du meuble de Milan en 2008. Le jardin, dont les matériaux sont mis en valeur par des effets de lumière, mettait idéalement en scène le mobilier d'extérieur original de la marque, dont fait partie le Net Chair. Le projet de ce fauteuil moderne, utilisable aussi en intérieur, est né de l'expérimentation du concept de confort sur des matériaux inhabituels. Le fauteuil semi-transparent, mesurant 60 x 55 x 100 cm, est entièrement réalisé en maille métallique, sans aucune structure interne. La robustesse, en contraste avec la légèreté immatérielle de son design, est garantie par les formes sinueuses issues du pliage de deux plaques d'acier réticulaire. Les points de jonction et de contact avec le sol ont été renforcés afin d'en garantir la stabilité. Ce projet mono-matériau s'avère également écologique.

www.moroso.it

Tomek Rygalik for Moroso (Italy)
2008
prototype

Ori.Tami

Multifunctional tatami
Multifunktions-Tatami
Tatami multifonction

 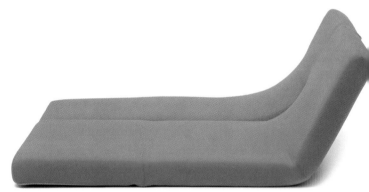

Ori.Tami is an example of how design becomes "eco" when it creates versatile and multifunctional objects, even with non-sustainable materials. The name comes from the combination of the Japanese words origami and tatami, the typical mat that futons are placed on for sleeping. With a few simple moves, the little base mattress converts into either a chaise longue, a couch or an armchair, according to need. Its chromium-plated steel structure is covered with polyurethane-foam padding and Lycra upholstering, which is particularly reinforced at the joints. Ori.Tami is packaged like a mattress, so its compact size during the transport phase further contributes to its sustainability.

Ori.Tami ist ein Beispiel dafür, wie Design auch „öko" sein kann, indem es vielseitige und multifunktionale Objekte entwickelt, auch wenn dafür keine nachhaltigen Materialien verwendet werden. Der Name setzt sich aus den japanischen Wörtern Origami und Tatami, der traditionellen Matte, auf die der Futon zum Schlafen ausgebreitet wird, zusammen. Mit wenigen einfachen Handbewegungen wird die Grundmatratze je nach Bedarf in eine Chaiselongue, ein Sofa oder einen Sessel verwandelt. Die Struktur besteht aus Chromstahl, die Polsterung aus Polyurethanschaumstoff. Der Überzug hingegen ist aus Lycra, während die Kontakt- und Biegestellen besonders verstärkt wurden. Ori.Tami wird wie eine Luftmatratze eingerollt. Das geringe Volumen und Gewicht des Produktes ist ein weiterer bemerkenswerter Faktor hinsichtlich seiner Nachhaltigkeit.

Ori.Tami montre comment le « design » devient « éco » lorsqu'il crée des objets versatiles et multifonctions, tout en utilisant des matériaux renouvelables. Son nom provient de la combinaison des termes japonais origami et tatami, le tapis de sol mythique sur lequel est posé le futon. En quelques gestes simples, le tapis de sol se transforme en chaise-longue, divan ou fauteuil, suivant les besoins. Sa structure est en acier chromé tandis que le rembourrage est en polyuréthane expansé; le revêtement est quant à lui en lycra, particulièrement renforcé sur les zones de contact et de pli. La réduction des volumes durant le transport (Ori.Tami est emballé comme un tapis de sol) est un facteur supplémentaire favorisant la viabilité écologique de ce produit.

www.campeggisrl.it

Giulio Manzoni for Campeggi (Italy)
2007

soft collection

Extendable furniture modules
Ausziehbare Einrichtungsmodule
Modules d'ameublement extensibles

This line of indoor and outdoor furniture is part of the permanent collection of the MoMA in New York. The Soft modules—including dividing walls, chairs, lamps and multi-use modular blocks—are constantly being adapted to new and temporary solutions, thanks to their beehive structure. This is what makes the modules both strong and transformable. Sizes can also vary enormously. For example: the dividing wall can stretch as wide as 16 ft, yet when folded it reduces to 2". A magnet-hooking system, easy to apply when needed, was designed to fix the modules together. The Soft line is 100% recyclable and available in two mono-material versions: paper or synthetic fabric (polyethylene).

Diese Einrichtungselemente, die sowohl Innen wie Außen verwendet werden können, befinden sich in der permanenten Designausstellung des Museum of Modern Art in New York. Die Module Soft – darunter auch Trennwände, zusammenstellbare Blöcke für verschiedene Verwendungszwecke, Sitzplätze und Lampen – können sich an neue und temporäre Lösungen anpassen. Möglich ist dies dank der wabenförmigen Struktur, die diese Module robust und veränderbar macht. Die Maße können enorm variieren: die Trennwand kann bis zu 5 m Länge erreichen, aber im gefalteten Zustand nur noch 5 cm. Magnetverbindungen ermöglichen bei Bedarf das fächerähnliche Öffnen der Module. Die Produktreihe Soft ist zu 100% recyclebar und in zwei verschiedenen Versionen erhältlich: aus Papier oder Kunstfaser (Polyethylen).

www.molodesign.com

Cette ligne d'éléments d'ameublement, intérieurs et extérieurs, est exposée en permanence au MoMA de New York. Les modules Soft (cloisons, blocs modulables à usage divers, sièges et lampes) s'adaptent à des besoins toujours nouveaux et temporaires. Leur structure en nid d'abeille donne de la robustesse aux modules et leur confère en même temps élasticité et transformabilité. Les dimensions peuvent considérablement varier : la cloison de séparation peut atteindre 5 m de long mais ne mesurera que 5 cm une fois repliée. Un système d'aimantation très facile d'utilisation a été mis au point pour permettre l'association de plusieurs modules. La ligne Soft, mono-matériau et 100% recyclable, est disponible en deux versions, papier ou tissu synthétique (polyéthylène).

Todd MacAllen and Stephanie Forsythe for molo (Canada)
2003

93

Starch Chair

Chair made of starch
Stuhl aus Kartoffelstärke
Fauteuil en amidon

Part-chair and part-sculpture, the explicitly-named Starch Chair belongs to the collection of English designer Max Lamb, who is known for his creations of hybrid handmade objects that hover somewhere between craftsmanship and industrial production processes. Made with the foam extracted from potato starch, not only is the chair completely biodegradable but also, in theory, edible. As it solidifies, the strings of starch create a rigid sculpture that can withstand considerable weight. It is up to the designer to establish its shape during the production phase. Rolling, overlapping and refolding the material creates an organic, linear form, producing furniture pieces that are at once eccentric and fully sustainable.

Der englische Designer Max Lamb, der für seine hybriden Entwürfe bekannt ist, schafft auch beim Starch Chair eine Verbindung zwischen Kunsthandwerk und industriellen Produktionsprozessen. Der Sessel Starch Chair wurde mit einem speziellen Schaum hergestellt, der durch Extrusionsverfahren aus Kartoffelstärke gewonnen wird. Bei diesem Verfahren verfestigen sich die Materialfäden und bilden eine starre Struktur, die auch größere Gewichte tragen kann. Der Schaum ist nicht nur vollkommen biologisch abbaubar, sondern theoretisch auch essbar. Während der Produktionsphase kann der Sessel jede beliebige Form annehmen: durch Aufrollen, Übereinanderlegen und Biegen der Kunststofffäden kann der Designer organische oder auch lineare Formen gestalten. So entstehen neue, exzentrische Ausstattungsgegenstände, die sich durch ihre Nachhaltigkeit auszeichnen.

Le designer anglais Max Lamb, connu pour ses créations artisanales hybrides en équilibre entre l'artisanat et les procédés de production industriels, ajoute à sa collection un fauteuil-sculpture au nom plus qu'explicite : Starch Chair. Réalisé avec une mousse obtenue de l'extrusion d'amidon de pomme de terre, le fauteuil est non seulement totalement biodégradable, mais aussi, en théorie, comestible. En se solidifiant, les fils de ce matériau créent une structure rigide capable de soutenir un certain poids. Ne reste plus qu'à son créateur d'en définir la forme lors de la production : en les enroulant, superposant et repliant, il obtient des formes organiques mais aussi linéaires et donne vie à des pièces d'ameublement excentriques et pleinement respectueuses de l'environnement.

Max Lamb (UK)
2006
prototype

Viking
Home-assembly armchair
Zerlegbarer Sessel
Fauteuil démontable

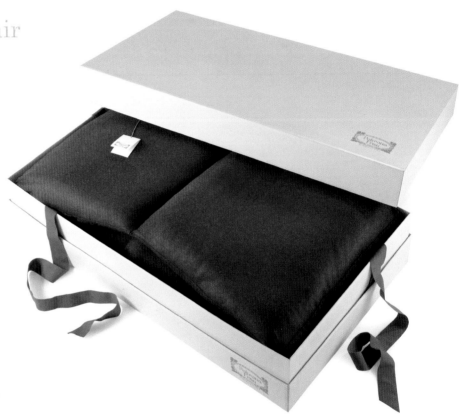

The Italian company Poltrona Frau has reconceived quality furniture by proposing a do-it-yourself version. The Viking chair is sold dismantled inside especially elegant packaging and its eight separate parts are easily assembled at home. Even the maintenance is simple. The structure is made of natural beech-wood and the seat is covered in completely hand-sewn leather, a trademark of the brand. The padding was carefully researched to compliment the ergonomic design. The Viking chair shows how interior furnishings appeal increasingly to a wise and modern public that accepts new, more sustainable styles of selling and use, without renouncing quality materials.

Mit Viking hat das italienische Unternehmen Poltrona Frau die Idee hochwertiger Ausstattung neu definiert, indem es diese Objekte in einer Do-it-yourself-Version anbietet. Viking wird zerlegt und in einer besonders eleganten Schachtel verkauft. Die acht Teile, aus denen der Sessel besteht, können zu Hause problemlos zusammengesetzt werden. Der Sessel besteht aus Naturbuche und das Sitzkissen wurde mit handgenähtem Leder überzogen. Um dem ergonomischen Design gerecht zu werden, wurde das Futter sorgfältig ausgewählt. Viking ist ein gelungenes Beispiel für Designmöbel, die sich immer mehr an ein modernes und vor allem umweltbewusstes Publikum richten, das, ohne auf edle Materialien zu verzichten, offen ist für neue und nachhaltige Formen des Verkaufs und der Verwendung.

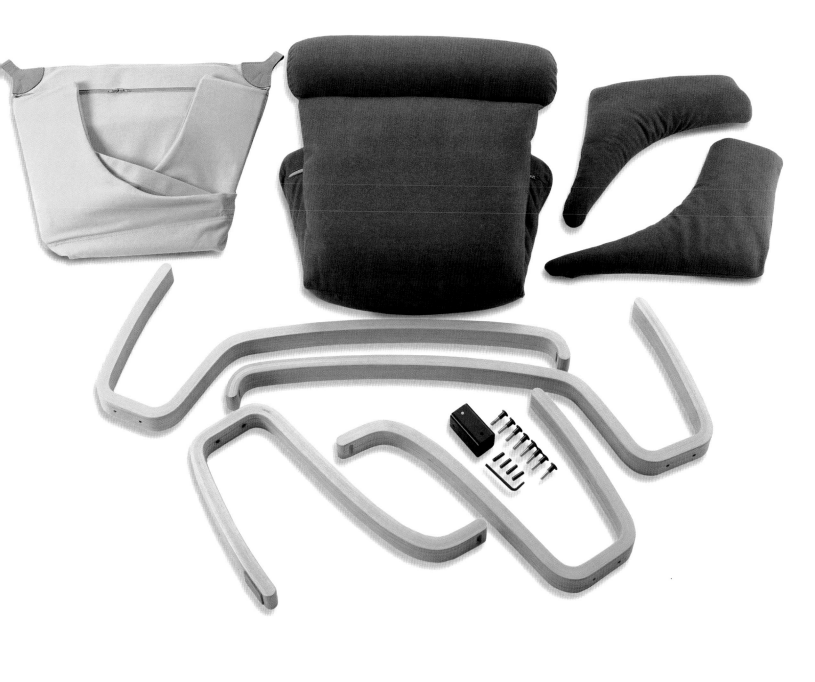

www.poltronafrau.it

Avec Viking, la société italienne Poltrona Frau a repensé l'ameublement de qualité en déclinant une version à faire soi-même. Le fauteuil Viking est vendu démonté, dans un emballage particulièrement élégant; les huit pièces qui le composent peuvent être assemblées chez soi sans difficulté et l'entretien n'en devient que plus facile. Le fauteuil possède une structure en hêtre naturel et une assise en cuir soigneusement cousue main, garantie habituelle de la marque. Le rembourrage a été particulièrement étudié pour coller au design ergonomique. Viking illustre la façon dont l'ameublement s'adresse de plus en plus à un public moderne et connaisseur, qui, sans devoir renoncer aux matériaux nobles, accepte des usages et styles de vente nouveaux et plus écologiques.

Ricerca e Sviluppo Poltrona Frau
for Poltrona Frau (Italy)
1990

Bendant Lamp

Customizable chandelier
Personalisierbarer Lampenschirm
Lustre personnalisable

There is perhaps no more intelligent expedient than transforming a product user into a co-designer. The subtle "petals" of this dynamic and lightweight chandelier made of recycled steel can be bent according to taste so that the fixture can take whatever shape the owner desires. What is more, its inclination can be changed as often as one likes, with a new game of light and shadow created each time. The chandelier is sustainable in each phase of its existence: from production—the steel is recycled directly in the production area, cut with a laser to greatly reduce waste and coated with eco-friendly paint—to transport—the packaging is two-dimensional so it takes up little space—to use— its transformable nature prolongs its life—and finally to disposal— the pieces are easily disassembled and ready to be recycled again.

Ein sicheres Mittel zum Erfolg ist es, den Käufer eines Produktes als Co-Designer einzuspannen. Bei diesem Leuchter aus recyceltem Stahl können die filigranen „Flügel" in jede gewünschte Form gebogen werden. Und dies nicht nur einmal, denn dieser dynamische und leichte Leuchtschirm kann beliebige Male neu geformt werden. Durch die jeweilige Neigung der Elemente können zudem immer neue Licht- und Schattenspiele geschaffen werden. Die Bendant Lamp ist ein hervorragendes Beispiel für die Prinzipien von Öko-Design: Bei der Produktion – der recycelte Stahl wird mit dem Laser geschnitten, wodurch das Abfallmaterial auf ein Minimum reduziert wird. Bei der Lackierung – es werden umweltverträgliche Farben verwendet. Beim Transport – die flache Verpackung ist äußerst Platz sparend. Bei der Verwendung – die vielfältigen Formmöglichkeiten verlängern seine Nutzungsdauer. Und schließlich bei der Entsorgung – die Teile sind sehr leicht zerlegbar und können recycelt werden.

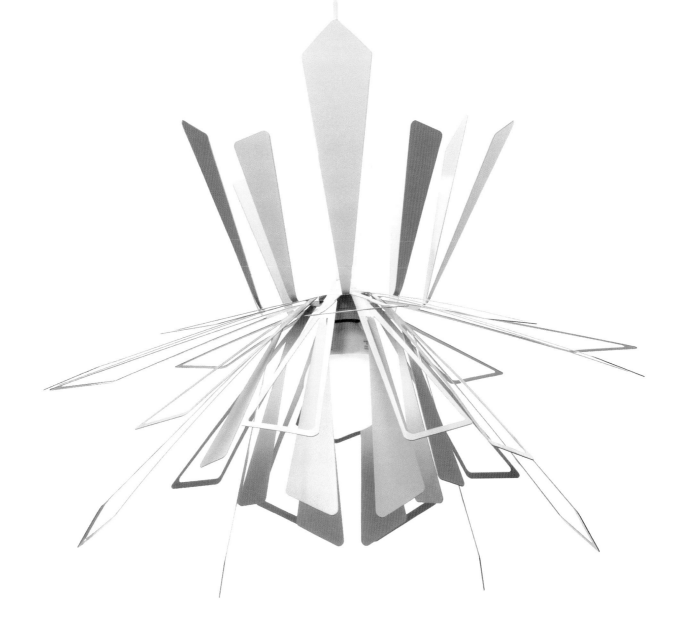

Il n'existe sans doute pas d'astuce plus maligne que d'élever l'utilisateur d'un produit au rang de co-designer. Les « pétales » aériens de ce lustre en acier recyclé, à l'aspect dynamique et léger, peuvent être pliés de manière à donner la forme désirée au lustre. Mais ce n'est pas tout : leur inclinaison peut varier selon l'envie et créer des jeux d'ombres et de lumières toujours différents. Le lustre est durable dans toutes ses phases d'existence : de la production (l'acier, recyclé directement dans les zones de production, est découpé au laser afin de réduire au maximum les rebuts de matériau, et verni à l'aide de colorants éco-compatibles) au transport (le packaging plat occupe peu d'espace), en passant par l'utilisation (sa capacité de transformation rallonge sa durée de vie), jusqu'au désassemblage (les pièces sont facilement démontables et prêtes à être recyclées).

www.mioculture.com

Jaime Salm for MIO (USA)
2007

CORON

Felt lamp
Filzlampe
Lampe en feutre

The CORON is all about essentials. Made from just a few elements, this lamp has a dynamic and modern design. The lampshade is made from just one sheet of wool felt rolled up to form a cone and secured with a wooden button. When the light is turned on, it is diffused and tinted by the shade, with no need for special bulbs. The lamp requires no special maintenance, its parts are easily replaceable and the shade can even be washed.

Schlichtheit ist das Merkmal der Lampe CORON. Die nur aus wenigen Teilen bestehende Lampe zeichnet sich durch ihr dynamisches und modernes Design aus. Der Lampenschirm besteht aus nur einem Filzbogen, der zu einem Kegel geformt wird. Mit einem Holzknopf wird die Form fixiert. Das ausgestrahlte Licht ist gedämpft und wird durch die Farbe des Filzes leicht abgetönt, ohne dass besondere Glühbirnen benötigt werden. Der Lampenschirm erfordert keine besondere Pflege und ist zudem waschbar. Er ist in verschiedenen Farben erhältlich und kann leicht ausgewechselt werden.

L'essentialité est le mot d'ordre chez CORON. Composée de peu d'éléments, cette lampe propose un design dynamique et moderne. L'abat-jour est simplement constitué d'une feuille de feutre enroulée sur elle-même en forme de cône et fixée par un bouton de bois. La lumière obtenue est colorée, suivant la teinte de l'abat-jour, sans avoir recours à des ampoules spécifiques. En plus d'être lavable, cette lampe ne requiert aucun entretien particulier. Les différents composants peuvent être remplacés très facilement.

www.mixko.co.uk

Nahoko Koyama for MIXKO (UK)
2005

Paper Basket

Waste basket
Papierkorb
Corbeille à papier

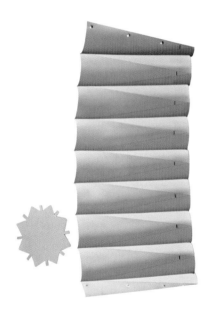

www.regenesi.com

matali crasset for Regenesi (Italy)
2008

As the name of its line, o-Re-gami, suggests, this product was inspired by the world of objects created out of paper. It is made, however, of regenerated leather, a material that has had little to do with reuse and recycling until now. The waste basket is made of two elements, base and walls, which are held together without glue. Paper Basket takes the knowledge of folding and cutting paper from the Japanese tradition to create an object with an engaging design, even in the simplicity of its form. Its two-dimensional packaging is another aspect that contributes to the sustainability of the product.

Der Name der Produktreihe, o-Re-gami, verweist bereits auf die Inspirationsquelle für dieses Designobjekt: die bekannten Faltfiguren aus Papier. Als Material wurde regeneriertes Leder verwendet, das bisher bei der Wiederverwendung und beim Recycling wenig Beachtung fand. Der Papierkorb besteht aus einem Boden und einem Korb, die ohne Leim zusammengehalten werden. Paper Basket nutzt die aus der japanischen Tradition stammende Kunst des Papierfaltens und des Papierschnitts zur Produktion eines schlichten Gegenstands, der formschöne Linien aufweist. Auch die zweidimensionale Verpackung ist funktional und trägt zur Nachhaltigkeit des Produktes bei.

Comme le suggère le nom de la ligne o-Re-gami à laquelle il appartient, ce produit s'inspire du monde des figures en papier plié. Le matériau utilisé est pourtant ici du cuir recyclé, une matière qui a jusqu'ici trouvé peu de place dans le monde du recyclage et de la récupération. Cette corbeille à papier est composée de deux éléments, la base et les parois, fixées sans colle. Paper Basket exploite la connaissance du pliage et du découpage issue de la tradition japonaise pour créer un objet aux lignes attrayantes et aux formes simplissimes. L'emballage à plat, très fonctionnel, s'ajoute à la durabilité du produit.

SoftBowl

Wool-felt vases
Filzvasen
Vases en feutre

SoftBowl is a line of containers and vases in wool felt made by one of Philadelphia's latest millinery shops. Benefits include their incredibly light weight and, most important, the fact that they can be composted. Each of the three models (Beehive, Wobowl and Swoop) is made entirely by hand with an attention to detail typical of handcrafted work. Because of this, and the natural materials used, SoftBowl production requires less than a tenth of the energy needed to make ceramic vases and containers.

SoftBowl ist ein Entwurf aus einem der modernsten Filz-Ateliers von Philadelphia und besteht aus einer Serie von Behältern und Blumentöpfen aus Filz. Sie sind nicht nur leicht, sondern vor allem kompostierbar. Jedes der drei verfügbaren Modelle (Beehive, Wobowl und Swoop) ist reine Handarbeit und wurde mit besonderer Liebe und Sorgfalt fürs Detail hergestellt. Der Einsatz von natürlichen Materialien und die Verarbeitung von Hand hat eine deutliche Reduzierung des Energiekonsums zur Folge. Die Herstellung von SoftBowl erfordert nämlich weniger als ein Zehntel der für die Herstellung von herkömmlichen Keramikvasen und -behältern nötigen Energie.

Ultime création d'un atelier de modiste de Philadelphie, SoftBowl est une ligne de récipients et de vases en feutre, légers et compostables. Chacun des trois modèles disponibles (Beehive, Wobowl et Swoop) est entièrement réalisé à la main, un soin particulier (typique du travail artisanal) étant apporté aux détails. Grâce au travail manuel et à l'emploi de matériaux naturels, la consommation d'énergie est considérablement réduite. En réalité, la production de SoftBowl requiert moins d'un dixième de l'énergie nécessaire à la réalisation de vases et récipients en céramique.

www.mioculture.com

Jaime Salm and Roger C. Allen for MIO (USA)
2007

FLAKE

Fabric modules
Papierflocken
Modules en tissu

www.woodnotes.fi

Mia Cullin for Woodnotes Oy (Finland)
2006

Finnish designer Mia Cullin came up with the idea of creating curtains, table cloths, place mats and three-dimensional structures out of small fabric modules shaped like snowflakes. Through slits at the base of each snowflake point, the modules attach together like origami creations so that shape, design and function change and adapt to the needs and creativity of the moment. A curtain, for example, can be divided into two parts to form a cover and a small mat. The modules are made of Tyvek, a flexible, rigid fabric that provides efficient insulation.

Die finnische Designerin Mia Cullin hatte die Idee, aus kleinen, flockenförmigen Stoffelementen Vorhänge, Tischdecken, Teppiche und dreidimensionale Strukturen zu entwerfen. Die einzelnen Elemente können an den Spitzen wie bei einem Origami beliebig zusammengesteckt werden. Form, Design und Funktion sind variabel und können an die jeweiligen Bedürfnisse angepasst werden. Der Kreativität sind keine Grenzen gesetzt: ein Vorhang kann z. B. in zwei Teile geteilt werden, um dann eine Decke oder einen Teppich zu bilden. Die Flexibilität der Module wird durch das verwendete Material Tyvek, einer papierfliesartigen Faser, erreicht. Dieses Material verfügt über eine hohe Festigkeit und Isolierfähigkeit.

La designer finlandaise Mia Cullin a eu l'idée de créer des rideaux, serviettes, tapis et structures tridimensionnelles à partir de petits modules de tissu, en forme de flocon de neige. Grâce aux incisions réalisées à la base des pointes, les modules s'emboîtent les uns dans les autres afin de varier la forme, le design et la fonction et de s'adapter aux besoins et à la créativité du moment : un rideau pourra par exemple être divisé en deux et former une couverture et un petit tapis. La flexibilité des modules est également possible grâce au matériau employé, le Tyvek, qui se caractérise par une rigidité importante et une capacité d'isolation efficace.

Split Bamboo
Natural coat rack
Natürlicher Kleiderständer
Porte-manteau naturel

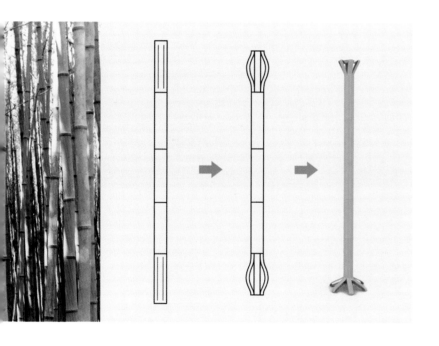

Not only is nature an inexhaustible fount of inspiration for design, but sometimes it can even become a piece of furniture. In the case of Split Bamboo, Jinhong Lin used bamboo reeds to create a coat rack, without changing the original shape. The formal and structural characteristics of this plant allow the reeds to be folded at both ends to form the hooks and the base. Indeed, if cut at a specific time during its growth, bamboo is particularly flexible and elastic. Split Bamboo shows how forms often exist in nature that, with a few adjustments, can fulfill the functions of everyday objects.

Die Natur ist nicht nur eine unerschöpfliche Quelle für Inspirationen, sie kann auch selbst zum Ausstattungsobjekt werden. Der Designer Jinhong Lin hat Split Bamboo, einen Kleiderständer aus Bambusrohr entwickelt, ohne dabei die natürliche Form des Rohrs zu verändern. Dank der Form und strukturellen Beschaffenheit können die beiden Rohrenden gebogen werden. Wenn Bambus in einer bestimmten Wachstumsphase geschnitten wird, weist er eine ausreichende Flexibilität und Elastizität dafür auf. Split Bamboo ist ein gutes Beispiel dafür, dass in der Natur vorkommende Formen mit kleinen Korrekturen die Funktionen vieler Alltagsgegenstände erfüllen können.

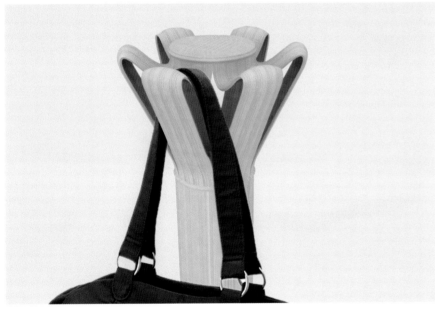

www.esign.lineoid.com

La nature est non seulement une grande source d'inspiration pour le monde du design, mais il lui arrive aussi de devenir objet de décoration. Dans le cas de Split Bamboo, Jinhong Lin a créé un porte-manteau à partir d'une tige de bambou, sans en modifier la forme originelle. Les caractéristiques formelles et structurelles de cette plante permettent de replier la tige sur elle-même à ses extrémités, afin de former le pied et les patères : s'il est coupé lors d'une phase précise de sa croissance, le bambou en devient relativement flexible et élastique. Split Bamboo démontre que la nature regorge souvent de formes qui, nécessitant peu d'ajustements, peuvent satisfaire à la fonction d'objets du quotidien.

Jinhong Lin for Tianjin Polytechnic University (China)
2008
prototype

117

Upon Floor

Coat racks
Garderobenständer
Portes-manteaux

www.stefan-diez.com

Stefan Diez for Schönbuch (Germany)
2006

Initially German designer Stefan Diez wanted to create a furnishing object out of wooden netting that could be flexible and multifunctional. The design included two versions, one for the ground and one for the wall. Several parts had to be laser-cut from a single piece of wood, with different thicknesses to create the curves. Out of this original idea, the designer developed the final project in sheet metal, which is more lightweight and versatile, and defined its function as a coat rack. The two versions of Upon Floor are produced in a single manufacturing plant with minimal variations in the production process, thereby considerably reducing the environmental impact.

Die ursprüngliche Idee des deutschen Designers Stefan Diez war die Herstellung eines Austattungsobjektes bestehend aus einem Holzgitter. Es sollte flexibel sein und gleichzeitig verschiedene Funktionen erfüllen. Das Projekt sah zwei Versionen vor: eine Ausführung für die Aufstellung am Boden, während eine zweite für die Wand bestimmt war. Aus einem einzigen Stück Holz sollten mit dem Laser mehrere Elemente in verschiedenen Dichten ausgeschnitten werden, um eine Biegung des Materials zu ermöglichen. Aus dieser ersten Idee entwickelte der Designer das Endprodukt aus Metall. Die Leichtigkeit und Vielseitigkeit des Materials ermöglicht unterschiedliche Verwendungen, wie beispielsweise als Wandgarderobe oder Garderobenständer. Beide Ausführungen von Upon Floor werden in einer Produktionsanlage hergestellt, so dass nur minimale Variationen im Verarbeitungsprozess erfolgen. Dadurch können die Umweltbelastungen deutlich vermindert werden.

L'idée initiale du designer allemand Stefan Diez était de réaliser un objet de décoration formé par une treille de bois, qui soit flexible et puisse assumer des fonctions diverses. Le projet prévoyait deux versions, une sur pied et une murale; les éléments d'épaisseurs différentes devaient être découpés au laser dans une même pièce de bois, afin de dégager des angles arrondis. De cette première idée, le designer a développé un projet final en métal, plus léger et modulable et illustrant sa fonction de porte-manteau.
Les deux versions de Upon Floor sont produites dans une seule usine :
la chaine subit un minimum de variations et réduit ainsi notablement l'impact de la production sur l'environnement.

Fontanella

Fountain
Brunnen
Fontaine

Designer Massimo Gattel developed the idea for this fountain by starting with a question: can the problem of water shortage be addressed by changing how a faucet works? The answer won third prize at the Mini Design Award 2008, whose theme was "Adding value to water." This unusual faucet is opened by turning the two parts of the metal pipe in opposite directions, like squeezing water from a piece of cloth. The pipe returns to its initial position after only seven seconds, while the waste water runs down along the sides of the stone. Like a little monument to water, Fontanella reminds us that this precious resource is not infinite and implores us in a symbolic way not to "squeeze it out to the last drop."

Bei der Herstellung dieses Brunnens ging der Designer Massimo Gattel von einer zentralen Frage aus: ist es möglich, auf das Problem der Wasserknappheit aufmerksam zu machen, indem man die Funktionsweise eines Wasserhahns verändert? Die Antwort brachte ihm den dritten Preis beim Mini Design Award 2008 mit dem Thema „Dem Wasser Bedeutung geben". Um diesen ungewöhnlichen Wasserhahn zu öffnen, genügt es, die beiden Metallrohre in entgegengesetzter Richtung zu drehen, wie bei einem Tuch, das man auswringt. Die Rohre kehren nach nur sieben Sekunden in ihre ursprüngliche Position zurück, während das Restwasser am Stein hinunter läuft. Wie ein kleines Wasserdenkmal erinnert Fontanella daran, dass diese wertvolle Ressource nicht unendlich ist. So fordert der Brunnen auf symbolische Weise dazu auf, das kostbare Gut nicht „bis auf den letzten Tropfen auszuwringen".

Pour la réalisation de cette fontaine, le designer Massimo Gattel est parti d'une seule question : modifier le fonctionnement des robinets permettrait-il de faire comprendre la rareté de l'eau? La réponse à cette question a remporté le troisième prix du Mini Design Award 2008, dont le thème était la valeur de l'eau. Pour ouvrir ce robinet insolite, il suffit de tourner en sens contraire les deux parties du tube métallique, comme en tordant un tissu. Le tube reprend sa position initiale après seulement sept secondes, tandis que l'eau descend le long de la pierre. Assimilable à un petit monument honorant l'eau, Fontanella rappelle que cette ressource est précieuse et ne sera pas disponible à l'infini. Il invite ici de manière symbolique à ne pas la « presser jusqu'à la dernière goutte ».

www.massimogattel.it

Massimo Gattel for Mini Design Award 2008 (Italy)
2008
prototype

Modular Bird House

Abodes for birds
Vogelhäuschen
Maisonnettes pour oiseaux

Known mainly for their modular architecture projects, 4 ARCHITECTURE entered the world of product design with an exceptionally small "urban" project. These modular birdhouses with their pleasing tear-drop shapes are produced by rapid prototyping through three-dimensional printing. This facilitates production in one transfer, without relying on hot soldering and more complicated assembly processes. Not only is the manufacturing faster this way, but energy consumption and material waste are notably reduced. The architects also thought of the needs of the winged community: the single modules can be aggregated to host more birds by taking their dimensions into account, since the size of the houses is decided by the buyer.

Die Gruppe 4 ARCHITECTURE ist hauptsächlich bekannt für ihre Projekte im Bereich der modularen Architektur. Ihre Premiere im Produktdesign feierten sie mit einem außerordentlich kleinen „urbanen" Projekt. Diese modularen Vogelhäuschen in Tropfenform wurden im so genannten Rapid Prototyping Verfahren mittels 3D-Druck hergestellt. Dieses Verfahren erfolgt in einem einzigen Durchlauf und erfordert keine aufwendigen Zusammensetzungsprozesse. Die Bearbeitung ist effizient und der Energieverbrauch sowie die Materialabfälle werden bedeutend verringert. Die Architekten haben auch an die Bedürfnisse der fliegenden Besucher gedacht: die einzelnen Module können zusammen aufgehängt werden und bieten so Unterschlupf für mehrere Vögel. Die Größe der Vogelhäuschen kann vom Käufer festgelegt werden.

Précédemment connue pour ses projets d'architecture modulaire, 4 ARCHITECTURE a fait son entrée dans le monde du design produit avec son projet « urbain » exceptionnellement petit. Ces maisonnettes modulables pour oiseaux, en jolie forme de goutte, sont produites en prototypation rapide grâce à des moules tridimensionnels. Cette technique permet la création de formes en un seul passage, sans avoir recours à des soudures à chaud ou à des procédés d'assemblage plus complexes. Le travail est ainsi plus rapide tandis que la consommation énergétique et les pertes de matériau sont remarquablement réduites. Les architectes ont aussi pensé aux besoins communautaires des volatiles : les modules unitaires peuvent être assemblés afin d'accueillir plusieurs oiseaux en fonction de leur taille, la dimension des maisonnettes étant définie par l'acheteur.

www.re4a.com

**Paul Coughlin, Joseph Tanney and Robert Luntz
for RESOLUTION: 4 ARCHITECTURE (USA)
2006**

Loco

Bench
Sitzbank
Banc

www.allplus.eu

Ivan Palmini for ALL+ (Republic of San Marino)
2007

Loco is a seating system with interchangeable parts that can be used to create a variety of solutions in both public and private spaces. The anodized aluminum structure facilitates the use of various materials for the seat and the back rest. Wood, leather, rubber and laminate offer a wide range of possibilities to adapt this bench to the surrounding environment and the desired use. Thanks to the bench's linear, mono-material structure, the company needs only one chain of production and assembly, thereby reducing the environmental impact of this phase. Since it can also be disassembled, Loco is easy to recycle.

Loco ist eine Sitzbank mit austauschbaren Elementen, wodurch sich vielfältige Variationen zur Gestaltung von öffentlichen Anlagen oder Innenräumen ergeben. Die Struktur aus eloxiertem Aluminium ermöglicht einen einfachen Austausch des Materials für die Sitzfläche und die Rückenlehne: Holz, Leder, Gummi, Laminat und Aluminium bieten viele verschiedene Möglichkeiten, um diese Bank an ihre Umgebung und den jeweiligen Zweck anzupassen. Dank der linearen und monomateriellen Struktur wird nur ein einziger Produktions- und Montageweg benötigt, wodurch sich die Umweltauswirkungen bereits in der Herstellungsphase verringern. Da die Bank auch zerlegt werden kann, wird das Recycling der Loco ebenfalls erleichtert.

Loco permet de créer des solutions diverses, dans les espaces publics comme en intérieur, grâce à un système d'éléments interchangeables. La structure en aluminium anodisé facilite le remplacement des pièces d'assise et du dossier tandis que bois, cuir, caoutchouc, laminé et aluminium offrent de larges possiblités pour adapter ce banc aux différents environnement et utilisations. Grâce à sa structure mono-matériau et épurée, la marque n'a besoin que d'une seule chaine de production et de montage, réduisant ainsi l'impact de cette phase sur l'environnement. Démontable, Loco facilite également son propre recyclage.

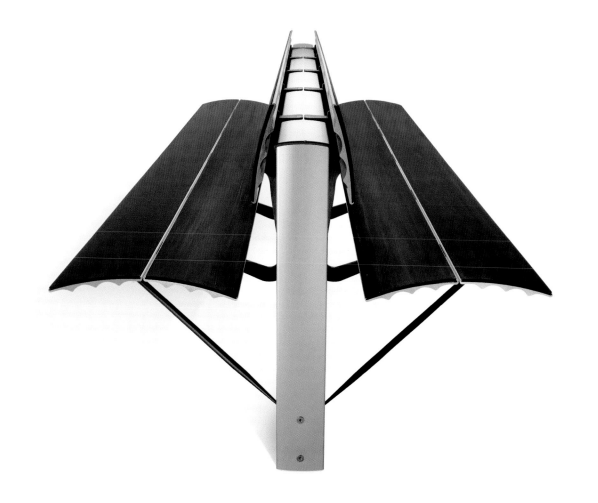

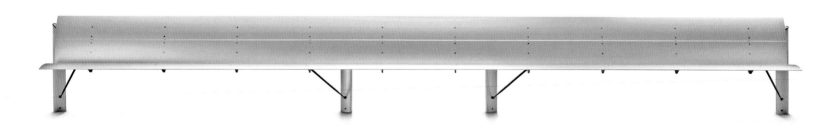

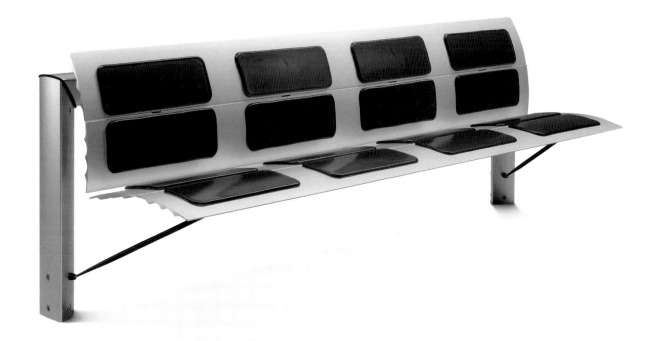

Introduction

Einleitung
Introduction

Over the centuries and the course of our socio-productive evolution, the words "light" and "energy" have acquired fundamental roles in everyday life, both for the production of goods and for social relationships. The growing need for energy has had two enormously important consequences: the increase in supply from non-renewable sources and the consequent aggravation of environmental conditions. In recent years, states and international bodies have started working together to stop the abuse of resources with laws, decrees and protocols. Two of the main objectives have been the reduction of CO_2 emissions and the spread of alternative energy sources.

The present selection is subdivided into five types: lighting, energy-saving systems, chargers, computers and their accessories, and telecommunications. The intention is to show that even small changes can contribute to the protection of resources and the environment. But it is not enough for single countries to promote and guarantee that protection. To be guided toward sustainable choices at the moment of purchase, ecological consciousness must first come from the individuals themselves.

Im Laufe der Jahrhunderte und im Zuge der gesellschaftlichen und produktiven Entwicklung haben „Licht" und „Energie" eine immer bedeutendere Rolle eingenommen. Die ständig wachsende Nachfrage nach Energie hat jedoch zwei gravierende Folgen: einen höheren Verbrauch von nicht erneuerbaren Energiequellen und die damit verbundene Umweltverschmutzung. Die Zusammenarbeit mehrerer Staaten und internationaler Organisationen führte in den letzten Jahren zu zahlreichen Gesetzen, Verordnungen und Protokollen mit dem Ziel, CO_2-Emissionen zu reduzieren und alternative Energien zu fördern.

Die ausgewählten Typologien Beleuchtung, Energiesparsysteme, Ladegeräte, Computer und Zubehör sowie Fernsprechtechnik sollen aufzeigen, dass bereits kleine Änderungen einen wertvollen Beitrag zur Schonung der Ressourcen und zum Umweltschutz leisten können. Dass einzelne Länder mit verschiedenen Maßnahmen das ökologische Bewusstsein fördern, ist jedoch nicht genug. Eine umweltbewusste Lebensweise muss in jedem einzelnen Menschen selbst entstehen.

Si autrefois les seaux n'étaient utilisés que pour transporter de l'eau, il semble également servir aujourd'hui à accumuler de l'énergie solaire, comme le prouve l'Energy Bucket. Le designer italien Stefano Merlo a pensé à doter ce seau d'un couvercle équipé de panneaux solaires. Ils rechargent des ampoules à DEL d'1 kW présentes à l'intérieur du seau en plastique. Un tel système lumineux peut être utilisé partout où la lumière manque, à l'intérieur comme à l'extérieur. Il peut être déplacé très facilement et son fonctionnement ne requiert pas de prise électrique.

www.stefanomerlo.com

Stefano Merlo (Italy)
2007
prototype

133

Light Wind

Wind-energy street lamp
Wind-Licht
Lampion à énergie éolienne

www.demakersvan.com

Judith de Graauw for Demakersvan (The Netherlands)
2006

From wind comes light. Inspired by the irrepressible wind mills of its homeland, Dutch company Demakersvan developed Light Wind, the first street lamp for private use powered by wind energy. Its large size hints at its functioning: the 6.5-ft-long blades that top the luminaire capture even the slightest motion of air, using a dynamo to transform it into light. The energy obtained is stored in a battery that can turn the lamp on when needed. Light Wind is made of wood, steel and fabric and can be used in any climatic condition, though will certainly achieve the best results in countries like the Netherlands where there is always plenty of wind.

Die niederländische Firma Demakersvan ließ sich von den in ihrem Heimatland typischen Windmühlen inspirieren und entwickelte Light Wind, die erste Lampe für den Außenbereich, die allein durch Windenergie angetrieben wird. Die 2 m langen, auf dem Beleuchtungskörper angebrachten Propellerblätter fangen jede kleinste Windbewegung auf und verwandeln sie über einen Dynamo in Licht. Die so gewonnene Energie wird in einer Batterie gespeichert, um anschließend die Laterne direkt oder nur wenn nötig einzuschalten. Light Wind besteht aus Holz, Stahl und Stoff und kann bei jedem Wetter eingesetzt werden. Die besten Ergebnisse werden allerdings in Ländern wie den Niederlanden erzielt, in denen es selten an Wind fehlt.

Du vent vient la lumière. En s'inspirant des nombreux moulins à vent que compte son pays, cette entreprise néerlandaise a développé Light Wind, le premier lampion à usage privé qui s'autoalimente par l'énergie éolienne. Ses dimensions volumineuses sont dues à son mode de fonctionnement : les pales, longues de 2 m et insérées sur le corps lumineux, capturent chaque infime déplacement d'air et le transforment en lumière par l'intermédiaire d'une dynamo. L'énergie recueillie est accumulée dans une batterie, pouvant servir à allumer directement le lampion tous les soirs ou seulement si nécessaire. Light Wind, composé de bois, d'acier et de toile, peut être utilisé sous toutes les conditions climatiques mais offrira les meilleurs résultats dans un pays comme les Pays-Bas où le vent ne manque jamais.

Mix

Desk/wall lamp
Tisch-/Wandleuchte
Lampe de bureau/murale

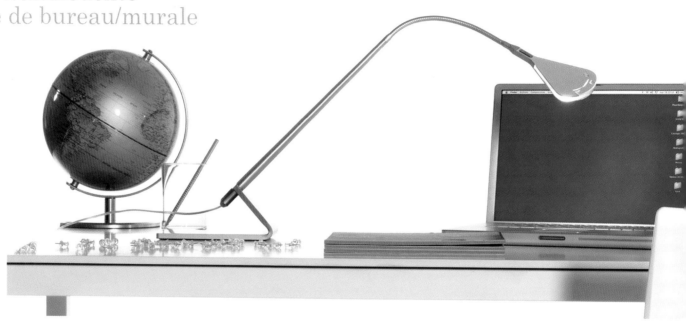

The type of light source and the easy disassembly of the components have earned this flexible aluminum lamp the prestigious prizes of both Light of the Future and Design Plus Frankfurt in 2006. Its base, in the desk version, and its support, in the wall version, are made of enameled folded sheet metal. The low energy consumption of the chip-on-board LEDs (5W) creates a pleasant light, but more importantly one that has considerable endurance. While a normal halogen bulb offers 2,000 hours of light on average, Mix reaches 50,000 hours. The lamp's head was optimized to facilitate the disassembly of its parts: the LEDs, the lens that channels light flow, the electrical circuit, the heat dissipater and the rotating filter, which regulates the color temperature, to adapt the light according to need. The Mix lamp can also be easily identified in the dark since its profile glows blue when it is turned off.

Die besondere Lichtquelle und die Einfachheit, mit der diese Lampe aus flexiblem Aluminium in ihre Einzelteile zerlegt werden kann, brachten ihr 2006 renommierte Auszeichnungen wie Light of the Future und Design Plus Frankfurt ein. Der Lampenfuß bei der Tischversion und die Halterung bei der Wandversion sind aus gebogenem, emailliertem Blech. Die Leuchtdioden-Technologie *Chip-on-Board* liefert ein angenehmes Licht bei einem niedrigem Stromverbrauch von nur fünf Watt. Am meisten beeindruckt jedoch die Lebensdauer. Während eine normale Halogenlampe im Durchschnitt 2000 Stunden Licht liefert, erreicht Mix 50 000 Stunden. Der Leuchtenkopf wurde optimiert und ermöglicht die einfache Zerlegung der Einzelteile: die Leuchtdioden, die Linse, die den Lichtfluss ausrichtet, der Stromkreis, der Kühlkörper und der Drehfilter, wodurch das Licht an die jeweiligen Bedürfnisse angepasst werden kann. Wegen ihrer blau leuchtenden Umrisslinie ist die Lampe Mix auch im Dunklen leicht zu finden.

Le type de source lumineuse et la facilité de désassemblage de ses composants ont valu à cette lampe en aluminium flexible les prestigieux prix Light of the Future et Design Plus Frankfurt en 2006. La base, dans la version de bureau, et le support, dans la version murale, sont en tôle pliée et vernie. Les LED *chip-on-board* créent une lumière agréable, à basse consommation énergétique (5W), mais surtout dont la durée est notable : tandis qu'une lampe halogène normale peut offrir en moyenne 2 000 heures de lumière, Mix atteint les 50 000 heures. La tête de la lampe a été optimisée pour faciliter son désassemblage : les LED, la lentille qui canalise le flux lumineux, le circuit électrique, le dissipateur de chaleur et enfin le filtre tournant, qui permet de régler la température de couleur pour adapter la lumière à ses besoins. Mix est facilement repérable même dans la nuit, car elle luit d'une couleur bleu.

www.luceplan.com

Alberto Meda, Paolo Rizzatto for Luceplan (Italy)
2005

Parans SP2

Natural lighting system
Innenbeleuchtung mit natürlichem Tageslicht
Système d'éclairage naturel

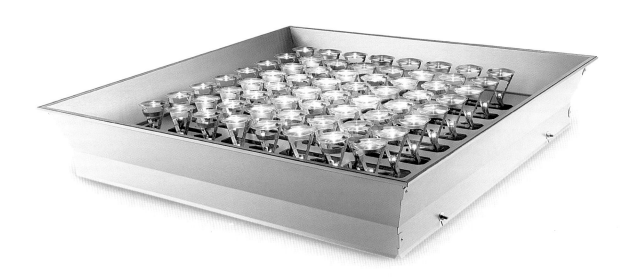

Parans is an indoor lighting system powered by solar energy. Panels are placed outside a building to capture sunlight, which is "transported," via a system of mobile reflectors, to indoor light fixtures that are specially designed with thin, flexible fiber optics. A micro computer that automatically moves the reflectors throughout the day guarantees a maximum use of light. The system is thus extremely efficient, because it increases the amount of light that can be transported from a distance, in addition to allowing buildings with few windows to enjoy natural light. Because of its innovative and sustainable design, Parans was counted by the WWF as one of the best companies in Sweden for addressing climatic and environmental issues in 2008.

Parans ist ein Innenbeleuchtungssystem, das Sonnenlicht nutzt. Die Sonnenstrahlen werden nicht in Energie umgewandelt, sondern direkt über ein faseroptisches Kabel weitergeleitet. Sonnenlicht-kollektoren an der Außenseite eines Gebäudes fangen das Sonnenlicht ein. Dieses wird von speziellen Linsen gebündelt und über flexible, dünne Lichtleiterkabel zu den für dieses Projekt entworfenen Deckenleuchten geleitet. Ein Mikrocomputer garantiert die maximale Nutzung des Lichts und verstellt die Linsen automatisch, so dass sie immer direkt zur Sonne ausgerichtet sind. Das Parans-System gewährleistet eine gute optische Effizienz, d.h. eine hohe Menge an befördertem Licht. So ist es möglich, auch in Räumen mit wenig Licht eine natürliche Beleuchtung zu genießen. Dank des innovativen Projekts wurde der schwedische Hersteller 2008 vom WWF zu den Unternehmen gezählt, die sich beispielhaft mit Klima- und Umweltfragen beschäftigen.

www.parans.com

Parans est un système d'éclairage intérieur utilisant la lumière du soleil. Des panneaux spécifiques installés à l'extérieur de l'édifice servent à capturer la lumière. Grâce à un système de réflecteurs mobiles, celle-ci est « transportée » vers les lampes, disposées selon les besoins le long de fibres optiques flexibles. L'exploitation maximale de la lumière est garantie par un micro-ordinateur qui déplace automatiquement les réflecteurs selon la course du soleil. Ce système garantit une bonne efficacité optique, c'est-à-dire une quantité élevée de lumière transportée à distance, et permet aux locaux privés de fenêtres de bénéficier de lumière naturelle. L'entreprise à l'origine de ce projet innovant et écologique compte depuis 2008 parmi les entreprises suédoises les plus attentives aux problématiques climatiques et environnementales, selon WWF.

Bengt Steneby for Parans Solar Lighting AB (Sweden)
2007

139

Sky

Photovoltaic street lamp
Solarzellen-Lampe
Lampion à cellules
photovoltaïques

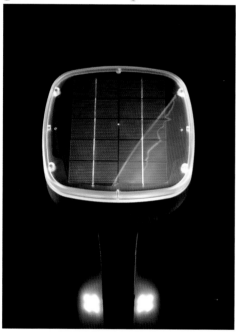

www.luceplan.com

Alfredo Häberli for Luceplan (Italy)
2007

Sky is an alternative-energy street lamp that was conceived by Alfredo Häberli, a designer who is particularly committed to researching highly technological sustainable solutions. Sky employs the latest generation of photovoltaic cells adapted for external use. The cells are gathered in the upper part of the lamp, or the area most exposed to solar radiation. They are charged all day and light up automatically at nightfall. This versatile system provides for three versions, two for the ground and one for the wall, all available with LEDs and rechargeable batteries, i.e. without the use of electrical cords or power. Even the careful choice of materials —aluminum for the structure and polycarbonate for the luminaire— demonstrates the designer's awareness of environmental issues.

Sky ist eine Outdoor-Leuchte, die mit Alternativenergie gespeist wird. Sie wurde von dem Designer Alfredo Häberli konzipiert, der sich intensiv mit hochtechnologischen und nachhaltigen Lösungen beschäftigt. Sky enthält modernste Fotovoltaikzellen, die für die Verwendung im Freien geeignet sind. Die Solarzellen sind auf der gesamten Oberfläche der Lampe angebracht. Tagsüber wird Sonnenenergie gespeichert, die bei Einbruch der Dunkelheit als intensive Beleuchtung abgegeben wird. Dieses vielseitige System ist sowohl als Standleuchte oder als Wandleuchte verfügbar. Beide Ausführungen können in der LED-Version mit wieder aufladbaren Batterien ohne elektrische Kabel, oder aber mit elektronischer Stromversorgung geliefert werden. Auch die sorgfältig ausgewählten Materialien – Aluminium für die Struktur und Polykarbonat für die Leuchtkörper – zeugen von der Sensibilität des Designers für Fragen des Umweltschutzes.

Sky, le lampion d'extérieur à énergie alternative a été pensé par Alfredo Häberli, un designer particulièrement impliqué dans la recherche de solutions durables hautement technologiques. Sky emploie des cellules photovoltaïques de dernière génération adaptées à l'usage en extérieur. Les cellules sont situées dans la partie supérieure de la lampe, la zone la plus exposée aux radiations solaires; elles se chargent ainsi durant la journée et diffusent leur lumière automatiquement lorsque la nuit tombe. Ce système versatile prévoit deux versions, au sol et murale, toutes deux disponibles avec des DEL à batterie rechargeable, sans fils électriques ou par alimentation électronique. Le choix attentif des matériaux (aluminium pour la structure et polycarbonate pour le corps lumineux) prouve la sensibilité du designer quant aux thématiques environnementales.

Solar Street Lamp
Street lighting system
Solar-Straßenbeleuchtung
Système d'éclairage public

For a city infrastructure that has become an increasing burden in terms of consumption, Serbian designer Nicola Knezevic designed a solar-energy street lighting system that is coordinated digitally. Energy is amassed during the day by a solar panel and a MoSESS system (Multi-Modal Sensor Systems for Environmental Exploration). The real innovation, however, is its use of a wireless computer network. The system channels excess energy to points that need it, since the street lamps are connected to the general electrical network. This technology therefore facilitates the flexible use of energy and provides for its application beyond the exclusive domain of street lighting.

Für städtische Behörden mit steigenden Energieverbrauch hat der serbische Designer Nicola Knezevic ein solarbetriebenes Straßenbeleuchtungssystem entwickelt, das digital gesteuert und koordiniert wird. Während des Tages wird die Energie über Sonnenkollektoren und dem so genannten MoSESS-System (Multi-Modal Sensor Systems for Environmental Exploration) gespeichert. Die echte Innovation liegt aber in einer speziellen Energiespartechnologie. Mittels unterirdischer Kabelverbindungen kann das System die überschüssige Energie, die beispielsweise die Lampen produzieren, an Orte senden, an denen Bedarf besteht. Diese Technologie erlaubt also Flexibilität in der Nutzung der Sonnenenergie, die somit nicht nur für die Straßenbeleuchtung, sondern auch für andere Zwecke verwendet werden kann.

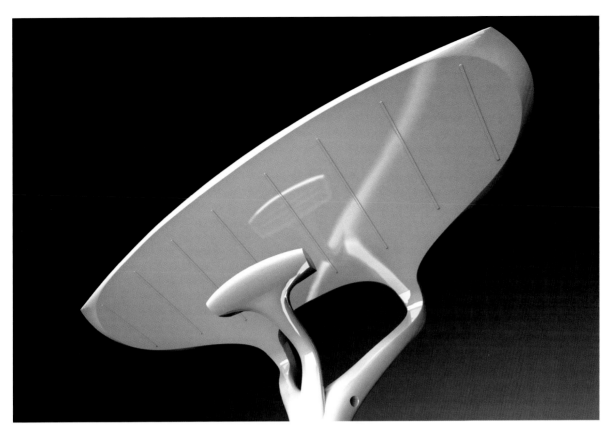

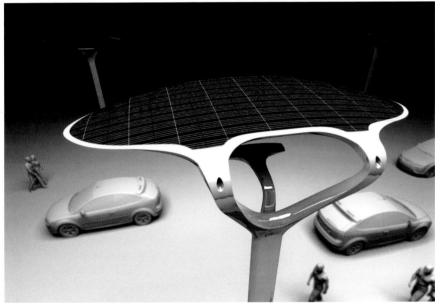

www.nikoladesign.com

Pour les infrastructures publiques plus gourmandes en termes de consommation, le designer serbe Nicola Knezevic a créé un système d'éclairage public à énergie solaire, géré numériquement. L'énergie est accumulée durant la journée par un panneau de cellules solaires et par le système MoSESS (Multi-Modal Sensor Systems for Environmental Exploration). La réelle innovation réside cependant dans l'usage d'un réseau informatique à liaison sans fil : ce système permet d'acheminer l'énergie excédentaire aux zones en déficit, car les lampadaires sont reliés au système électrique général. Cette technologie permet ainsi d'exploiter l'énergie en toute flexibilité et d'appliquer ce système dans des domaines autres que l'éclairage public.

Nikola Knezevic for Nikoladesign (Serbia)
2003

145

systemX

Lighting modules
Beleuchtungsmodule
Modules d'éclairage

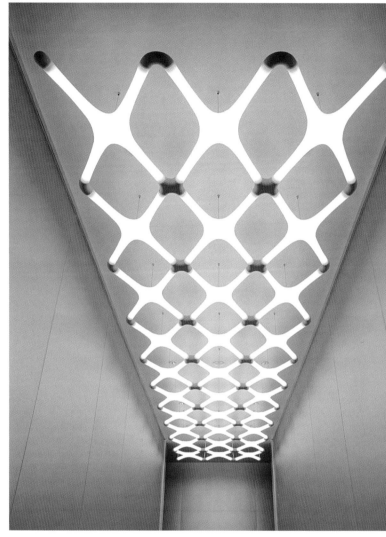

systemX is a flexible lighting system that can be transformed according to the dimensions of a space, just like the inherent nature of light. The base modules can be used to create different shapes, vertically or horizontally, thereby adapting to the needs of the environment. The innovative aspect of the lighting modules goes beyond simply their visual impact, which is strongly sculptural. Particular attention has also been paid to the visual and installation needs of the product by ensuring that systemX can be used with fluorescent bulbs, both for warm and cool light.

systemX ist ein flexibles Beleuchtungssystem, das sich wie Licht dem Raum und seinen Dimensionen anpassen kann. Die Basis-Module des Systems erlauben die Bildung neuer Formen, die sich senkrecht oder waagerecht ausbreiten. Das Design ist innovativ und entfaltet mit seiner Gitterstruktur nicht nur eine besondere visuelle Wirkung, sondern hat auch einen skulpturalen Charakter. Bei der Entwicklung von systemX wurden auch visuelle und technische Anforderungen beachtet, so können Leuchtstoffröhren sowohl für Warm- als auch für Kaltlicht verwendet werden.

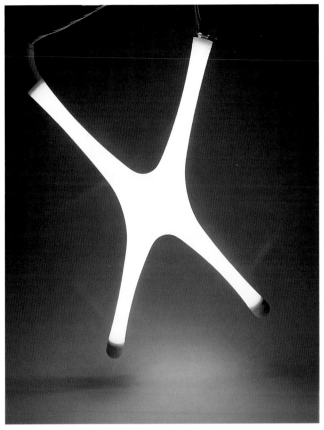

www.yamagiwa-lighting.com

systemX est un système lumineux flexible qui, comme la lumière par sa nature intrinsèque, se transforme selon les espaces et la dimension. Les modules de base qui le constituent permettent de créer des formes variées, verticales ou horizontales, en s'adaptant aussi aux besoins de chacun. Son aspect innovant ne se limite pas seulement à son impact visuel, fortement sculptural : une attention particulière a été portée aux nécessités d'éclairage et d'installation du produit. SystemX utilise des lampes fluorescentes et permet d'obtenir une lumière froide ou chaude.

Ross Lovegrove for Yamagiwa (Japan)
2005

Zeno

Combined lighting system
Beleuchtungssystem
Système d'éclairage combiné

Zeno is a suspended or ceiling lighting system that optimizes consumption through the intelligent use of both solar and artificial light. The solar light is conducted along fiber optics inside the lamp, which contains two sources of artificial light: one direct and fluorescent, the other indirect and halogen. When meteorological variations or normal alternations between day and night require it, the solar light is integrated by the other two lights. A frosted-glass refracting lens is positioned at the center of the large, visually impressive disk in which the light sources are housed. The concentrated light reflected by the lens improves the chromatic output and the intensity of the light according to the strength desired.

Zeno ist ein Beleuchtungssystem, bei dem auf intelligente Weise Sonnenlicht in Verbindung mit Kunstlicht eingesetzt und der Energieverbrauch optimiert wird. Ein außen am Gebäude installierter Lichtsammler speist das Tageslicht in Glasfaserkabel ein und leitet es zu der innovativen Pendelleuchte weiter. Im Inneren der Lampe befinden sich zwei künstliche Lichtquellen, eine direkt einstrahlende Leuchtstoffröhre und eine indirekt einstrahlende Halogenlampe. Wenn sich durch bestimmte Wetterbedingungen oder beim Übergang von Tag zu Nacht die Lichtverhältnisse verändern, wird das Sonnenlicht durch die anderen beiden Lichtquellen ergänzt. Im Zentrum der Scheibe, in der sich drei verschiedene Lichtquellen befinden, wurde eine Reflektionsfläche aus sandgestrahltem Glas installiert. Dank des konzentriert zurückgestrahlten Lichts kann die Farb- und Lichtintensität je nach gewünschter Leistung eingestellt werden.

Exploitant de manière intelligente les lumières solaire et artificielle, Zeno est un système d'éclairage à suspension ou de plafond, capable d'optimiser sa consommation. La lumière solaire est acheminée par des fibres optiques situées dans la lampe, où se trouvent deux sources (fluorescente et halogène) de lumière artificielle. Suivant les variations météorologiques ou l'alternance normale du jour et de la nuit, la lumière solaire est intégrée aux deux autres. Une lentille de réfraction en verre sablé orne le centre de ce large disque à l'impact visuel fort. Grâce à la lumière concentrée de chacune des trois sources, reflétée par la lentille, il est possible d'améliorer le rendu chromatique et l'intensité lumineuse du système, en fonction des besoins.

www.elementi.luceplan.com

**Diego Rossi and Raffaele Tedesco
for Elementi di Luceplan (Italy)
2004**

149

GROW.2

Energy-efficient wall covering
Energiesparende Hausverkleidung
Revêtement économiseur d'énergie

Still in the prototype phase, GROW.2 is the evolution of a design exhibited at the MoMA: a covering for external walls that accumulates both solar and wind energy. Its form is inspired by nature, with flexible photovoltaic panels arranged across the surface to appear, and move in the wind, like leaves of ivy. The movement thus produced is captured and transformed into energy. The panels are made of 100% recycled polyethylene and the photovoltaic cells can be recycled. Thanks to their flexible modular structure, the panels adapt to all types of buildings and are easy to replace. In fact, each "leaf" can be removed if it fails to work, without interrupting the functioning of the entire system.

GROW.2 ist die Fortsetzung eines am Museum of Modern Art ausgestellten Projektes. Bei diesem Prototypen handelt es sich um eine Fassadenverkleidung zur Nutzung von Solar- und Windenergie. Die Form dieser flexiblen Fotovoltaikpaneele wurde von der Natur inspiriert. Sie werden wie Efeublätter ausgerichtet und bewegen sich im Wind. Die dadurch entstehende Bewegung wird in Energie umgewandelt. Die Paneele bestehen aus 100% Recycling-Polyethylen, während die fotovoltaischen Zellen wieder verwertbar sind. GROW.2 kann an jede Gebäudeform angepasst werden und ist leicht austauschbar. Bei Beschädigung wird das einzelne „Blatt" entfernt, ohne dass der Betrieb des ganzen Systems unterbrochen werden muss.

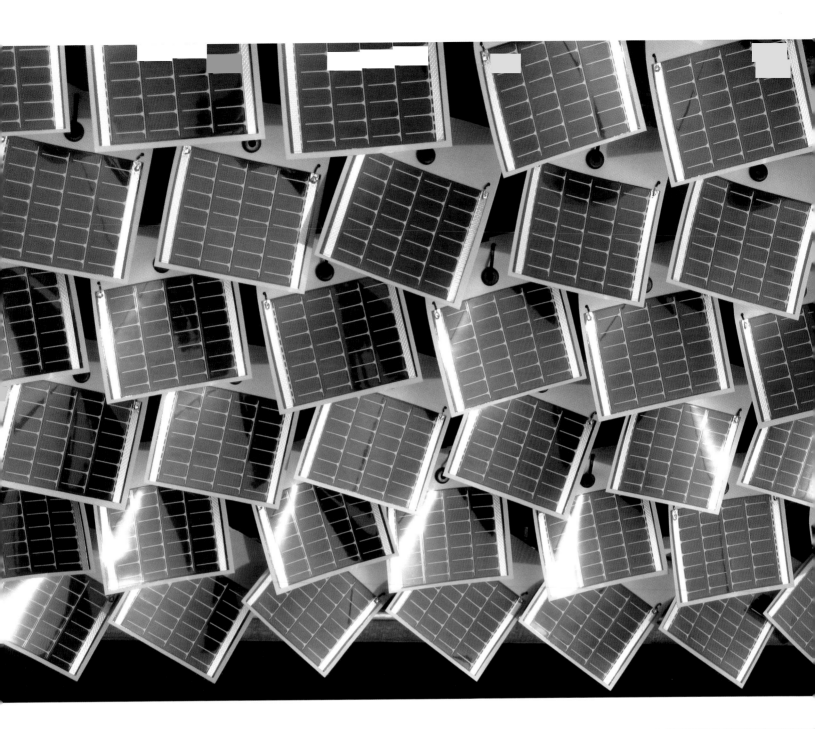

Évolution d'un projet exposé au MoMA, GROW.2 (encore au stade de prototype) est un revêtement mural extérieur permettant l'accumulation d'énergie solaire et éolienne. Imitant la nature, les panneaux photovoltaïques flexibles s'installent sur la surface du mur comme des feuilles de lierre et bougent aussi au gré du vent. Le mouvement ainsi créé est capturé et transformé en énergie. Les panneaux sont constitués de polyéthylène 100% recyclé, tandis que les cellules photovoltaïques sont, à leur tour, recyclables. Grâce à des modules flexibles, cette structure est adaptable à tous les types d'édifices et facilement remplaçable : chaque « feuille » peut en fait être retirée en cas de dommage sans interrompre le fonctionnement du système dans son ensemble.

www.solarivy.com

Samuel Cabot Cochran for Sustainably Minded Interactive Technology, LLC (USA)
2008
prototype

River Glow

Water monitoring system
Wasserüberwachungssystem
Système de surveillance des eaux

A mechanism with an impressive visual impact was designed to create this water monitoring system. Pollution detectors are immersed in water and connected to floating LEDs that, according to whether or not the water is over pollution limits, activate a red or green light that colors the surrounding water. The LEDs, which use low-tech sensors that consume very little energy, are powered by flexible, thin-film photovoltaic modules that capture solar energy during the day and keep River Glow on for about five hours at night. This creative device therefore transmits a simple, direct message to the whole population, not just the technicians who work in the field.

Für die Kontrolle der Wasserverschmutzung wurde ein optisches System entwickelt, bei dem die Schadstoffsensoren unter Wasser liegen und mit schwimmenden LEDs verbunden sind. Je nach Schadstoffgehalt im Wasser leuchten diese LEDs bei Dunkelheit rot bzw. grün auf und färben das Wasser in ihrem Umkreis in der entsprechenden Farbe ein. In den LEDs befinden sich Low-Tech-Sensoren mit einem niedrigen Stromverbrauch. Betrieben werden die LEDs über eine dünne und flexible fotovoltaische Folie, die tagsüber die Sonnenenergie speichert und der Anlage eine Autonomie von fünf Stunden verleiht. Das innovative und kreative System River Glow informiert nicht nur die Techniker in diesem Sektor, sondern auch die Bewohner über den Grad der Wasserverschmutzung.

Pour la fabrication de ce système de surveillance des eaux, un mécanisme à fort impact visuel a été créé. Les détecteurs de substances polluantes sont immergés dans l'eau et reliés à des DEL flottantes qui de nuit, en fonction du dépassement du seuil de pollution, activent une lumière rouge ou verte colorant l'eau qui l'entoure. Les DEL, qui utilisent des capteurs low-tech à basse consommation d'énergie, sont alimentées par des films photovoltaïques fins et flexibles qui capturent l'énergie solaire durant la journée et servent à alimenter le River Glow pendant cinq heures. Grâce à un moyen créatif, le message, simple et direct, n'atteint pas seulement le personnel concerné mais aussi l'ensemble de la population.

www.thelivingnewyork.com

**David Benjamin and Soo-in Yang
for The Living (USA)
2006
prototype**

153

SolarStore

Water heating system
Solarheißwassersystem
Système de chauffe-eau

It looks like a large hot water bag, but in fact the water is cold when first poured in and is heated inside using solar energy. The bag has a capacity of 34 oz and a surface area of some 6.5 sq ft when full. Its dark external PVC layer lets the sun's rays filter through an inner tube that connects to a lighter internal layer, which accumulates heat while remaining insulated, thanks to the so-called zebra effect. The temperature can thus reach up to 175°F. SolarStore reduces carbon dioxide emissions by 0.2 tons a year with respect to traditional water-heating systems and is an extremely cost-effective alternative, even when compared to other solar energy systems. The initial cost is already paid off after about six months of use, as the manufacturer claims. SolarStore could become a precious water-heating tool in countries with limited access to common energy sources. Since it is inflatable, it can also be comfortably rolled up and used for camping holidays.

Es sieht aus wie eine überdimensionale Wärmeflasche, aber es ist ein aufblasbarer Sonnenkollektor. Das kalte Wasser wird in den Behälter gefüllt und durch Sonnenenergie erhitzt. Der Behälter hat eine Kapazität von 30 Litern und eine Oberfläche von etwa 2 m². Die dunkle Außenhaut aus PVC filtert die Sonnenstrahlen durch einen Luftschlauch zu einer helleren Innenschicht. Der so genannte Zebra-Effekt sammelt die Wärme und isoliert sie gleichzeitig, so dass die Temperatur bis zu 80°C erreicht. Bei einer Reduzierung der Kohlenstoffdioxid-Emissionen von etwa 0,2 Tonnen pro Jahr gegenüber herkömmlichen Wassererhitzungssystemen bietet SolarStore eine kostengünstige Alternative. Den Angaben des Herstelles zufolge amortisieren sich die Anschaffungskosten bereits in sechs Monaten. SolarStore könnte ein Hilfsmittel in Ländern werden, in denen die Nutzung von Energiequellen eingeschränkt ist. Aber er ist auch ein praktischer Begleiter, denn er passt in einen Rucksack.

www.idc.uk.com

Cette poche volumineuse accueille de l'eau initialement froide et la chauffe grâce à l'énergie solaire. Elle offre une capacité de 30 l lorsqu'elle est pleine et une superficie d'environ 2 m². La surface extérieure en PVC sombre laisse passer les rayons du soleil à travers une poche d'air, vers une couche interne plus claire, qui accumule la chaleur grâce au fameux effet « zèbre ». Ainsi, la température peut atteindre jusqu'à 80°C. Avec une réduction des émissions d'anhydride carbonique d'environ 0,2 tonnes par an par rapport aux systèmes traditionnels utilisés pour chauffer l'eau, SolarStore représente une alternative extrêmement économique par rapport à d'autres systèmes utilisant l'énergie solaire : selon l'entreprise productrice, la dépense initiale est amortie en six mois d'utilisation. SolarStore pourrait devenir un instrument précieux dans les pays où l'accès aux sources d'énergie est limité. Gonflable, il peut être enroulé et utilisé en vacances ou en camping.

Stephen Knowles for Industrial Design
Consultancy Ltd (UK)
2008

155

Solio Classic

Solar-energy battery charger
Solarladegerät
Chargeur à énergie solaire

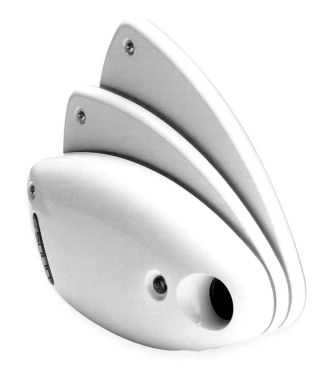

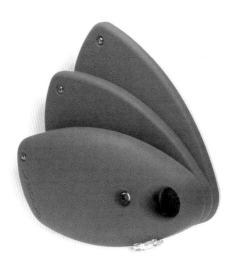

Solio is the first example of a series of innovative "clean" technologies that has incorporated an elegant design with sophisticated engineering to appeal to its user. Thanks to its interchangeable sockets, this lightweight (6 oz) and compact (5" x 2.5" x 1.5") battery charger can be used for a variety of cell phones, PDAs, MP3 players, digital cameras, GPS systems and game consoles. Solio's ergonomic body is composed of three solar panels, which powers its internal, high capacity battery, replaceable at the end of its life-cycle. For every hour of direct sun, Solio will provide about 15 minutes of talk time for most gadgets. Solio may also be powered from a computer, or a wall socket—and will hold its charge for up to one year.

Solio ist eines der ersten Beispiele unter den innovativen "sauberen Technologien", dass ein elegantes Design sowie innovative Bautechniken aufweist. Das Gerät ist sehr leicht (165 g) und kompakt (120 x 65 x 34 mm). Solio ist ein Solarladegerät, das dank einer Vielzahl von Adaptern für Handys, Smartphones und CD-Player, digitale Kameras, GPS-Systeme und Spielkonsolen verwendet werden kann. Wie Blütenblätter lässt sich die ergonomische Schale auffalten und speichert mit ihren Solarzellen Energie. Die enthaltene Hochleistungsbatterie kann am Ende ihrer Lebensdauer zudem ersetzt werden. Bereits eine Sonnenstunde liefert genug Energie für etwa 15 Minuten Gesprächszeit auf den meisten Geräten. Solio kann auch über einen Computer oder eine Steckdose aufgeladen werden und die gewonnene Energie bis zu einem Jahr lang speichern.

Solio est l'archétype d'une série de technologies « propres » et innovantes, attirant l'utilisateur par un design élégant et une mécanique sophistiquée. Grâce à des embouts et adaptateurs interchangeables, ce chargeur léger (168 gr) et compact (120 x 65 x 34 mm) s'adapte à une grande variété de téléphones portables, smartphones, lecteurs MP3, appareils photo numériques, GPS et consoles de jeux. La coque ergonomique de Solio est constituée de panneaux solaires alimentant une batterie interne de capacité importante et remplaçable en fin de vie. Une heure d'ensoleillement direct garantit 15 minutes de marche sur la plupart des appareils. Solio peut aussi être rechargé par l'intermédiaire d'un ordinateur ou depuis une prise murale et conserver sa charge jusqu'à un an.

www.solio.com

Better Energy Systems (USA)
2004

USBCELL

USB rechargeable battery
Aufladbare Batterie mit USB-Stecker
Pile rechargeable à port USB

A battery that can be easily recharged through a computer: this is the principle upon which Moixa Energy based its design of an alternative to its current batteries. The USB interface allows the battery to exploit the power of a computer. Problems tied to the disposal of alkaline batteries are thereby avoided and pieces normally used for rechargeable batteries, like the transformer, are made superfluous. Once the battery stops working, it can be sent back to the manufacturer to be regenerated. The USBCELL can be recharged some 500 times a year with a minimal loss of power. The numbers alone justify the project's validity: every year more than 15 billion alkaline batteries are released into the environment.

Stellen Sie sich vor, Sie besitzen eine Batterie, die einfach und bequem am Computer wieder aufgeladen werden kann. Dies ist das zugrundeliegende Prinzip der USBCELL der britischen Firma Moixa Energy. Dank der USB-Schnittstelle nutzt die Batterie den im Computer vorhandenen Strom. Zu den Vorteilen dieser Lösung gehört, dass die aufwendige Entsorgung von Alkalibatterien vermieden wird oder dass etwa die Herstellung eines Transformators, der bei wiederaufladbaren Batterien üblicherweise benötigt wird, entfällt. Die USBCELL kann circa 500 Mal pro Jahr mit einem nur geringen Leistungsverlust vom Hersteller aufgeladen werden. Die enormen Produktionsmengen von Wegwerf-Batterien sprechen für sich: jedes Jahr landen mehr als 15 Milliarden Alkalibatterien auf den Abfalldeponien.

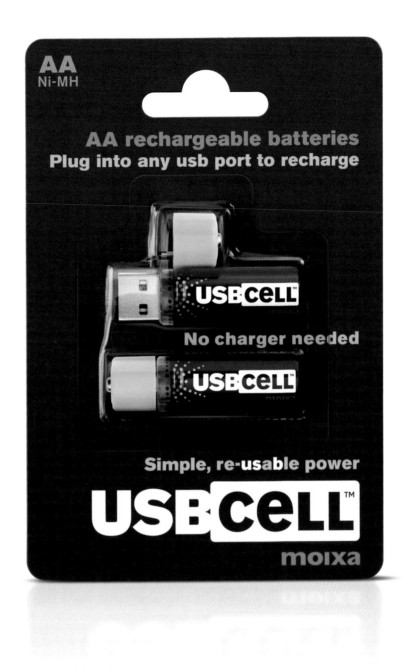

Imaginez une pile facilement rechargeable par l'intermédiaire d'un ordinateur. C'est le principe de fonctionnement du projet réalisé par Moixa Energy, une alternative aux piles actuelles. Grâce à l'interface USB, la pile exploite le courant de l'ordinateur et évite ainsi les problèmes liés à l'arrivée des piles alcalines dans les décharges ou rend inutile la production d'éléments tels que les transformateurs nécessaires aux piles rechargeables. Une fois les possibilités de recharge épuisées, la pile peut être renvoyée au producteur où elle sera régénérée. USBCELL peut être rechargée près de 500 fois par an sans quasiment perdre ses qualités initiales. Les chiffres liés à la production de piles suffisent à faire comprendre la validité de ce projet : chaque année, les déchargent reçoivent plus de 15 milliards de piles alcalines.

www.usbcell.com

British Design Duo (Simon Daniel and Chris Wright) for Moixa Energy Limited (UK)
2007

XO

Computer for kids
Computer für Kinder
Ordinateur pour enfants

The "One Laptop per Child" (OLPC) project is primarily aimed at developing countries with the goal of producing low-cost, sustainable computers for kids. The XO computer does not reflect the cliché of "low cost = low quality." On the contrary, it uses the best technologies and open-source software on the market. Since the computer must also withstand difficult climatic conditions like sand, excessive sun and high rates of humidity that could compromise its ability to function, it has a reinforced external layer and can be recharged with either electricity, solar energy or a manual crank, according to the model. The interest generated by the project has developed into a dense network of supporters, including Google and Amazon.

Das Projekt „One Laptop per Child" (OLPC) war vorwiegend für Entwicklungsländer vorgesehen mit dem Ziel, kindgerechte, kostengünstige und nachhaltige Computer herzustellen. Für den XO gilt allerdings nicht, dass niedrige Kosten gleichbedeutend sind mit schlechter Qualität. Für den Lerncomputer wurden die neusten Technologien und eine Open-Source-Software verwendet. Da der Computer auch schwierigen Bedingungen ausgesetzt sein kann, wie z. B. Sand, starke Sonneneinstrahlung und Feuchtigkeit, wurde das Gehäuse besonders robust gestaltet. Je nach Modell kann der Computer durch Strom, Sonnenenergie oder sogar von Hand mit Hilfe einer Kurbel wieder aufgeladen werden. Das Projekt weckte großes Interesse und erfuhr eine breite Unterstützung von einflussreichen Unternehmen, wie Google oder Amazon.

www.laptop.org

Principalement destiné aux pays en voie de développement, le projet « One Laptop per Child » (OLPC – Un ordinateur par enfant) a pour but de produire des ordinateurs adaptés aux enfants : à coût réduit et respectueux de l'environnement. XO, le nom de l'ordinateur, est bien loin du lieu commun « petit prix = mauvaise qualité », car il utilise les meilleures technologies présentes sur le marché et des logiciels open-source. Comme il doit résister à des conditions climatiques difficiles (sable, soleil excessif ou taux d'humidité élevé) qui en compromettent le fonctionnement, son boîtier est particulièrement renforcé et, suivant les modèles, se recharge à l'électricité, à l'énergie solaire mais aussi manuellement, par l'intermédiaire d'une manivelle. L'intérêt général du projet a su développer un large réseau de défenseurs, dont Google et Amazon.

Yves Béhar for fuseproject (USA)
2007

161

Dyson Airblade™

Electric hand dryer
Händetrockner
Sèche-mains électrique

For those who have always thought hot-air hand dryers are effective, the Airblade™ will come as a surprise. With its innovative design, this hand dryer emits a powerful burst of non-heated air that blows at a good 400 mph and is discharged from an opening the width of a strand of hair. In just 10 seconds, the air accomplishes the same it takes standard devices much longer to do with less satisfying results. Moreover, the air passes through a special filter that eliminates the bacteria normally found in public washrooms. With no hot air to produce, the Airblade™ also consumes up to 80% less energy than conventional dryers.

Wer bisher dachte, dass mit Heißluft betriebene, elektrische Händetrockner die wirksamsten seien, wird ganz schön ins Staunen kommen. Der auch im Design innovative Airblade™ erzeugt einen leistungsstarken, nicht erhitzten Luftstrom, der mit einer Geschwindigkeit von 640 km/h durch eine nur 0,3 mm große Öffnung – das entspricht dem Durchmesser eines Haares – geleitet wird. Dadurch wird in nur 10 Sekunden das gleiche Resultat erzielt, das bei herkömmlichen Geräten in bedeutend mehr Zeit und nicht immer auf zufrieden stellende Weise erreicht wird. Ein spezieller Filter beseitigt außerdem die Bakterien, die normalerweise in öffentlichen Toiletten vorkommen. Da keine Heißluft benötigt wird, verbraucht der Händetrockner im Vergleich zu konventionellen Geräten bis zu 80% weniger Strom.

On a tort de croire que les sèche-mains électriques à air chaud sont efficaces. Le puissant jet d'air non-chauffé émis par cet appareil, innovant même dans le design, circule à plus de 640 km/h par une ouverture de seulement 0,3 mm (l'épaisseur d'un cheveu). Il permet ainsi à l'air d'atteindre en 10 secondes seulement le même résultat que les appareils standard, qui eux mettent beaucoup plus de temps pour une qualité moindre. De plus, l'air passe par un filtre spécial qui élimine les bactéries généralement présentes dans les toilettes. Sans production d'air chaud, la consommation énergétique diminue jusqu'à 80% par rapport aux appareils conventionnels.

www.dysonairblade.com

Dyson Ltd (UK)
2007

BH-701

Bluetooth jewelry
Bluetooth-Headset
Bluetooth-bijou

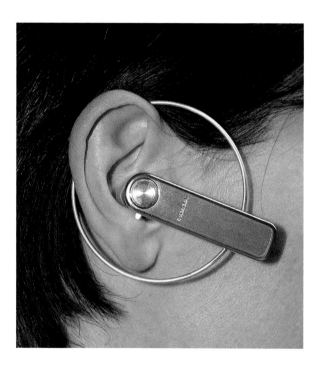

www.nokia.com

Heli Sade for Nokia (Finland)
2007

The more you like something, the longer it lasts. Taking these words to heart, Nokia designed an elegant Bluetooth earpiece for its female public that looks just like a piece of jewelry. Its multiple functions are all contained inside a linear parallelepiped with a metallic finish that accentuates its sober but chic design. The Bluetooth device sits in the center of a stainless steel ring, which turns into a sort of earring during communication since it is positioned partly behind the ear for greater comfort. Alternatively, when attached to its chain, this lightweight piece of hi-tech jewelry—weighing only 0.5 oz—transforms into an elegant pendant. Since it is no longer just a technological object, the chances are better that it will last, in the full sense of ecodesign.

Je mehr man sie lieb gewinnt, desto länger überdauern sie die Zeit. In diesem Sinne hat Nokia für die moderne Frau ein elegantes Bluetooth-Headset entwickelt, das wie ein Schmuckstück aussieht. Seine zahlreichen Funktionen sind in einem filigranen Empfängerteil mit metallenem Finish integriert, das das schlichte und raffinierte Design hervorhebt. Für einen besseren Tragekomfort verläuft der Edelstahlbügel zum Teil hinter dem Ohr. Mit dem passenden Trageriemen verwandelt sich das 13,3 g leichte High-Tech-Accessoire in einen eleganten Anhänger. Mit seinem ansprechenden Design ist eine lange Lebensdauer des Headsets im Sinne der Nachhaltigkeit garantiert.

Plus on les aime, plus ils durent. En prenant ces mots au pied de la lettre, Nokia a créé pour son public féminin une élégante oreillette Bluetooth aux allures de bijou. Ses nombreuses fonctions tiennent dans un parallélépipède linéaire aux finitions métallisées accentuant son design sobre et chic. Durant la communication, le cercle en acier inox, sur lequel l'oreillette est insérée, englobe en partie l'arrière de l'oreille pour un meilleur confort et une apparence boucle d'oreille. Au bout du cordon, ce bijou hi-tech très léger (seulement 13,3 g) se transforme en un élégant pendentif. Loin de n'être qu'un simple objet technologique, sa durée de vie rallongée est assurée, dans l'esprit total de l'écodesign.

Stickers

Post-a-Phone

Last number redial
Mute function
Call indicator
Personalization

Connector

Contains: Post-a-Phone handset, 2m cable with connector and self-adhesive stickers

Total weight 45g

Priestman Goode

Le low-tech prouve qu'il peut offrir des alternatives fonctionnelles et écologiques aux produits techniques. Postaphone est un téléphone fixe pensé pour remplacer en urgence un appareil cassé. L'avantage de ce produit réside en fait dans ses dimensions ultra fines qui lui permettent de tenir dans une enveloppe format A5 et ainsi d'être envoyé rapidement en cas de besoin. Léger et compact, mais surtout simple d'utilisation, il peut être personnalisé grâce à plusieurs commandes préenregistrées. À la différence de ses congénères plus anciens, il est fabriqué avec des matériaux recyclés (plastique et carton) et peut également être connecté à Internet.

www.priestmangoode.com

Paul Priestman for Priestmangoode (UK)
2007

169

Remade

Cellular phone
Konzept-Handy
Téléphone portable

Sustainability and ultra-modern design have given shape to this cell phone prototype made entirely of recycled materials. Aluminum and PET, found in cans and bottles respectively, were used for the body, while the keypad was made from old tires. The electronic part, which is usually what impacts the environment the most, is made of reused components. Finally, special technology was designed for the display to ensure high energy savings. Classified by Greenpeace as one of the first phone companies to take environmental politics into account, Nokia presented this prototype at the 2008 Mobile World Congress in Barcelona.

Nachhaltigkeit und ultramodernes Design haben die Form dieses Handy-Prototyps beeinflusst, den Nokia 2008 auf dem Mobile World Congress in Barcelona vorgestellt hat. Das Mobiltelefon wurde ausschließlich aus recycelten Materialien hergestellt. Sein Gehäuse besteht aus Aluminium und PET, die aus Dosen bzw. Flaschen gewonnen wurden, während für die Tastatur alte Reifen benutzt wurden. Auch für die elektronischen Elemente, die normalerweise die größten Auswirkungen auf die Umwelt haben, wurden umweltschonende Lösungen gefunden. Eine speziell für das Display entwickelte Technologie gewährleistet hohe Energieeinsparungen. Nokia wurde von Greenpeace zu den ersten Unternehmen gezählt, die sich für den Umweltschutz engagieren.

Le respect de l'environnement et un design ultra moderne ont donné naissance à ce prototype de portable intégralement fabriqué avec des matériaux recyclés. L'aluminium et le PET de la coque sont respectivement issus de canettes et de bouteilles, tandis que le clavier a été produit avec de vieux pneus. Pour la partie électronique, celle dont l'impact environnemental est généralement majeur, les composants utilisés sont issus du recyclage. Une technologie spécialement pensée pour l'écran garantira des économies d'énergies notables. Classée par Greenpeace parmi les trois premières entreprises de téléphonie à avoir pris en compte les politiques environnementales, Nokia a présenté ce prototype à l'occasion du World Mobile Congress de Barcelone, en 2008.

www.nokia.com

Tom Arbisi, Duncan Burns, Andrew Gartrell, Raphael Grignani, Simon James, Rhys Newman, Pawena Thimaporn and Pascal Wever for Nokia (Finland)
2008
prototype

Transportation

Transport
Transports

Introduction

Einleitung
Introduction

Problems with transport have long been linked with the consumption of non-renewable resources like oil. The fact that this model was introduced with the industrial revolution more than two centuries ago shows how our dependence on fossil fuels is a legacy of the past that must be overcome, as the new environmental situation requires. In fact, transport needs related to both urban nomadism and the transfer of goods have been transformed over the years as local and international communication networks have grown more dense.

There is no lack of alternative solutions, as this chapter indicates. New models show, for instance, how it is possible to avoid owning a vehicle thanks to a system of sharing (Bikedispenser). In addition to these already developed but still infrequently used models are countless innovations in the world of energy, like the use of electric energy (Segway i2) and hydrogen (ENV). Structural advances have also been made, so that the means can be more compact (One) or can even be used for more than one purpose (Aquaduct).

This section is subdivided into alternative means of transport, bicycles, two-wheeled motor vehicles, watercrafts, aircrafts and services.

Die Problematik beim Personen- und Warenverkehr besteht in der Ausschöpfung von Energiequellen, wie z. B. Erdöl, die nicht erneuerbar sind. Dieses System, das zur Zeit der industriellen Revolution entstand, zeigt, dass die Abhängigkeit von fossilen Brennstoffen eine Hinterlassenschaft der Vergangenheit ist, die nicht zuletzt wegen der veränderten Umweltbedingungen überholt werden muss. Die Anforderungen an die urbane Mobilität bzw. an den Transport von Waren haben sich entscheidend verändert. Gleichzeitig haben sich die nationalen und internationalen Kommunikationsnetze verdichtet.

An alternativen Lösungen mangelt es jedenfalls nicht, wie in diesem Kapitel aufgezeigt wird. Der Kauf eines Transportmittels ist dank neuer Modelle (Bikedispenser), bei denen das Fortbewegungsmittel mit anderen Benutzern geteilt wird, nicht mehr notwendig. Zu diesen bereits entwickelten, aber noch wenig genutzten Modellen kommen weitere Innovationen hinzu: im energetischen Bereich die Verwendung von Strom (Segway i2) und Wasserstoff (ENV), im strukturellen Bereich die Kompaktheit der neuen Transportmittel (One) – oder sogar die Verwendung von Verkehrsmitteln für mehrere Zwecke gleichzeitig (Aquaduct).

In diesem Kapitel werden alternative Verkehrsmittel, Fahrräder, Motorräder, Personenwagen, Wasserfahrzeuge, Flugtransportmittel und Dienstleistungen vorgestellt.

La problématique du transport est depuis toujours liée à la consommation des ressources non renouvelables, comme le pétrole. Face au nouveau contexte environnemental, ce modèle né il y a plus de deux siècles, héritage de la révolution industrielle, démontre combien la dépendance aux énergies fossiles doit être repensée. Au fil du temps, les besoins en déplacement, liés au nomadisme urbain comme au transport de marchandises, se sont transformés et les réseaux de communication locaux et internationaux se sont multipliés.

Les solutions alternatives ne manquent pas, comme l'indique ce chapitre. De nouveaux modèles montrent par exemple qu'il est possible de contourner la possession d'un moyen de transport grâce à un système de partage (Bikedispenser). À ces modèles déjà développés mais encore peu utilisés, s'ajoutent d'innombrables innovations dans le domaine énergétique – l'emploi d'énergie électrique (Segway i2) et d'hydrogène (ENV) –, dans le domaine structurel – la compacité des moyens de transport (One) – ou carrément l'utilisation de ces derniers à des fins encore plus poussées (Aquaduct).

Les divisions prévues dans ce chapitre englobent les moyens de transport alternatifs, vélos, deux-roues, voitures, moyens de transport aquatiques et aériens et enfin les services.

easyglider X6
Electric scooter
Elektro-Roller
Trottinette électrique

Bicycles and scooters have long been the ecological means of individual transport *par excellence*. The easyglider, a multifunctional electric scooter, offers an alternative that is just as sustainable. In fact, the 360 kW electric motor allows the scooter to reach 12.5 mph with minimal emissions since it recharges itself whenever it goes downhill. Because of its compact size (64 x 38.5 x 20"), it is easy to transport by car and use in more heavily-trafficked areas when needed. However, the designers did not forget about the scooter's potential for fun. Not only can the easyglider be used by skateboarders or inline skaters by removing the foot rest, but it is also available in a version for kids.

Fahrräder und Roller sind seit jeher die umweltfreundlichsten Fortbewegungsmittel überhaupt. easyglider ist ein multi-funktionaler Elektro-Roller, der eine innovative Alternative bietet. Mit 360 kW erreicht der Elektromotor eine Geschwindigkeit von bis zu 20 km/h bei sehr niedrigen Emissionen, da er sich beim Bergabfahren von selbst wieder auflädt. Durch seine geringen Abmessungen (162 x 98 x 51 cm) kann er leicht im Auto transportiert und bei Bedarf in verkehrsintensiven Gebieten benutzt werden. Die Erfinder haben bei der Planung auch den Spaßfaktor mitberücksichtigt: wenn man das Fußbrett entfernt, kann der easyglider auch als Skateboard oder mit Inline-Skates benutzt werden. Der easyglider ist auch in einer Ausführung für Kinder erhältlich.

Vélos et trottinettes sont les moyens de transport individuel écologique par excellence. easyglider, trottinette électrique multi-fonction, offre une alternative tout aussi durable : le moteur électrique de 360 kW permet en réalité à la trottinette d'atteindre les 20 km/h. Les émissions sont réduites car la batterie se recharge dans les descentes. Grâce à ses dimensions réduites (162 x 98 x 51 cm), la trottinette peut être emmenée partout en voiture pour l'utiliser lorsque le trafic est plus dense. Ses créateurs ont également travaillé son aspect amusant : sans plateau, easyglider peut tracter les adeptes du skate-board ou du roller et une version enfant est également disponible.

www.easy-glider.com

raumprodukt, David Weisser for Easy-Glider AG (Switzerland)
2008

Segway i2

Electric chariot
Zweiradroller
Transporteur électrique

www.segway.com

Segway Inc. (USA)
2006

The Segway® Personal Transporter (PT) i2 is an electric means of transport that can be used indoors or outdoors. It can travel 24 miles at a speed of 12.5 mph. The i2 was inspired by the design of ancient chariots and consists of two wheels, a footrest and handlebars. Balance is guaranteed by a stabilization system that responds to the rider's movements, picked up by five sensors located inside the footrest. The rider starts and stops simply by leaning forward or backward; a wireless InfoKey controller turns the PT off. The use of electric energy and a good relationship between the amount of material input and the weight of the rider (or MIPS) makes the i2 a decisively sustainable and handy urban vehicle.

Segway® Personal Transporter (PT) i2 ist ein elektrisches Personentransport-mittel, das sowohl Draußen wie Drinnen benutzt werden kann. Der Segway kann 38 km bei einer Geschwindigkeit von 20 km/h zurück legen. Das Design für i2 wurde von Rennwagen der Antike inspiriert und besteht aus zwei Rädern, einem Fußbrett und einem Lenker. Das Gleichgewicht wird durch ein Stabilisierungssystem gewährleistet und erfasst mit fünf Sensoren am Fußbrett jede Körperbewegungen des Fahrers. Die Fortbewegung erfolgt allein durch Gewichtsverlagerungen. Bei einer Vorwärtsbewegung des Oberkörpers fährt das Gerät an, während das Anhalten durch eine Bewegung nach hinten erfolgt. Ein kabelloses InfoKey Steuergerät schaltet den Roller aus. Die Verwendung von Strom und ein vorteilhaftes Verhältnis zwischen der Menge an verwendetem Material und dem Gewicht der zu transportierenden Person (genannt MIPS) macht aus i2 ein ausgesprochen äußerst praktisches Transportmittel für die Stadt.

Le Transporteur personnel (TP) Segway® i2 est un moyen de transport électrique, utilisable en intérieur comme en extérieur. Il peut parcourir 38 km à la vitesse de 20 km/h. L'i2 s'inspire du design des chars antiques et comprend deux roues, un marchepied et un guidon. L'équilibre est garanti par un système de stabilisation répondant aux mouvements détectés par cinq capteurs insérés dans le guidon : avancer et s'arrêter ne demandent qu'un déplacement du corps vers l'avant ou vers l'arrière ; une InfoKey met le TP hors tension. L'utilisation de l'énergie électrique offre un bon rapport consommation – poids de la personne transportée (ou MIPS), ce qui fait de l'i2 un moyen de transport urbain résolument facile d'accès et respectueux de l'environnement.

Aquaduct

Bicycle-purifier
Fahrrad mit Wasserfilter
Vélo-dépurateur

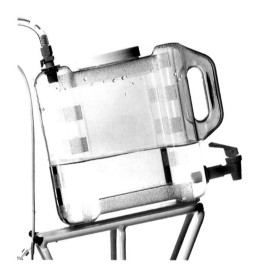

www.ideo.com

**Adam Mack, John Lai, Eleanor Morgan,
Paul Silberschatz, Brian Mason for IDEO (USA)**
2008
prototype

A water purifier that is also a means of transport or, vice versa, a bicycle that filters water. This, in short, is the project conceived by American studio IDEO for developing countries and particularly for women, who are usually the ones responsible for collecting the daily water supply. Using a special bike outfitted with a carbon filter and two tanks, water is pumped from one tank to the other, passing through the filter, thanks to the power triggered by the rider's pedaling action. With just a little physical exercise and, above all, at no cost, the water is purified of polluting elements during its transport. Aquaduct is an environmental and ethically sustainable project. Although it is not yet in production, the hope is that it will inspire the creation of yet more alternative water-purification systems.

Das Fahrrad Aquaduct wurde von dem amerikanischen Studio IDEO für die Verwendung in Entwicklungsländern konzipiert. Es handelt sich um eine Wasseraufbereitungsanlage, die gleichzeitig ein Fortbewegungsmittel ist oder umgekehrt ein Fahrrad das Wasser aufbereitet. Es ist vor allem für Frauen gedacht, deren Aufgabe die tägliche Wasserversorgung der Familie ist. An diesem speziellen Fahrrad sind zwei Tanks angebracht. Die beim Treten erzeugte Kraft pumpt das Wasser vom Haupttank über den Kohlenstofffilter in den Vordertank. Mit minimalem physischem Kraftaufwand wird so das verunreinigte Wasser während des Transports gereinigt und trinkbar gemacht. Auch wenn dieses umweltfreundliche Fahrrad noch nicht produziert wird, ist es eine wichtige Inspiration für die kostengünstige Produktion von Wasseraufbereitungssystemen.

Un dépurateur d'eau également moyen de transport ou inversement, un vélo qui purifie l'eau : voici la synthèse du projet des Américains d'IDEO, conçu pour les pays en développement et plus particulièrement pour les femmes, souvent responsables de l'approvisionnement quotidien en eau. En exploitant la mécanique de vélos auxquels on intègre deux réservoirs et un filtre au carbone, l'eau est pompée d'un réservoir à l'autre à travers le filtre grâce à la force de l'utilisateur. Par un simple exercice physique et surtout sans aucun coût, l'eau est purifiée des souillures durant le transport. Aquaduct est un projet durable sur les plans environnemental et éthique et bien que la production n'ait pas encore commencé, celui-ci pourrait entraîner la production de systèmes alternatifs pour l'épuration de l'eau.

CityCruiser

Velocipede-taxi
Fahrradtaxi
Taxi-vélocipède

www.veloform.com

Dipl.-Ing. Stefan Kruschel; Dr. Franz for Veloform
GmbH (Germany)
2000 and 2006

Halfway between a rickshaw and an electric bicycle, the CityCruiser is powered by the driver's muscle strength, with a supplementary electric motor for long stretches. Two 12-Volt batteries help it reach a speed of about 7 mph without the release of harmful emissions. In addition to the driver, the vehicle has space for two passengers plus luggage. The CityCruiser is built with sustainable materials: recyclable polyethylene for the cab and metal for the chassis. The use of more than one material, however, does not impede its recycling, since it was produced according to the dictates of design for components. Otherwise cumbersome for its dimensions (10 x 3.5 x 6 ft), it can thus be easily transported to dealers.

CityCruiser ist eine Kombination aus Rikscha und Elektrorad, der die Muskelkraft des Fahrers nutzt, die auf längeren Strecken durch zwei 12-Volt-Batterien unterstützt wird. Ohne Abgabe von Emissionen kann so eine Geschwindigkeit von 11 km/h erreicht werden. Außer dem Fahrer bietet der CityCruiser noch zwei weiteren Personen mitsamt ihren Koffern Platz. Die Kabine besteht aus Recycling-Polyethylen, während der Rahmen aus recyceltem Metall gebaut wurde. Die Verwendung von mehreren Materialien steht einer einfachen Endverwertung nicht im Wege, da das Fahrradtaxi gemäß den Grundsätzen des Bauteiledesigns zusammengesetzt wurde. So wird auch der Transport zu den Verkaufsstellen erleichtert, der sonst auf Grund der Maße (185 x 305 x 110 cm) sehr umständlich wäre.

À mi-chemin entre le rickshaw et le vélo électrique, le CityCruiser exploite la force musculaire du conducteur, couplée à un moteur électrique sur les trajets plus longs. Grâce à deux batteries de 12 Volts, on peut atteindre une vitesse de 11 km/h sans aucune émission nocive. En plus du conducteur, ce moyen de transport accueille deux passagers avec bagages. Le CityCruiser est construit avec des matériaux recyclés : le carénage externe est réalisé en polyéthylène recyclé tandis que le châssis qui le supporte est en métal. L'utilisation de plusieurs matériaux n'empêche pas son recyclage final, car le véhicule est réalisé selon les préceptes du design de composants. Le transport vers les points de vente, peu encombrant par ses dimensions (185 x 305 x 110 cm), est ainsi plus simple.

FLUIDA.IT

Folding bicycle
Faltrad
Vélo pliable

Like all city bikes, FLUIDA.IT provides a last hope for those having to brave urban traffic. Flexible, lightweight and compact, this velocipede, unlike other products belonging to the same category, is optimized for all the phases of its use. Not only can the pedals and handlebar be folded, reducing the space they take up, but the seat also doubles as a lock. The most innovative components, however, are the wheels: with two different sizes, the bulk of the bicycle is reduced by 50%, resulting in a saving of material without compromising either gear speed or road holding.

FLUIDA.IT ist ein Rettungsanker für jene, die den städtischen Verkehr bezwingen müssen. Flexibilität, Leichtigkeit und Kompaktheit charakterisieren dieses Stadtrad. Im Gegensatz zu anderen Produkten der gleichen Kategorie wurde es für die verschiedenen Benutzungsphasen optimiert: während die Pedale und das Lenkrad gefaltet werden können und so weniger Platz einnehmen, erfüllt der Sattel eine doppelte Funktion, da er gleichzeitig auch als Schloss dient. Die innovativsten Bauteile sind jedoch die Räder: die verschiedenen Größen erlauben eine Raumeinsparung von 50%. Trotz der Materialeinsparung ist weder die Fahrgeschwindigkeit noch die Straßenlage beeinträchtigt.

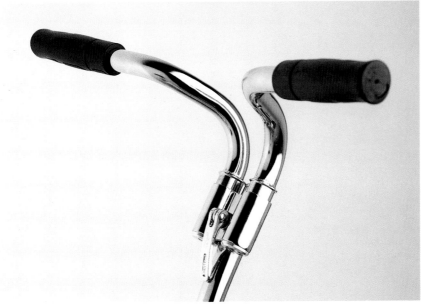

www.fluida.it

Comme tous les vélos de ville, FLUIDA.IT est une bouée de sauvetage pour qui doit affronter la circulation urbaine. Flexibilité, légèreté et compacité caractérisent ce vélo qui, à la différence des produits appartenant à la même catégorie, a été optimisé dans toutes ses phases d'utilisation : tandis que les pédales et le guidon peuvent être repliés, réduisant ainsi l'espace occupé, la selle possède la double fonction de cadenas. La partie la plus innovante est le design des roues : de dimensions diverses, elles permettent de réduire l'encombrement de 50% et d'économiser ainsi des matériaux, sans entraver la rapidité ni la tenue de route.

Marco Gaudenzi, Isao Hosoe, Takeo Hosoe, Nicola Pari for Fluida S.r.l. (Italy)
2000

One

Folding bicycle
Faltrad
Vélo pliable

The Brompton folding bicycle has become a legend amid city traffic. Now, with One, Thomas J. Owen shows how this basic idea can be developed. Made of aluminum and carbon fiber, this prototype is even more manageable and easy to transport. Once the bike is folded up, it forms a cylinder complete with handle to hide the "dirty" parts inside. There is even a version with an electric motor. One is therefore presented as the evolution of a sustainable product that offers an efficient and dynamic alternative to increasingly slow and crowded urban traffic.

Das Brompton-Faltrad gehört zu den Klassikern im städtischen Verkehr. Mit dem Modell One zeigt Thomas J. Owen, dass die Grundidee noch weiter ausgebaut werden kann. Dieser Prototyp aus Aluminium und Kohlenstofffaser ist handlicher und einfacher zu transportieren. Im gefalteten Zustand hat das Fahrrad die Form eines Zylinders mit Handgriff, wobei die "schmutzigen" Teile im Inneren verborgen werden. Der Erfinder stellte sogar eine mit Elektromotor ausgestattete Version vor. Das Modell One präsentiert sich als die Weiterführung eines nachhaltigen Produktes, das eine effiziente und dynamische Alternative zum immer überfüllteren und langsameren Stadtverkehr darstellt.

www.thomasjowen.co.uk

Le vélo pliable Brompton est d'ores et déjà une légende de la circulation citadine. Avec One, Thomas J. Owen démontre qu'une idée basique peut toujours être développée : réalisé en aluminium et fibre de carbone, ce prototype en devient encore plus maniable et facile à transporter. Le vélo, une fois plié, prend la forme d'un cylindre doté d'une poignée; il protège son utilisateur des parties salies par la route. Le créateur propose même une version dotée d'un moteur électrique. One se présente ainsi comme la dernière évolution d'un produit écologique, offrant une alternative efficace et dynamique à une circulation urbaine de plus en plus dense.

Thomas J. Owen (UK)
2006
prototype

Atlantic Zero Emission

Hydrogen scooter
Wasserstoff-Roller
Scooter à hydrogène

Like all hydrogen-powered vehicles, which release water vapor in place of polluting gases into the air, the Atlantic Zero Emission scooter is still a prototype and will stay that way until suitable infrastructures are created to support the use of non-fossil fuels. The hydrogen propulsion system produces 6 kW of power, provides a fuel distance of about 90 miles of city driving and can reach a speed of about 50 mph. Aesthetically, the scooter, presented by the Italian company Aprilia in 2004, maintains the shape and design of the other models in the Atlantic series. Even the size of its fuel-cell tank is the same as scooters that use fossil fuels, showing that the design of a vehicle does not have to depend on the kind of fuel it uses.

Der Roller Atlantic Zero Emission, der in seiner Ästhetik die Formen und Linien der Atlantic-Reihe beibehält, wurde 2004 vom italienischen Unternehmen Aprilia vorgestellt. Wie alle Verkehrsmittel mit Wasserstoff-Antrieb gibt der Roller keine schädlichen Abgase, sondern nur Wasserdampf in die Umwelt ab. Bis zur Errichtung von Anlagen, die für nicht-fossile Kraftstoffe geeignet sind, bleibt dieser Roller allerdings ein Prototyp. Der Wasserstoffantrieb liefert 6 kW Leistung, besitzt eine Reichweite von 150 km im städtischen Verkehr und kann eine Geschwindigkeit von 85 km/h erreichen. Das Tankvolumen der Brennstoffzelle entspricht dem von Rollern, die mit fossilen Brennstoffen angetrieben werden. Atlantic Zero Emission zeigt eindrucksvoll, dass anspruchsvolles Design nicht vom verwendeten Kraftstoff abhängig sein muss.

www.aprilia.com

Comme tous les moyens de transport alimentés à l'hydrogène relâchant de la vapeur d'eau, en lieu et place de gaz polluants, le scooter Atlantic Zero Emission n'est encore qu'un prototype. Il le restera d'ailleurs jusqu'à ce que des infrastructures adaptées à l'usage des carburants non fossiles soient créées. La propulsion à hydrogène développe 6 kW de puissance, garantit une autonomie de 150 km en usage urbain et peut atteindre une vitesse de 85 km/h. D'un point de vue esthétique, le scooter, présenté par la société italienne Aprilia en 2004, conserve les formes de la série Atlantic. Les dimensions du réservoir destiné aux piles à combustible sont les mêmes que celles des réservoirs à essence; ceci prouve que le design ne dépend en aucun cas du type de carburant utilisé.

**Aprilia in collaboration with Mes-Dea
(Italy – Switzerland)
2004
prototype**

ENV

Hydrogen motorcycle
Wasserstoffbetriebenes Motorrad
Moto à hydrogène

The world of two wheels has opened its doors to hydrogen motors. The ENV (Emissions Neutral Vehicle) project, developed by the English company Intelligent Energy in 2005, represents the first application of fuel-cell, or combustible-cell, technology to motorcycles. A bike can reach up to 50 mph with a hydrogen motor, which is based on the use of PEM (Proton Exchange Membrane) fuel cells; inside the motor, the cells overlap in various layers to make the most of the space available. Not only is hydrogen one of the few combustibles that does not cause pollution, it actually generates a precious resource. The waste produced by combustion is in fact pure water, which can either evaporate or be consumed—as occurred during the Apollo space mission. While the ENV is still a prototype, it shows how the sustainable technology it employs is ready to be produced and commercialized.

Die Motorradwelt öffnet ihre Tore dem Wasserstoffmotor. Das Projekt ENV (Emissions Neutral Vehicle), das 2005 von der englischen Firma Intelligent Energy entwickelt wurde, ist eine der ersten Prototypen mit der fuel cell-Technologie (Brennstoffzelle). Der Wasserstoffmotor, der eine Geschwindigkeit von bis zu 80 km/h ermöglicht, basiert auf der Verwendung von PEM-Zellen (Polymer-Elektrolyt-Membran). Im Motorinneren werden die Zellen aufgrund des geringen Platzes übereinander geschichtet. Wasserstoff ist einer der wenigen Brennstoffe, die die Umwelt nicht belasten, sondern auch ein kostbares Gut liefern: das Abfallprodukt ist nämlich reines Wasser. Dieses kann man verdampfen lassen oder trinken, so wie es auf der Apollo Raumfahrtmission gemacht wurde. ENV ist zwar noch ein Prototyp, aber diese umweltfreundliche und nachhaltige Technologie ist reif für die Produktion und Vermarktung.

Le monde du deux-roues ouvre ses portes au moteur à hydrogène. Le projet ENV (Emissions Neutral Vehicle), développé en 2005 par la société anglaise Intelligent Energy, constitue l'une des premières applications de la technologie « full cell » (l'utilisation de cellules combustibles) dans le secteur. Le moteur à hydrogène permet d'atteindre les 80 km/h grâce aux cellules PEM (Proton Exchange Membrane); celles-ci sont superposées dans le moteur afin d'optimiser l'espace restreint. L'hydrogène est un des rares combustibles non polluants. Il génère de plus un bien précieux : sa combustion ne rejette que de l'eau pure, pouvant ensuite être transformée en vapeur ou consommée (comme ce fut le cas lors de la mission spatiale Apollo). ENV n'est encore qu'un prototype mais il démontre cependant combien la technologie durable utilisée ici ne demande qu'à être exploitée et commercialisée.

www.intelligent-energy.com

Seymourpowell for Intelligent Energy (UK)
2005
prototype

Air Car Eureka

Compressed-air car
Druckluftauto
Automobile à air comprimé

It may be hard to believe, but the concept of the compressed-air car goes back to 1687 when French mathematician and physicist Denis Papin conducted the first studies on the subject. Some two-hundred years later, the French brothers Andraud and Tessier de Motay developed the first vehicle to use this technology. Today, ever more companies are conducting research into this non-polluting fuel. Particularly worthy of attention is the Spanish company Air Car Factories, which is carrying out various sustainable transportation projects, including the multipurpose vehicle Eureka. The benefits of this "historic" technology are both environmental and financial. Not only are production costs reduced by 20% because of the small number of components used, but the fuel is easy to procure and transport. What is more, the air tank can be recycled without the negative fallout on the environment that takes place with the batteries of traditional cars.

Das Konzept für das Druckluftauto geht bereits auf das Jahre1687 zurück, als der französische Mathematiker und Physiker Denis Papin erste Forschungen auf diesem Gebiet unternahm. Etwa zwei Jahrhunderte später entwickelten die Franzosen Andraud und Tessier de Motay das erste Auto mit Drucklufttechnologie. Heutzutage betreiben immer mehr Unternehmen Forschungen mit diesem umweltverträglichen Brennstoff. Besondere Beachtung verdient dabei das spanische Unternehmen Air Car Factories, das bereits nachhaltige Projekte realisierte, darunter auch das Auto mit Einraumkarosserie Eureka. Diese Technologie ist umweltfreundlich und kostengünstig. Durch die Reduzierung von Bauteilen können die Produktionskosten um 20% gesenkt werden und der Brennstoff ist leicht zu beschaffen und zu transportieren. Außerdem kann der Lufttank ohne negative Auswirkungen auf die Umwelt recycelt oder entsorgt werden.

www.aircarfactories.com

Aussi incroyable que cela puisse paraître, le concept de voiture à air comprimé remonte à 1687, lorsque le mathématicien et physicien français Denis Papin réalisa les premières recherches sur le sujet. Environ deux siècles plus tard, les Français Andraud et Tessier de Motay développèrent la première voiture utilisant cette technologie. Aujourd'hui, le nombre d'entreprises approfondissant leurs recherches sur ce carburant non polluant ne cesse de croître. L'espagnol Air Car Factories compte parmi les plus remarquables, avec ses différents projets de transport durable, dont le monospace Eureka. Les avantages de cette technologie « historique » sont non seulement environnementaux mais aussi économiques : grâce au nombre limité de composants, les coûts de production sont réduits de 20% tandis que le carburant est facile à trouver et à transporter. De plus, le filtre à air peut être recyclé ou retiré sans retombées négatives sur l'environnement, contrairement aux batteries des voitures traditionnelles.

Sergio de la Parra for Air Car Factories S.A. (Spain)
2008
prototype

201

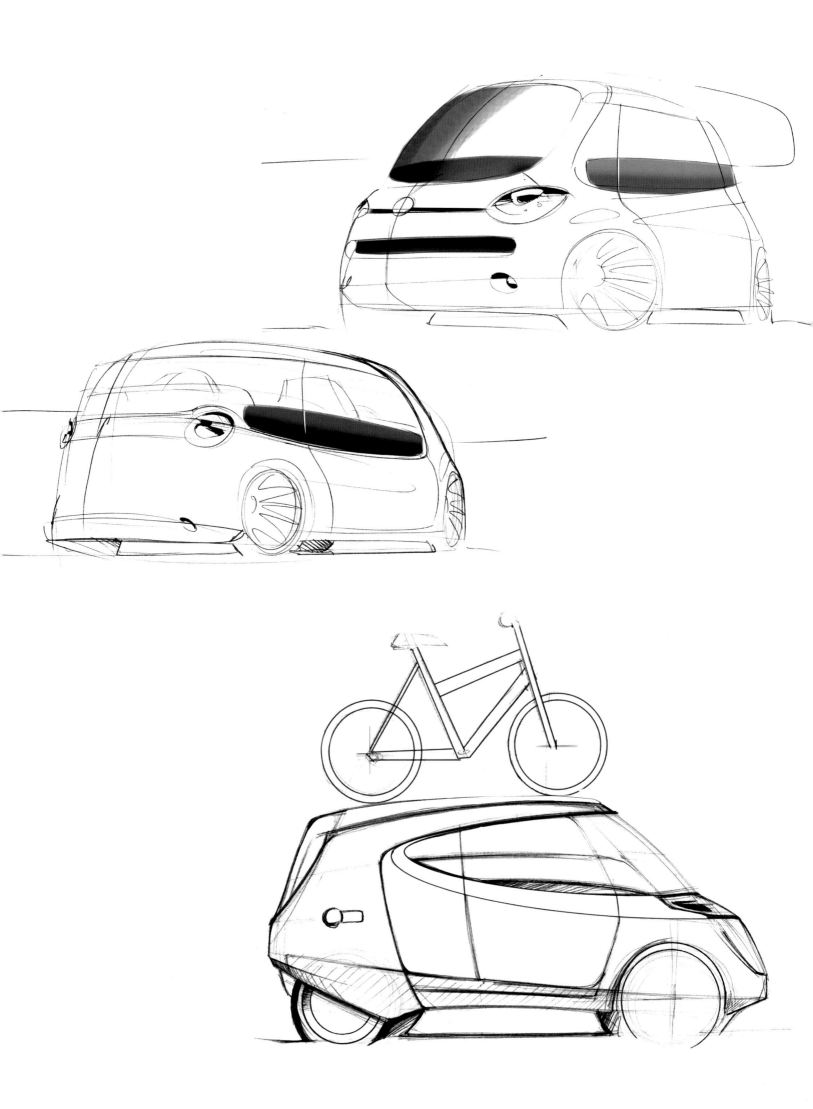

Phylla

Solar-energy city car
Solarzellenbetriebener Stadtwagen
Citadine à énergie solaire

Presented in 2008 by the Regione Piemonte, Fiat Research Center and the Polytechnic Institute of Turin, the Phylla—Greek for "leaf"—is a city car that responds to various sustainable approaches. Not only does it use alternative energy sources, but it is recyclable and some of its parts are even biodegradable. Flexible photovoltaic panels provide a fuel distance of 11 miles. However, with the use of rechargeable electric batteries, the car can be driven up to 124 miles. Less than 10 ft long and around 5 ft wide, it weighs only 1650 lbs, can reach 80 mph and accelerates to 30 miles in just 6 seconds. The developers also took the dismantling phase into consideration by incorporating materials that are easy to recognize and separate, thereby facilitating recycling. Phylla therefore emerges as a "technological laboratory" that experiments with innovative solutions for sustainable urban mobility.

Der Kleinwagen Phylla – das Wort stammt aus dem Griechischen und bedeutet „Blatt" – wurde 2008 von der Regione Piemonte, dem FIAT-Forschungszentrum und der Technischen Hochschule Turin vorgestellt. Der Wagen erfüllt mehrere Anforderungen an Nachhaltigkeit: er wird durch Alternativenergien angetrieben, ist vollständig recycelbar und einige seiner Bestandteile, wie bspw. die Karosserie oder die Reifen, sind biologisch abbaubar. Die Photovoltaikzellen ermöglichen eine Reichweite von 18 km, bei Benutzung der Elektrobatterien sogar bis zu 200 km. Der Kleinwagen ist weniger als 3 m lang und rund 1,5 m breit. Aufgrund des geringen Gewichts von 750 kg erreicht Phylla eine Höchstgeschwindigkeit von 130 km/h und beschleunigt von 0 auf 50 km/h in 6 Sekunden. Die Entwickler planten eine umweltbewusste Entsorgung und wählten ein Design, dass die Wiederverwertung der verschiedenen Materialien erleichtert. Phylla fungierte als „technologisches Labor", in dem innovative Lösungen für einen umweltfreundlichen, urbanen Verkehr getestet wurden.

Présentée en 2008 par la région Piémont, le Centre de recherche
FIAT et l'École polytechnique de Turin, Phylla, du grec « feuille »,
est une voiture citadine répondant à diverses approches
environnementales : elle emploie une source d'énergie alternative,
elle est recyclable et certains de ses éléments sont biodégradables.
Les panneaux photovoltaïques flexibles garantissent une
autonomie de 18 km mais la voiture peut parcourir jusqu'à 200 km
avec une batterie électrique. Mesurant moins de 3 m de long et
large d'à peine 1,5 m, son poids est très réduit (750 kg). Elle peut
atteindre les 130 km/h avec une accélération proche des 50 km en
6 secondes. Les créateurs ont été également attentifs à la phase de
désassemblage pour permettre le recyclage des différents
matériaux, faciles à identifier et à séparer. Phylla se présente ainsi
comme un « laboratoire technologique » expérimentant des
solutions innovantes pour une mobilité urbaine éco-durable.

www.crf.it

Centro Ricerche Fiat (Italy)
2008
prototype

Czeers

Solar-energy boat
Solarboot
Bateau à énergie solaire

www.czeers.com

**David Czap and Nils Beers for Czeers Solarboats
(The Netherlands)**
2007
prototype

The Czeers is one of the first of its kind: a speedboat for racing powered by solar energy. Its surface is entirely covered by photovoltaic panels, allowing the electric motor to reach a strength of 80 kW and a speed of 30 knots (34.5 mph). The cutting-edge qualities of this 33 ft.-long boat include a linear, futuristic design and an LCD touch-screen control system. The prototype was created in 2006 and proved its value by winning the world competition for solar-propulsion boats, the "Frisian Solar Challenge", by going some ten hours longer than the other boats.

Czeers ist ein mit Solarenergie betriebenes Motor-Rennboot. Sämtliche Flächen des Bootes sind mit Solarzellen bedeckt. Diese speisen den Elektromotor, der eine Leistung von 80 kW und eine Geschwindigkeit von 30 Knoten (55 km/h) erreichen kann. Das Boot besitzt zahlreiche moderne Merkmale: lineares und futuristisches Design auf 10 m Länge, Bedienelemente wie ein LCD-Touchscreen zur einfachen Steuerung sowie sorgfältig ausgewählte Materialien, wie z. B. Kohlenstoff für den Bootskörper. Der 2006 fertig gestellte Prototyp hat die weltweit größte Regatta für solarzellenbetriebene Boote, die „Frisian Solar Challenge", mit etwa 10 Stunden Vorsprung auf die anderen Boote gewonnen.

Parmi les premiers de son genre, Czeers est un bateau de compétition à moteur, alimenté à l'énergie solaire. Sa surface est entièrement recouverte de panneaux photovoltaïques qui permettent au moteur électrique d'atteindre une puissance de 80 kW et une vitesse de 30 nœuds (55 km/h). Sa modernité réside dans le design linéaire et futuriste de ses 10 m de long et le système de contrôle touch screen sur écran LCD. Le prototype réalisé en 2006 a déjà démontré sa valeur en remportant la compétition mondiale des bateaux à propulsion solaire, le « Frisian Solar Challenge », avec une avance d'environ dix heures sur les autres bateaux.

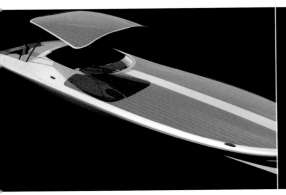

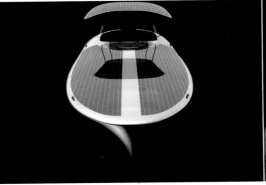

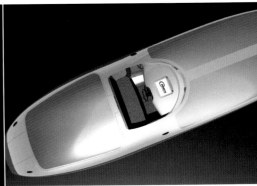

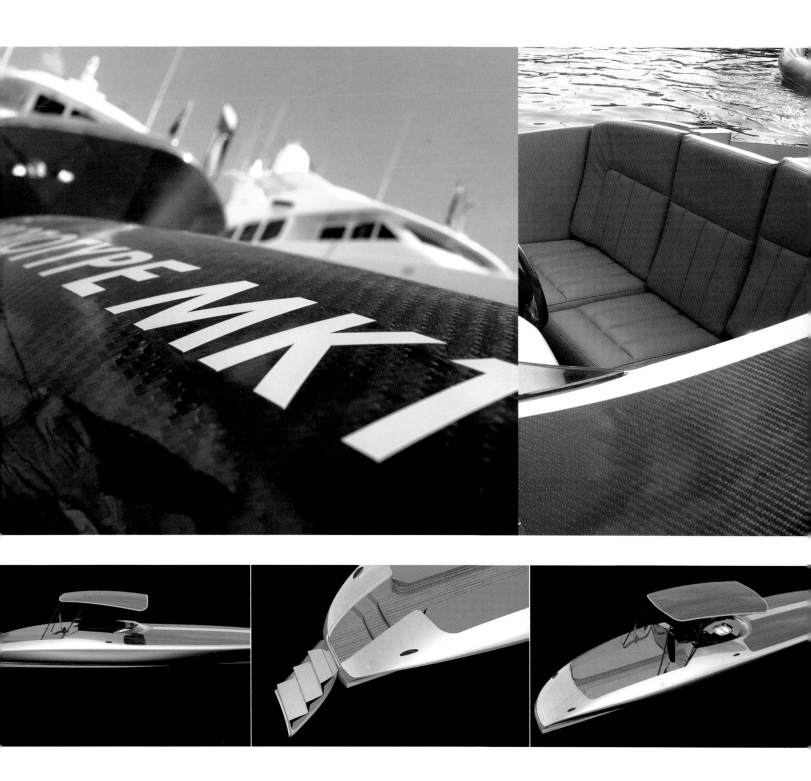

Lanikai

Inflatable kayak
Aufblasbarer Kajak
Kayak gonflable

www.clearbluehawaii.com

Andres Segreta for Clear Blue Hawaii (USA)
2003

Lanikai is an inflatable kayak that can be put back in its own bag when deflated. It is 10-ft long when blown up, weighs little more than 22 lbs and is easily transported—great for those who love to travel far off the beaten track. Lanikai is made with 840-denier nylon, a very durable material. To make this sport even more attractive, the kayak's hull was made partly out of a transparent material so the rower can enjoy a unique view. Lanikai is one of several products made by a company that has long searched for sustainable solutions to problems of transport and manageability of individual watercrafts.

Lanikai ist ein aufblasbarer Kajak mit einer Länge von fast 3 m und einem Gewicht von rund 10 kg. Wenn er nicht benutzt wird, kann er Platz sparend in einer Aufbewahrungstasche verstaut werden. Die für dieses Modell charakteristische Kompaktheit und Leichtigkeit ermöglichen einen komfortablen Transport. Diese Eigenschaften sind besonders nützlich, wenn man abgelegene Orte erreichen möchte. Lanikai besteht aus sehr widerstandsfähigem und beständigem Nylon 840 Denier, das eine lange Lebensdauer des Produktes gewährleistet. Eine weitere Besonderheit ist der durchsichtige Rumpf, der den Insassen eine einzigartige Sicht auf die Unterwasserwelt bietet. Lanikai ist eines von vielen Produkten des Unternehmens Clear Blue Hawaii, das für seine nachhaltigen Lösungen bei Transport und Handlichkeit bekannt ist.

Lanikai est un kayak gonflable qui tient dans un sac lorsqu'il est dégonflé. Compact et léger, sa longueur d'environ 3 m et son poids à peine supérieur à 10 kg le distinguent des autres kayaks et facilitent son transport, une caractéristique intéressante pour qui aime se rendre hors des sentiers battus. Lanikai est fabriqué en matériau très résistant, le nylon 840 deniers, qui en garantit la durée de vie. Pour rendre l'activité encore plus attrayante, le fond est en partie réalisé en matière transparente afin de jouir d'une vue unique. Lanikai est l'un des nombreux produits d'une entreprise qui recherche depuis toujours des solutions viables aux problèmes de transport et de maniabilité des embarcations individuelles.

PlanetSolar

Solar-energy catamaran
Solar-Katamaran
Catamaran à énergie solaire

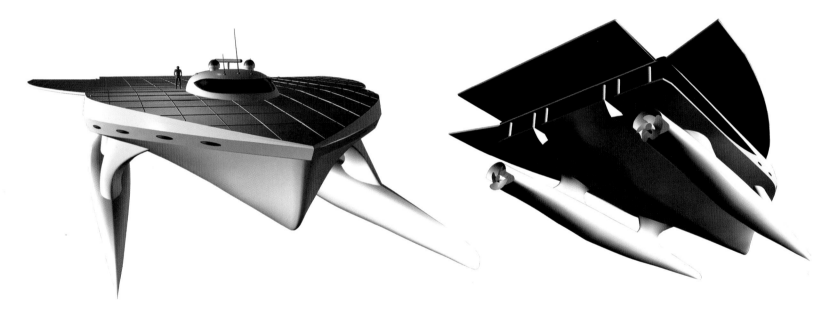

In 2004, a team of naval physicists, engineers and builders began a series of studies on the use of solar energy in the nautical world, as a challenge to the skeptics. This futuristically-designed catamaran was one of the first prototypes to be completed. Ninety-eight feet long, with solar panels covering a total surface area of 1542 sq ft, it is designed to reach a speed of 15 knots. The product will be launched in 2010 with a memorable undertaking: a 120-day voyage across the world, hugging the equator. A promotional campaign will take place alongside the docking of the catamaran at each planned stop to raise awareness of natural energy sources as valid alternatives to combustible fossil fuels.

Entgegen aller Skepsis startete 2004 ein Team von Physikern, Ingenieuren und Schiffsbauern eine Untersuchungsreihe zur Nutzung von Solarenergie in der Schifffahrt. Das Ergebnis ist ein Katamaran mit futuristischem Aussehen. Dieser Prototyp ist 30 m lang und auf einer Fläche von 470 m^2 mit Sonnenkollektoren bedeckt. Die Bauweise ermöglicht eine Geschwindigkeit von bis zu 15 Knoten (28km/h). Das Projekt verfolgt das anspruchsvolle Ziel einer Weltumseglung entlang des Äquators in 120 Schifffahrtstagen allein auf Solarenergiebasis. Während dieser langen Reise, geplant für 2010, wird eine Werbekampagne das Anlegen des Katamarans bei den jeweiligen Zwischenstationen begleiten. Ziel ist es, das Publikum auf das Potential von natürlichen Energiequellen als wertvolle Alternative zu fossilen Brennstoffen aufmerksam zu machen.

Défiant tout scepticisme, une équipe de physiciens, ingénieurs et constructeurs navals ont initié en 2004 une série de recherches sur l'utilisation de l'énergie solaire dans le milieu nautique. L'un des premiers prototypes réalisés est ce catamaran au design futuriste : long de 30 mètres, totalement recouvert de panneaux solaires, pour une surface totale de 470 m², il est programmé pour atteindre une vitesse de 15 nœuds (28 km/h). Le projet sera lancé en 2010 dans le cadre d'une entreprise mémorable : un tour du monde le long de l'équateur en 120 jours. Une campagne de promotion accompagnera l'arrivée du catamaran aux escales prévues le long du trajet, afin de sensibiliser le public sur le potentiel des sources naturelles d'énergie comme alternative valable aux combustibles fossiles.

www.planetsolar.org

Craig Loomes for Craig Loomes Design (New Zealand)
2009
prototype

Solar Impulse

Photovoltaic-energy airplane
Solarflugzeug
Avion à énergie photovoltaïque

Around the world, about a million tons of gas are consumed each hour. Hence, designs involving renewable energy sources are constantly being pushed to new horizons. Solar Impulse, an airplane that runs on solar energy, is the fruit of that research in the aeronautical world. Although the two prototypes created, HB-SIA and HB-SIB, are not the first of their kind, they represent a true challenge since they were conceived to fly both during the day and at night. After the first tests and a 36-hour flight, the HB-SIA model will repeat a classic in the history of aviation: crossing the Atlantic. The HB-SIB will subsequently circle the world in five legs. Totally revolutionary, with a wingspan of 208 ft and a weight of some 3500 lbs, Solar Impulse is a powerful symbol that will serve as an inspiration to discover the advantages of renewable energies.

Jede Stunde wird weltweit etwa eine Million Tonnen Erdöl verbraucht. Forschungen im Bereich der erneuerbaren Energiequellen sind daher an der Tagesordnung. Ein Beispiel dieser Forschung im Luftfahrtbereich ist Solar Impulse, ein durch Sonnenenergie angetriebenes Flugzeug. Die beiden hergestellten Prototypen HB-SIA und HB-SIB sind zwar nicht die ersten Flugzeuge dieser Art, sie gehören jedoch zu den ehrgeizigsten Projekten, da sie im Gegensatz zu Anderen für den Tag- und Nachtflug konzipiert wurden. Auf einer Fläche von 200 m² wurden auf den Flügeln und auf der Höhenflosse Solarzellen angebracht, mit denen das Flugzeug dank der vier Motoren von jeweils 10 PS eine Höhe von 8500 m und eine Geschwindigkeit von 70 km/h erreichen kann. Nach Ausführung der ersten Tests und eines 36-stündigen Flugs wird das HB-SIA mit einem Atlantiküberflug einen großen Klassiker der Luftfahrt wieder aufleben lassen. Das HB-SIB wird hingegen eine Erdumrundung mit fünf Zwischenlandungen in Angriff nehmen. Mit einer Flügelspannweite von 63,40 m und einem Gewicht von 1600 kg ist das revolutionäre Solar Impulse ein starkes Symbol, das zur Entdeckung der Vorteile erneuerbarer Energien anregen wird.

www.solarimpulse.com

Un million de tonnes de pétrole sont consommées chaque heure dans le monde. C'est pourquoi les projets liés aux sources d'énergies renouvelables s'orientent vers des horizons toujours nouveaux. Solar Impulse, l'avion propulsé uniquement à l'énergie solaire, est le fruit de ces recherches dans le domaine aéronautique. Les deux prototypes réalisés, le HB-SIA et le HB-SIB, ne sont pas les premiers du genre, mais représentent un réel défi car, à la différence d'autres prototypes, ils ont été conçus pour voler de nuit comme de jour. Leurs 200 m² de cellules photovoltaïques fixées sur l'aile et le stabilisateur horizontal doivent permettre de voler à 70 km/h et d'atteindre une altitude de 8 500 m, avec quatre moteurs de 10 CV chacun. Après les vols-tests et l'accomplissement d'un vol de 36 heures, le HB-SIA rééditera les grandes classiques de l'histoire de l'aviation : la traversée de l'Atlantique. Ensuite, le HB-SIB tentera le tour du monde en cinq étapes. Totalement révolutionnaire, avec son envergure de 63,40 m pour un poids de 1 600 kg, le Solar Impulse est un symbole fort pour inciter à recourir davantage aux énergies renouvelables.

Solar Impulse (Switzerland)
2003
prototype

215

Bikedispenser

Bicycle distribution system
Fahrradverleihsystem
Distributeur de vélos

In response to urban nomadism and the environmental issues related to it, Springtime came up with a service that offers a mode of rapid transit without recourse to private cars or public buses. The first automatic bicycle distribution system was installed in two Dutch cities in 2007. Through the use of a simple rechargeable prepaid card, one can withdraw a bike from a transit location like a station and return it to the dispenser when finished. The bicycles are arranged just 6.5" apart, making Bikedispenser the most compact storage system in the world. The introduction of a service that completely replaces the use of fuel transport is an important step against the main causes of pollution and city traffic.

Als Antwort auf das wachsende Bedürfnis nach freier Fortbewegung in der Stadt und den damit verbundenen Umweltproblemen entwickelte die holländische Firma Springtime eine Lösung, die auf die Benutzung von Privatautos oder öffentlichen Bussen verzichtet. Der Bikedispenser ist ein automatisches Fahrradverleihsystem und wurde 2007 erstmals in zwei holländischen Kleinstädten realisiert. Dank einer aufladbaren Fahrradverleihkarte kann das Fahrrad an Orten des öffentlichen Verkehrs wie Bahnhöfen ausgeliehen werden. Nach der Benutzung wird das Fahrrad einfach wieder in den „Automaten" abgestellt. Die Fahrräder haben einen Abstand von nur 17 cm voneinander. Bikedispenser ist dadurch das kompakteste Fahrradaufbewahrungssystem weltweit. Die Einführung einer solchen Dienstleistung, bei der keine mit Treibstoff angetriebenen Verkehrsmittel benutzt werden, ist ein wichtiger Beitrag für die Schonung der Umwelt.

En réponse aux formes de nomadisme urbain et aux problématiques environnementales qui leur sont liées, Springtime a créé un service offrant la possibilité de se déplacer rapidement, sans devoir recourir à sa voiture ou aux transports publics. Le premier système de distribution automatique de vélos a été installé en 2007 dans deux villes néerlandaises. Grâce à une simple carte rechargeable prépayée, il est possible de retirer un vélo dans des lieux publics à forte fréquentation, comme les gares, et de le réinsérer dans le distributeur en fin d'utilisation. Les vélos sont rangés à seulement 17 cm les uns des autres, caractéristique faisant du Bikedispenser le système de stockage le plus compact au monde. L'introduction d'un service substituant totalement l'usage de moyens de transport nécessitant du carburant est une avancée importante contre les principales causes de pollution et de circulation urbaine.

www.bikedispenser.com

Springtime and Post&Dekker for Bikedispenser.com BV (The Netherlands)
2007

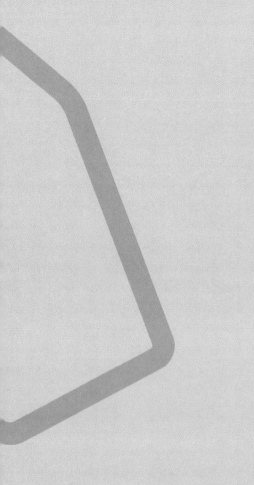

Clothing & accessories

Bekleidung & Accessoires
Habillement & accessoires

Introduction

Einleitung
Introduction

The clothing and accessories industries are more subject to rapid and continuous change than any other. Indeed, to stay in fashion and keep up with the times, we tend to leave perfectly fine, usable clothes in the closet, simply because tastes and trends have changed.

The fashion consumer can, however, make sustainable choices without feeling out-of-style or appearing anonymous. The products selected for this chapter have precisely that intention: to show that eco-friendly clothes and accessories are every bit as good as a traditional ones. In fact, more and more major labels and fashion houses are paying attention to environmental issues (Patagonia, Adidas), while other companies have been sustainable from the beginning (I'm Not A Plastic Bag, Marbella).

The main strategies adopted by the fashion world that are shown here are dematerialization—like the reduced Dopie thong sandal that is practically just a sole—and the use of recycled materials (ornj bags and BOOTLEG) and non-synthetic materials (Eco-chic), which favor greater skin tolerance. But ecodesign also means optimizing, minimizing and directly involving the consumer, as with the idea of selling a pattern to create several different bags using the fabric of the pattern itself (Sac à faire).

The chapter is arranged by type: footwear, bags, clothing and various accessories.

Die Modebranche unterliegt schnellen und fortwährenden Änderungen. Kleider, die noch in gutem Zustand sind bleiben im Kleiderschrank hängen, einfach nur, weil sich der persönliche Geschmack oder der allgemeine Trend geändert hat.

Der Verbraucher kann jedoch eine nachhaltige Entscheidung treffen, ohne dabei das Gefühl zu haben, nicht mehr dem Trend zu folgen oder unscheinbar zu wirken. Mit den in diesem Kapitel ausgewählten Produkten soll aufgezeigt werden, dass umweltfreundliche Mode oder Accessoires der klassischen Mode in nichts nachstehen. Im Gegenteil, immer mehr Unternehmen und Modehäuser schenken dem Umweltschutz besondere Beachtung (z. B. Patagonia, Adidas), während andere von Beginn an nachhaltige Produkte entwickelten (z. B. I'm Not A Plastic Bag, Marbella).

Die wichtigsten in der Modebranche angewandten Strategien sind die Entmaterialisierung wie die Flip-Flops Dopie, die auf ein Minimum reduziert wurden und praktisch nur noch aus einer Sohle bestehen, die Verwendung von Recycling-Materialien (ornj bags und BOOTLEG) oder der Einsatz von nicht synthetischen Materialien (Eco-chic), die eine bessere Hautverträglichkeit bieten. Ökologisches Design bedeutet aber auch Optimierung, Minimierung und die direkte Einbeziehung der Käufer, wie z. B. bei Sac à faire, wo das Schnittmuster gleichzeitig der Stoff für die Herstellung von mehreren Taschen ist.

Das Kapitel enthält folgende Typologien: Schuhe, Taschen, Kleidung und Accessoires.

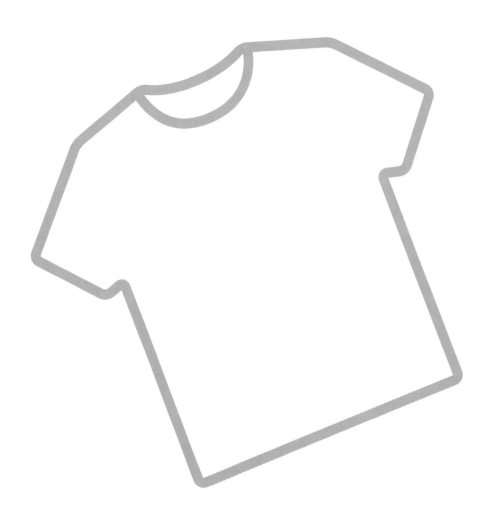

Les secteurs de l'habillement et des accessoires sont les plus sujets aux changements rapides et cycliques. Pour être toujours à la mode et se montrer dans l'air du temps, on tend souvent à laisser au placard des vêtements encore en bon état, car les goûts et tendances ont simplement changé.

Le consommateur peut cependant opérer un choix durable, sans pour cela sortir des codes de la mode ou se fondre dans la masse. Les produits sélectionnés dans ce chapitre ont justement l'intention de démontrer qu'un vêtement ou un accessoire eco-friendly n'a rien à envier à d'autres produits. Au contraire, les grandes marques et créateurs de mode sont de plus en plus nombreux à s'intéresser aux thématiques environnementales (Patagonia, Adidas), tandis que d'autres sont initialement nées dans cette optique durable (I'm Not A Plastic Bag, Marbella).

Vous retrouverez ici les principales stratégies adoptées par le secteur de la mode : dématérialisation (comme c'est le cas pour Dopie, qui réduit au minimum les tongs, au point de n'en faire quasiment qu'une semelle) ou utilisation de matériaux issus du recyclage (ornj bags et BOOTLEG) et non synthétiques (Eco-chic), qui favorisent une meilleure tolérance par l'épiderme. Mais écodesign signifie aussi optimiser, minimiser et impliquer directement l'acheteur, idée exploitée par la vente d'un patron permettant de réaliser plusieurs sacs en utilisant le tissu même du patron (Sac à faire).

Le chapitre est organisé suivant les types de produits : chaussures, sacs, vêtements et accessoires divers.

Crocs

Shoes for every season
Schuhe für jede Jahreszeit
Chaussures de toute saison

Often it is not the material that makes a product sustainable but its use, or even its reuse. This is the case with Crocs, which are made entirely of Croslite, a resin patented expressly for this purpose. On the one hand, the use of just one material minimizes cost and waste. On the other hand, their flexible structure allow Crocs to turn into winter footwear with the simple insertion of special padding. Parts can be substituted individually if needed, without having to throw the whole shoe away. Indeed, Crocs have become a cult object. Not only are they exceptionally lightweight, sturdy and odor-resistant, but they also respond to the comfort and health needs of the foot. With SolesUnited, the manufacturing company also came up with a way for Crocs to be recycled. Through this unique program, used footwear is collected and reused as the main material for a new production of shoes, which in turn are distributed throughout developing countries.

Oft ist es nicht das Material, das einem Produkt Nachhaltigkeit verleiht, sondern vielmehr die Verwendung bzw. Wiederverwendung. Dies ist der Fall bei Crocs, die vollkommen aus Croslite bestehen, einem exklusiv für Crocs patentierten Harztyp. Bei Produkten, die nur aus einem einzigen Material bestehen, sind die Kosten der Herstellung und die Abfallmengen sehr gering. Zudem können Crocs dank ihrer flexiblen Struktur einfach durch Einsetzen eines entsprechenden Futters in Winterschuhe verwandelt werden. So können die Teile, aus denen der Schuh besteht, einzeln ausgetauscht werden, ohne dass man gleich den ganzen Schuh wegwerfen muss. Crocs sind innerhalb kurzer Zeit zum Kultobjekt geworden. Sie sind besonders leicht, widerstandsfähig und bilden keine unangenehmen Gerüche. Sie entsprechen den Komfort- und Gesundheitsbedürfnissen der Füße. Erwähnenswert ist ein besonderes Projekt der Herstellerfirma zur Wiederverwertung der Crocs: SolesUnited. Die getragenen Crocs werden eingesammelt und als Rohstoff für die Schuhproduktion wieder verwendet. Diese neu hergestellten Schuhe werden dann in Entwicklungsländern verteilt.

Souvent, ce n'est pas le matériau qui rend le produit renouvelable, mais son utilisation ou plutôt sa réutilisation. C'est le cas des chaussures Crocs, entièrement fabriquées en Croslite, une résine spécialement brevetée : si d'une part la production d'un seul matériau minimise les coûts et les pertes, de l'autre, la structure flexible des Crocs permet d'en faire des chaussures d'hiver en ajoutant simplement la doublure prévue à cet effet. Les différentes parties de ces chaussures peuvent si nécessaire être changées individuellement, ce qui permet de garder certains éléments. Devenues cultes en peu de temps, les Crocs sont particulièrement légères, résistantes et anti-odeurs, tout en répondant aux besoins de confort et d'hygiène du pied. SolesUnited, l'entreprise productrice, a également pensé à leur réutilisation dans le cadre d'un programme spécial : les sabots usagés sont récupérés et réutilisés comme matière première pour une nouvelle production de chaussures, à leur tour distribuées dans les pays en voie de développement.

www.crocs.com

Crocs (USA)
2004

Dopie

Recyclable thong sandal
Recycelbare Flip-Flops
Tongs recyclables

Dopie's design key-word is essentiality. The very concept of the thong, itself a reduced form of footwear, has been re-devised and is even further exemplified by its main components: the strap and the sole. Indeed, the latter is refolded to create the thong itself, which acts to protect and block the foot. The strap is inserted into two slits in the sole, thereby simplifying the recycling of both components. Dopie shoes are made with a minimal use of resources and a recyclable material—ethylene-vinyl-acetate (EVA)—apart from the Velcro used to adjust the strap.

Das Schlüsselwort beim Design von Dopie lautet: Minimalismus. Das reduzierte Konzept der traditionellen Flip-Flops wurde hier überarbeitet und bei den Hauptbestandteilen Riemen und Sohle noch minimalistischer ausgeführt. Die Sohle wurde so geformt, dass sie von den ersten beiden Zehen gehalten wird. Diese Falte sorgt gleichzeitig für den Schutz und die Stabilität des Fußes. Der Riemen wurde durch zwei Schnitte in die Sohle eingesetzt. Auf diese Weise wird das Recycling der beiden Bestandteile vereinfacht. Dopie werden mit einem Mindestaufwand an Ressourcen und aus dem Kunststoff EVA (Ethylenvinylacetat) hergestellt. Daneben wird nur noch ein Klettverschluss zur Einstellung des Riemens benötigt.

Le maître-mot de Dopie est l'essentialité. Le concept de la tong, forme assez réduite en soi, a été retravaillé jusque dans ses principaux composants, la sangle et la semelle. Le repli, qui retient le pied, fait de cette chaussure une tong tout en constituant un réel élément de protection. La sangle est insérée dans deux fentes de la semelle, facilitant ainsi le recyclage des deux matériaux. La fabrication des Dopie nécessite un minimum de ressources et un matériau recyclable, l'acétate d'éthyle vinyle ou EVA (sans compter le velcro qui permet d'ajuster la sangle).

www.terraplana.com

Dopie for Terra Plana (UK)
2008

F50 Tunit

Modular soccer shoes
Modulare Fußballschuhe
Chaussures de foot modulaires

Adidas took the occasion of the 2006 World Cup to create the first modular soccer shoe. Consisting of three elements (chassis, upper and studs), the F50 Tunit was produced for a limited edition of 32 versions, one for every participating country in the championship. Each of the three parts was fully optimized: the chassis is more lightweight, with significantly less material, and it was carefully conceived to cushion impact at the points of greatest pressure (heel and ball); the upper guarantees good perspiration and cooling; and the removable studs allow for one base pair of shoes to be changed according to the conditions of the game. Indeed, with a totally flexible design, the F50 Tunit can be easily personalized.

Im Rahmen der Fußballweltmeisterschaft 2006 entwarf Adidas den ersten modulierbaren Fußballschuh. Dieser besteht aus drei Modulen: Chassis, Schaft und Stollen. Das Modell F50 Tunit wurde als limitierte Edition in 32 Versionen hergestellt, eine für jedes Teilnehmerland. Alle drei Module wurden aufs Höchste optimiert: das Chassis ist leichter, da die verwendete Materialmenge auf ein Minimum reduziert wurde. Es soll insbesondere die Druckpunkte an empfindlichen Stellen wie Ferse und Vorderfuß dämpfen; der Schaft gewährleistet einen guten Luftdurchlass und gute Kühlung, während die abnehmbaren Stollen die Anpassung an die verschiedenen Spielbedingungen ermöglichen. Durch das flexible Design kann F50 Tunit den Bedürfnissen seines Trägers optimal angepasst werden.

À l'occasion de la Coupe du Monde 2006, Adidas a créé la première chaussure de foot modulaire : constituée de trois éléments démontables (châssis, chausson et crampons), la F50 Tunit a été réalisée en édition limitée et en 32 versions, une pour chaque pays participant au championnat. Chacun des trois éléments a été optimisé : le châssis est plus léger car la quantité de matériau a été réduite de moitié, et tout particulièrement pensé pour amortir les chocs sur les points de pression maximale (talon et avant-pied); le chausson garantit une bonne circulation de l'air et les crampons amovibles permettent d'utiliser une seule paire de chaussures de base, à modifier selon les conditions de jeu. Grâce à son design totalement flexible, la F50 Tunit peut facilement être personnalisée.

adidas AG (Germany)
2006

Sugar & Spice

Modular shoes
Zusammensetzbare Schuhe
Chaussures à assembler

Sugar & Spice is a sustainable product for two reasons. First, versatility: the shoes consist of four modules that are inserted into one another like a series of Chinese boxes, and they can be worn with or without the outsole. Second, choice of materials: 70% natural latex rubber for the outsole, 15% recycled EVA (polyethylene vinyl acetate) for the footbed, and pigskin leather for the upper. Unlike other modular shoes on the market, Sugar & Spice's four parts are sold separately in case of damage. The Patagonia homepage also reports all the data on the emissions generated and the materials used for its many intelligently designed shoes.

Die Nachhaltigkeit beim Freizeitschuh Sugar & Spice zeigt sich in der sorgfältigen Auswahl der Materialien und in der Vielseitigkeit. Er besteht aus vier Einzelteilen, die ineinander gefügt werden und auch ohne den Außenschuh getragen werden können. Als Materialien wurden 70% pflanzliches Gummi, 15% Recycling-EVA (Ethylenvinylacetat) für die Sohle und Schweineleder für das Obermaterial verwendet. Im Gegensatz zu anderen zusammensetzbaren Schuhen auf dem Markt können die einzelnen Elemente von Sugar & Spice separat gekauft werden, falls eines kaputt sein sollte. Wer weitere Informationen erhalten möchte, findet auf der Webseite von Patagonia alle Daten zu den Emissionen und den verwendeten Materialien.

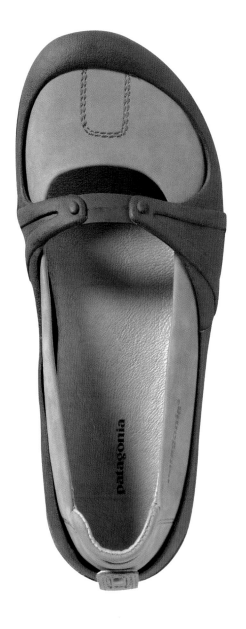

www.patagonia.com

Choix des matériaux et versatilité sont les éléments faisant de Sugar & Spice un produit durable. Celle-ci est composée de quatre éléments à insérer les uns dans les autres comme des poupées russes et la semelle externe supplémentaire est totalement facultative. Les matériaux choisis sont constitués à 70% de caoutchouc d'origine végétale, à 15% d'EVA (polyéthylène vinylacétate) recyclé pour la semelle et de la croute de porc pour l'empeigne. A la différence d'autres chaussures du marché développant ce concept, les quatre éléments de Sugar & Spice peuvent être achetés séparément en cas d'endommagement. La page d'accueil du site de Patagonia informera les intéressés des données concernant les émissions engendrées et les matériaux employés pour la production de ces chaussures intelligentes.

Deborah Andersen for Patagonia Footwear (USA)
2006

BUCCIA

Convertible bags
Platzsparende Taschen
Sacs transformables

www.mhway.it

Makio Hasuike for MH WAY (Italy)
2004

Just by opening the large zipper of a BUCCIA bag, briefcase or knapsack, it converts into a flat sheet. This way, it takes up hardly any space when stored and not in use. The bags are made of lightweight materials (polyester and foam polyethylene) and special care was taken in the details of critical points like the handles, which are made of leather for extra durability. With BUCCIA, the company's designer and founder Makio Hasuike wanted to create something that was fully in tune with his philosophy, a line of aesthetically pure and flexible objects whose most obvious decorative element is, precisely, the zipper.

Durch einfaches Öffnen des Reißverschlusses werden die verschiedenen Modelle der Produktlinie BUCCIA in eine flache, zweidimensionale Form verwandelt. Auf diese Weise können sie, wenn sie nicht gebraucht werden, ohne großen Platzbedarf verstaut werden. Die Produkte, die aus Polyester und geschäumten Polyethylen bestehen, wurden mit einem besonderen Auge für Details entwickelt. Um Risse an stark beanspruchten Stellen, wie z. B. dem Handgriff, zu vermeiden, werden diese aus Leder gefertigt. Mit BUCCIA wollte Makio Hasuike, Designer und Gründer der Firma, in völligem Einklang mit seiner Philosophie eine Produktreihe entwickeln, die ästhetisch rein und flexibel sein sollte und auffälligstes Element eben der Reißverschluss ist.

Ouvrez la fermeture éclair des sacs, serviettes et sacs à dos de la ligne BUCCIA pour faire apparaître des feuilles « profilées » parfaitement plates. Lorsque vous ne les utilisez pas, ces sacs prennent un minimum de place. Produits à l'aide de matériaux légers (polyester et polyéthylène expansé), certains détails ont été particulièrement soignés comme les éléments importants tels que l'anse, fabriquée en cuir pour une solidité optimale. En accord total avec sa philosophie, Makio Hasuike, designer et fondateur de la marque, a voulu créer avec BUCCIA une ligne d'objets esthétiquement purs et flexibles, dont l'élément esthétique le plus évident est à l'évidence la fermeture éclair.

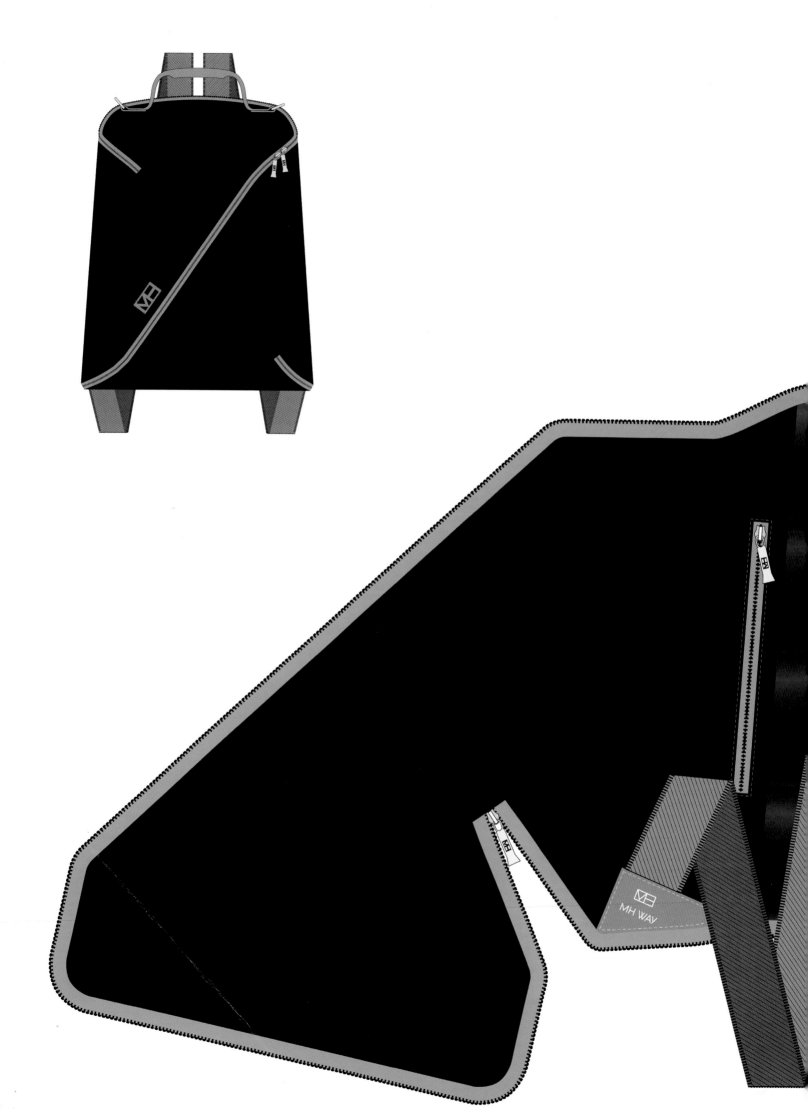

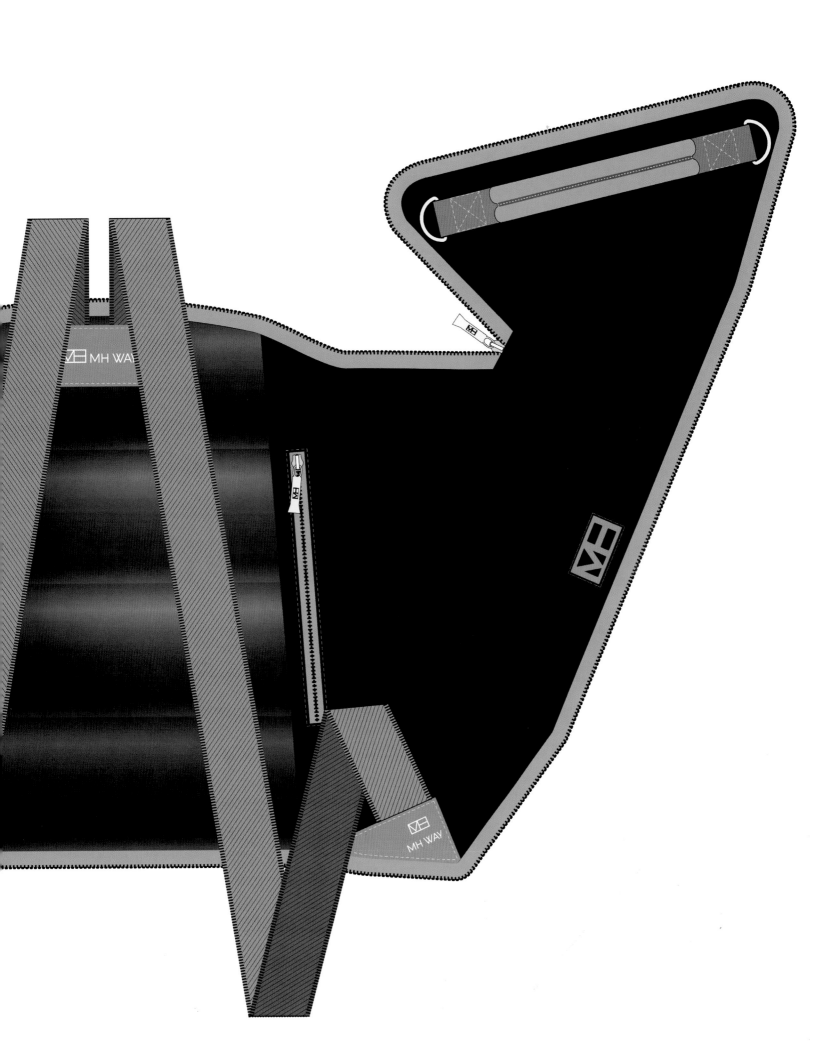

I'm NOT A Plastic Bag

Cotton shopping bag
Stofftasche
Cabas en coton

I'm NOT A Plastic Bag was the first shopping bag made entirely of cotton and as such is a cult object that opened the way to a series of bags in natural materials. The redundancy of the printed message is purposefully provocative. The simple affirmation of what the bag is not is meant as an admonishment for people to use shopping bags made of biodegradable or reusable materials rather than plastic and thereby reduce their negative impact on the environment. Considering that 170 plastic bags per capita are discarded each year, the trend promoted by this shopping bag is a remarkable result.

I'm NOT A Plastic Bag ist die erste Einkaufstasche, die vollkommen aus Baumwolle hergestellt wurde. Sie zählt zu den Kultobjekten der Ökobewegung und hat den Weg für Naturfaser-Taschen geebnet. Das aufgedruckte Motto ist gewollt provozierend: die einfache Aussage darüber, was die Tasche eben nicht ist, will dazu auffordern, keine Plastiktüten mehr zu verwenden, sondern Tüten, die biologisch abbaubar sind oder aus wieder verwertbaren Materialien bestehen. Dadurch können die Auswirkungen auf die Umwelt deutlich vermindert werden. Wenn man bedenkt, dass pro Person etwa 170 Plastiktüten pro Jahr die Umwelt belasten, setzt dieser durch den Shopper lancierte Trend ein wirkungs-volles Zeichen.

www.anyahindmarch.com

Anya Hindmarch (UK)
2007

I'm NOT A Plastic Bag est le premier cabas entièrement fabriqué en coton. Devenu culte, il a ouvert la voie à toute une série de sacs en matériaux naturels. Le message imprimé est volontairement provocateur : en refusant simplement d'être en plastique, ce sac invite à l'utilisation de matériaux biodégradables ou réutilisables et réduit ainsi l'impact sur l'environnement. Si l'on considère qu'un habitant jette environ 170 sacs dans la nature chaque année, la tendance lancée par ce cabas marque une avancée remarquable.

MARBELLA

Recycled-material bags
Taschen aus Recycling-Material
Sacs en matériaux recyclés

www.demano.net

Meck Osten for demano (Spain)
2006

Demano products have become international cult objects that are helping raise awareness about environmental themes in a creative way, especially for the younger public. Founded in Barcelona in 1998, Demano was one of the first companies to actually pay attention to ecological problems. It all started after three Brazilian women noticed the great number of advertising posters around the Spanish city and decided to create bags using colored PVC rectangles. Following the success of the first models, they added new materials: scraps from local textile companies, old umbrellas and polyester—pretty much anything that would otherwise be destined for the dump. With charming shapes and skilful color combinations, Demano has given life to a vibrant line of sustainable design accessories.

Demano-Produkte sind internationale Kultobjekte. Sie sensibilisieren auf kreative Weise vor allem das jüngere Publikum für Umweltfragen. Demano wurde 1998 in Barcelona gegründet und gilt als eines der ersten Unternehmen, das sich eingehend mit Umweltproblemen beschäftigte. Die drei brasilianischen Gründerinnen bemerkten die großen Mengen an Werbebannern, die in der spanischen Stadt ausgehängt wurden. Aus diesen farbigen PVC-Rechtecken fertigten sie Taschen. Nach dem Erfolg der ersten Modelle kamen neue Materialien hinzu wie z. B. Abfallprodukte aus der Textilindustrie, alte Regenschirme und Polyester, bzw. all jene Materialien, die sonst auf den Müllhalden gelandet wären. In der Folgezeit entwarf Demano eine ganze Reihe von Accessoires mit ansprechenden Formen und Farbkombinationen, die dem Prinzip der Nachhaltigkeit von Ökodesign entsprechen.

Les produits Demano contribuent de manière créative à la sensibilisation du public aux questions environnementales. Née à Barcelone en 1998, Demano fut l'une des premières entreprises réellement à l'écoute des problématiques écologiques : c'est en observant les grandes quantités d'affiches publicitaires exposées dans la ville espagnole que trois Brésiliennes eurent l'idée de confectionner des sacs en réutilisant ces rectangles colorés en PVC. Après le succès des premiers modèles, de nouveaux matériaux furent intégrés, comme les rebuts des entreprises textiles locales, de vieux parapluies et du polyester, autrement dit tous les matériaux normalement destinés à envahir les décharges. Grâce à des formes attrayantes et de savants mélanges de couleur, Demano a réussi à donner vie à une ligne créative d'accessoires au design écologique.

ornj bags

Industrial-material bag
Tasche aus Industriematerial
Sac en matériau industriel

www.ornjbags.com

David Shock for davidshockdesigns (USA)
2008

These days, the recycling of industrial materials for the production of accessories is all the rage. For its part, ornj created a fun, modern line of bags out of the colored plastic fences used on construction sites. Like other materials of this type, these fences were doomed to be discarded once their primary, short-lived function had ceased, regardless of their durability. Noting the user-friendliness and high performance of the material, designer David Shock decided to use it to create a laundry bag. The project was so successful that he has since repeated it for three more models in a recent line. ornj has received increasing requests for products like this, which are made with recycled materials and offer lasting resistance while still respecting aesthetics, fully in tune with the times.

Das Recycling von Industriematerial zur Herstellung von Modeaccessoires liegt im Trend. Für ornj wurden orangefarbene Plastikzäune, die von Baustellen bekannt sind, für eine ansprechende und moderne Taschen-kollektion wieder verwendet. Wie bei anderen ähnlichen Materialien steht diesen Absperrzäunen, nachdem sie ihre Funktion erfüllt haben, nur noch ein kurzes Leben vor ihrer Entsorgung bevor – ungeachtet des robusten und langlebigen Materials. Der Designer David Shock nutzte die einfache Verwendung und die vielen verschiedenen Möglichkeiten, die das Material bot. Nach dem erfolgreichen Entwurf eines Wäschekorbs griff er wieder auf dieses Material zurück, um drei Modelle einer neuen Produktreihe herzu-stellen. Die Nachfrage nach Produkten aus wieder verwerteten Materialien, die beständig sind, ohne dabei den ästhetischen Aspekt zu vernachlässigen, nimmt immer weiter zu.

Le recyclage de matériaux industriels pour la production d'accessoires est en plein essor. ornj utilise les grillages en plastique de couleur que l'on emploie sur les chantiers pour donner corps à une ligne moderne et originale de sacs à main. Comme d'autres matériaux similaires et malgré une résistance à toute épreuve, ces grillages ont, au-delà de leur fonction première, une durée de vie assez courte et sont destinés à la décharge. Grâce à leur facilité d'utilisation et leurs performances élevées, le designer David Shock a eu la bonne idée de les utiliser pour les trois modèles de la ligne, après le succès d'un premier sac à linge, réalisé avec ce matériau. En plein accord avec les tendances actuelles, la demande de produits similaires, issus du recyclage et durables dans le temps (sans altération des qualités esthétiques), ne cesse d'augmenter.

Sac à faire

DIY bags
Do-it-yourself-Tasche
Sacs à faire soi-même

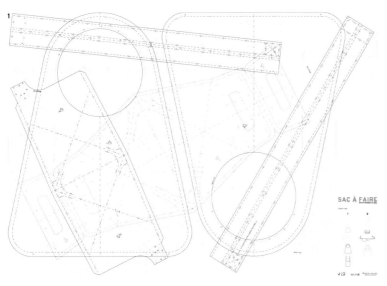

The ready-to-wear and the do-it-yourself come together in the Sac à faire. Born as the thesis project of a young Austrian designer, the Sac à faire is a veritable craft kit for making bags that consists of just one diagram and ten patterns. Its originality lies in the fact that there is no need to buy separate materials, since the bags are made with the fabric of the diagram itself. This synthetic material, HDPE (high-density polyethylene), seems almost like paper and is easy to fold and sew. It also has what it takes to last, as it is extremely sturdy, waterproof, washable and iron-friendly. "Wear it proudly, because you made it yourself!" says the website, underlining the benefits of self-production, not least of which is the advantage of reducing the financial and environmental waste of unsold objects.

Sac à faire vereint erstmals die Konzepte Prét-à-porter und Do-it-yourself. Der Do-it-yourself-kit für Taschen entstand zunächst als Doktorarbeit der jungen österreichischen Designerin Marlene Liska und enthält Skizzen von zehn verschiedenen Modellen. Die Besonderheit dabei ist, dass kein Stoff separat gekauft werden muss, da die Taschen aus dem Material, auf dem sich die Skizzen befinden, hergestellt werden können. Dieses synthetische Material HDPE (Polyethylen hoher Dichte) ähnelt Papier und lässt sich sehr leicht falten und nähen. Außerdem besitzt es alle Eigenschaften, um eine lange Lebensdauer des Produktes zu gewährleisten: es ist robust, wasserundurchlässig, waschbar und bügelbar. „Wear it proudly, because you made it yourself!" besagt die Webseite. Dieses Motto unterstreicht die Vorteile der Eigenherstellung kostengünstig und umweltfreundlich.

www.sacafaire.net

Le prêt-à-porter et les loisirs créatifs se sont rencontrés dans Sac à faire. À l'origine d'un projet de thèse d'une designer autrichienne, Sac à faire est un vrai kit pour fabriquer son propre sac et contient uniquement des patrons prévus pour dix modèles. Sa particularité réside dans le fait qu'il n'est pas nécessaire d'acheter de tissu, car les sacs sont élaborés à partir du matériau même du patron. Ce matériau synthétique, l'HDPE (polyéthylène haute densité), ressemble à du papier tout en étant facile à plier et à coudre. Il possède de plus toutes les caractéristiques lui permettant de vaincre les épreuves du temps : extrêmement robuste, imperméable, lavable et facile à repasser. « Wear it proudly, because you made it yourself ! » (Portez-le dignement, c'est vous qui l'avez fait !) indique le site Web, soulignant ainsi que l'autoproduction permet d'éviter les pertes économiques et environnementales des articles invendus.

Marlene Liska (Austria)
2006

Solar Beach Tote

Solar-paneled beach bag
Solar-Strandtasche
Sac de plage à panneaux solaires

The Solar Beach Tote is a beach bag that can also recharge electrical appliances. The thin solar panel on the front of the bag is composed of 52 micro cells that accumulate energy. Through a socket on the side, the bag can recharge the battery of a common cell phone in 2-4 hours. The bag is made entirely of recycled PET, which makes it both waterproof and environmentally-friendly. The company is in fact especially careful about environmental costs and only uses materials that come from Texas or North Carolina, where its factories are located. The Solar Beach Tote is therefore an interesting response to multiple ecodesign criteria.

Solar Beach Tote ist eine Strandtasche, die elektrische Geräte aufladen kann. Eine dünne Schicht aus 52 Solarzellen speichert die Sonnenenergie. Über den auf der Seite angebrachten Stecker können so handelsübliche Handys in 2 bis 4 Stunden aufgeladen werden. Die Tasche besteht ausschließlich aus recyceltem PET, das ihr gleichzeitig Wasserundurchlässigkeit verleiht. Die Auswirkungen auf die Umwelt sind bei diesem Produkt besonders gering. Schon bei der Auswahl des Recycling-Materials bewies das amerikanische Herstellerunternehmen besondere Sensibilität für Fragen des Umweltschutzes. Es werden ausschließlich Materialien aus Texas und North Carolina benutzt, wo sich auch die Produktionswerke befinden. Solar Beach Tote erfüllt verschiedene Kriterien von Ökodesign.

www.rewarestore.com

Le Solar Beach Tote est un sac de plage capable de recharger les appareils électriques. Le panneau solaire très fin disposé à l'avant du sac contient 52 microcellules permettant l'accumulation d'énergie. Grâce à la prise située sur le côté, le sac peut ainsi recharger la batterie d'un téléphone portable en 2 à 4 heures. Le sac est entièrement fabriqué en PET recyclé, matériau qui le rend imperméable en plus de lui garantir un faible impact sur l'environnement. Particulièrement attentive aux coûts environnementaux, la société récupère ce matériau exclusivement dans la zone de production, c'est-à-dire au Texas et en Caroline du Nord, où se situent les usines. Le Solar Beach Tote devient ainsi une réponse intéressante aux multiples critères de l'écodesign.

Reware (USA)
2006

Eco-chic
Haute couture and sustainability
Haute Couture und Nachhaltigkeit
Haute-couture et développement durable

www.gattinoni.net

Guillermo Mariotto for Gattinoni (Italy)
2008

With the 2008 spring-summer collection, high fashion became the mouthpiece of the eco-friendly world. Venezuelan couturier Guillermo Mariotto, creative director of Italian fashion house Gattinoni, presented 43 designs on the runway created with natural, biodegradable and recycled materials. Among the pieces in the collection, Bio-sposa, a wedding dress, merits particular attention for its use of PLA fiber, a derivative of cornstarch. The particularly luminous reflections of the garments created this way and the design, in no way inferior to clothes made of traditional textiles, make the aesthetic potential of this type of resource obvious. The message speaks for itself: even the high-fashion world can actively participate in protecting the environment and call upon its customers to buy mindfully and consciously.

Bei den Modenschauen Frühjahr/Sommer 2008 standen die Modelle der Haute Couture ganz im Zeichen der Umweltverträglichkeit. Der venezolanische Designer Guillermo Mariotto, Creative Director des italienischen Modehauses Gattinoni, präsentierte auf dem Laufsteg 43 Modelle aus natürlichen, biologisch abbaubaren und recycelten Materialien. Unter den Kollektionsmodellen verdient das Hochzeitskleid Bio-sposa besondere Beachtung. Es wurde aus einer aus Maisstärke gewonnenen Kunststofffaser (PLA) gefertigt. Die besonderen Lichtreflexe dieser Entwürfe und das Design, das Kreationen aus klassischen Stoffen in nichts nachsteht, haben das ästhetische Potential dieser innovativen Materialien aufgezeigt. Die Botschaft dabei spricht für sich selbst: auch Haute Couture kann aktiv zum Umweltschutz beitragen, und die Kunden dazu anregen, aufmerksamer und bewusster einzukaufen.

Avec la collection printemps-été 2008, les podiums sont devenus les porte-paroles des mouvements pour l'environnement. Le styliste vénézuélien Guillermo Mariotto, directeur de création de la maison italienne Gattinoni, a proposé lors de son défilé 43 modèles en matériaux naturels, biodégradables et recyclés. La collection recèle des trésors dont l'un mérite une attention particulière : la robe de mariée Bio-sposa, réalisée en fibre de PLA, un dérivé de l'amidon de maïs. Les reflets particulièrement lumineux des modèles ainsi créés et le design, qui n'a rien à envier aux tissus traditionnels, ont mis en évidence le potentiel esthétique de ce type de ressources. Le message est clair : même la haute-couture peut participer activement à l'éveil des consciences et inviter ses propres clients à acheter en faveur du développement durable.

naturevsfuture®

Clothing line
Kleiderkollektion
Ligne de vêtements

Because of the use of dyes and highly-valued animal furs and skins, and the ways that new-generation technical textiles are produced, the fashion industry, like others, can have negative consequences on the environment. There are also the ethical questions regarding the working conditions in some areas of the world where products are made. naturevsfuture® is a collection of clothes made mainly from natural and secondary materials from urban or manufacturing waste. In addition to the classic wool and organic cotton, there is also hemp, soy, bamboo, SeaCell® and lyocell (obtained from algae and cellulose respectively), and Ingeo, a derivative of corn. The choice of materials is based exclusively on the sensorial and functional characteristics required by the item of clothing.

Wie viele andere Bereiche wirkt sich auch die Modebranche negativ auf die Umwelt aus, z. B. durch die Anwendung bestimmter Färbemittel, durch die Verarbeitung von Leder und Pelzen und die damit verbundene Bedrohung einiger Tierarten, sowie durch die Produktionsverfahren bei der Herstellung modernster Textilien. Hinzu kommen ethische Fragen in Bezug auf die Arbeitsbedingungen in einigen Produktionsländern. Die Kollektion naturevsfuture® verwendet vor allem natürliche Materialien oder Sekundärmaterialien. Neben den klassischen Fasern Wolle und Bio-Baumwolle wurden vor allem folgende Rohstoffe eingesetzt: Hanf, Soja, Bambus, SeaCell® und Lyocell, die aus Algen bzw. Zellulose gewonnen werden und schließlich die aus Mais hergestellte Ingeo-Faser. Die Wahl des Materials erfolgte ausschließlich nach sensorischen und funktionalen Kriterien, die das Kleidungsstück erfüllen soll.

Comme d'autres secteurs, la mode peut aussi avoir des conséquences négatives sur l'environnement. Colorants, utilisation de peaux et fourrures d'animaux rares et modalités de production des tissus techniques nouvelle génération sont autant de menaces. S'ajoutent ensuite à celles-ci les questions étiques liées aux conditions de travail dans certaines régions du monde. La collection naturevsfuture® emploie surtout des matériaux naturels ou des matières secondaires provenant de déchets urbains ou de chutes industrielles. Les matériaux classiques comme la laine et le coton Bio côtoient chanvre, soja, bambou, SeaCell® et lyocell, respectivement dérivés d'algues et de cellulose, ainsi que l'Ingeo, issu du maïs. Le choix des matériaux s'effectue exclusivement selon les caractéristiques sensorielles et fonctionnelles voulues pour chaque pièce.

www.naturevsfuture.com

Nina Valenti for naturevsfuture® (USA)
2002

BOOTLEG

Inner-tube belt
Gürtel aus einem Fahrradschlauch
Ceinture en chambre à air

The re-use potential of materials in the accessories industry is becoming increasingly evident, giving life to new combinations. Old bicycle inner tubes, for example, were the inspiration for Italian designer Dario Toso's BOOTLEG belts. The inner tubes are collected directly from resellers and reconditioned, at which point they are ready for a second life cycle. Even the logo's printing on the belt buckles with the use of low-impact water-based ink was conceived in terms of sustainability. BOOTLEG was originally a do-it-yourself object that spread across the internet as an open-source project. Just by following the instructions and buying the buckle, you can make the belt you like and learn the value of reuse at the same time.

Recycelte oder wieder verwendete Materialien zur Gestaltung von Modeaccessoires werden immer beliebter und führen zu immer neuen Synergien. Im Fall der BOOTLEG-Gürtel inspirierte sich der Designer Dario Toso an alten Fahrradschläuchen. Die Schläuche werden direkt bei den Händlern eingesammelt und können nach der Aufbereitung für einen neuen Verwendung eingesetzt werden. Nachhaltigkeit spielte auch beim Logo auf der Gürtelschnalle eine wichtige Rolle: es besteht aus umweltfreundlicher Farbe auf Wasserbasis. BOOTLEG entstand ursprünglich als Do-it-yourself-Objekt, das im Internet als Open-Source-Projekt angeboten wurde. Mit dem Kauf der Schnalle und unter Beachtung der Anleitungen konnte man seinen Wunschgürtel kreieren und dabei direkt den Wert der Wiederverwendung erkennen.

www.bootleg.it

Le potentiel de réutilisation des matériaux dans le secteur des accessoires devient de plus en plus évident et donne vie à de nouvelles synergies. Dans le cas de la ceinture BOOTLEG, le designer italien Dario Toso s'est inspiré de chambres à air usagées de vélos. Celles-ci sont récupérées directement chez les revendeurs ; une fois remises en état, elles sont prêtes à vivre une nouvelle vie. L'empreinte de la marque sur la boucle est aussi pensée en termes durables, en employant une encre à base d'eau dont l'impact environnemental est faible. BOOTLEG est à l'origine un objet à faire soi-même, le projet ayant été diffusé sur internet en open-source : en suivant les instructions et en n'achetant que la boucle, on pouvait réaliser la ceinture désirée et comprendre directement la valeur du recyclage.

Dario Toso for Cinelli - Gruppo S.p.a. (Italy)
2008

ic! berlin

All-steel glasses
Sonnenbrille aus Federstahl
Lunettes mono-matériau

ic! berlin offers a line of sun and eye glasses for men, women and children with a unique and ingenious design. The frames that have made them famous are made entirely out of steel. Their parts clasp together, without the use of glue or screws, which means they are perfectly recyclable. The flexibility of the material also makes them practically indestructible. Cut from a 0.02"-thick steel plate, the glasses are slender and ultra-lightweight. This innovative technology has helped to produce a line that is "simple and nude, sexy because it's extremely intelligent and functional," as defined by the team that created it. Because of the ergonomic design, the glasses can be adapted to the features of the face for maximum comfort. They can also be personalized with a vast array of interchangeable temples.

ic! berlin bietet eine Linie von Sonnen- und Sehbrillen für Männer, Frauen und Kinder mit einem einzigartigen und genialen Design. Die Rahmen – das Markenzeichen von ic! Berlin – bestehen allein aus Federstahl. Sie werden durch ein patentiertes Stecksystem zusammengesetzt, ohne die Verwendung von Klebstoff oder Schrauben. Dank der Flexibilität des Materials sind die Brillen praktisch unzerstörbar und äußerst langlebig. Die durch Wasserstrahltechnik aus einer 0,5 mm dünnen Stahlplatte geschnittenen Brillen sind dünn und ultraleicht. Diese Technologie ermöglichte die Herstellung einer durch das Entwicklerteam wie folgt definierten Produktreihe: „eine einfache und nackte aber auch sinnliche Linie, weil sie extrem intelligent und funktionell ist". Die Brillen sind ergonomisch, da sie sich an die Gesichtszüge anpassen und maximalen Komfort bieten.

www.ic-berlin.de

ic! berlin propose une ligne de lunettes de soleil et de vue, pour hommes, femmes et enfants, au design unique et étonnant. Les montures mono-matériau qui ont fait leur célébrité sont totalement en acier; leurs composants sont encastrés, sans collage ni vis, ce qui en facilite le recyclage. La flexibilité de l'acier les rend quasiment indestructibles. Découpées au jet d'eau dans une plaque d'acier de 0,5 mm d'épaisseur, la finesse et l'ultra-légèreté de ces lunettes est étonnante. L'utilisation de cette technique a permis de créer une ligne « simple et nue, fonctionnelle et sexy par son intelligence extrême », comme la définit son équipe de réalisation. Les lunettes sont ergonomiques car elles s'adaptent aux traits du visage pour un confort optimal, et personnalisables grâce à leur large gamme de branches de rechange.

Ralph Anderl, Kathrin Schuster, Bernhard Schwarzbauer for ic! berlin (Germany) 2008

261

Sushehat

Transformable hat
Vielseitiger Hut
Chapeau transformable

Asian style is the inspiration for both the form and packaging of Sushehat. Designed by Peter De Vries for a 2003 exhibition on the Japanese Empire in Hamburg, this hat can take on a full nine different shapes simply by folding the edges and tying the bow. The hat's materials consist of paper mixed with hemp, cotton, boiled wool and velour-felt. The packaging, much smaller than a normal hat box, is printed with instructions on how to create the nine models. While it may only have one function, Sushehat is an accessory that can be endlessly changed and renewed.

Sushehat lehnt sich sowohl beim Namen als auch bei seiner Verpackung an den asiatischen Stil an. Der Hut wurde 2003 von Peter De Vries im Rahmen einer Ausstellung über das Japanische Kaiserreich in Hamburg vorgestellt. Durch einfaches Falten und Umschlagen kann der Hut neun verschiedene Formen annehmen. Die verwendeten Materialien sind gemischtes Hanfpapier, Baumwolle, Samt und Filz. Auf der Verpackung, die gegenüber herkömmlichen Hutschachteln in der Größe stark reduziert wurde, ist die Anleitung für die verschiedenen Trageversionen aufgedruckt. Obwohl die Funktion immer die eine bleibt, verwandelt sich Sushehat in ein vielseitiges Accessoire, das immer wieder auf neue Weise benutzt werden kann.

Autant par son nom que par la forme de son emballage, Sushehat est résolument oriental. Pensé par Peter De Vries à l'occasion de l'exposition sur l'Empire Japonais qui s'est tenue à Hambourg en 2003, le chapeau peut prendre jusqu'à neuf formes : il suffit simplement d'en plier ou en tourner les bords. Les matériaux utilisés sont constitués d'un mélange de papier et de chanvre, du coton, de la laine bouillie, du velours et du feutre. Les instructions pour réaliser les neuf modèles sont imprimées sur l'emballage, dont les dimensions sont très réduites comparées aux chapeaux habituels. Même si sa fonction reste unique, Sushehat n'en demeure pas moins un accessoire facilement versatile et toujours nouveau.

www.sushehat.de

Peter De Vries (Germany)
2003

263

Toys

Spielzeug
Jouets

Introduction

Einleitung
Introduction

As important as it is for toys to be educational, their environmental impact should not be neglected. Not only do toys often have a short life, but they can even transfer harmful substances upon contact, for example because of toxic dyes. The public is generally very aware of this subject, yet truly sustainable alternatives within this industry remain considerably obscured. It is in fact possible these days to buy toys with a predilection for natural dyes or materials that derive from seasonally renewable sources, like PlayMais®, or that prevent overproduction and waste by providing do-it-yourself guidelines, like Foldschool.

In selecting the toys and games for this chapter, solutions that educate kids about environmental issues (Play Rethink) and clean technologies (H-RACER) were also taken into consideration.

These choices show how the world of toys can adopt approaches that are multiple, various and often unexpected.

Der Lerneffekt ist bei Spielzeug sehr wichtig, aber auch die Umweltbelastungen verdienen Beachtung. Einerseits haben Spielsachen oft nur eine kurze Lebensdauer, und andererseits können sie bei Körperkontakt schädliche Stoffe abgegeben, wie z. B. durch die verwendeten Farben. Die Öffentlichkeit ist für gewöhnlich sehr interessiert an diese Themen, aber über nachhaltige und umweltfreundliche Alternativen ist nur wenig bekannt. Heute können Spielsachen gekauft werden, die natürliche Farbstoffe enthalten oder aus jahreszeitlich erneuerbaren Materialien bestehen, wie z. B. PlayMais® oder Produkte, die Kindern die Möglichkeit geben, Formen und Design selbst zu bestimmen, wie Foldschool.

In diesem Kapitel werden auch Spiele präsentiert, bei denen sich die Kinder mit Umweltproblemen (Play Rethink) oder sauberen Technologien (H-RACER) spielerisch auseinandersetzen.

Die Auswahl zeigt die vielfältigen, unterschiedlichen und oft auch überraschenden Ansätze, die bei der Produktion von Spielzeug angewendet werden.

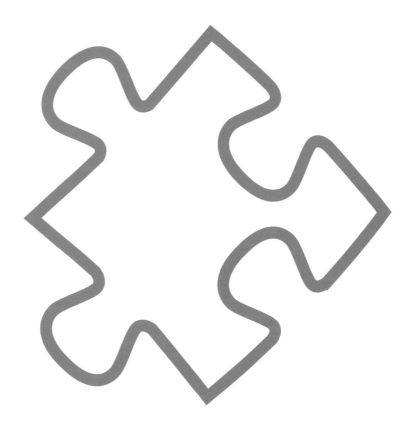

Même si la fonction éducative des jouets est très importante, leur impact sur l'environnement ne doit pas pour autant être négligé : ils ont souvent une durée de vie assez courte et peuvent relâcher des substances au contact par exemple de colorants toxiques. L'opinion publique est généralement très sensible à cette thématique mais souvent peu informée des alternatives véritablement durables présentes dans ce secteur. Il est aujourd'hui possible d'acheter des jouets privilégiant des colorants naturels ou des matériaux dérivant de sources renouvelables de manière saisonnière (comme PlayMais®), ou qui donnent à l'enfant la possibilité d'en déterminer la forme et le design, comme Foldschool.

La sélection de jouets de ce chapitre prend aussi en considération des solutions qui éduquent l'enfant à la thématique environnementale (Play Rethink) et aux technologies propres (H-RACER).

Ces choix démontrent que les approches du monde du jouet sont souvent multiples, variées et inattendues.

Creatures
Recycled toys
Recycling-Spielsachen
Jouets recyclés

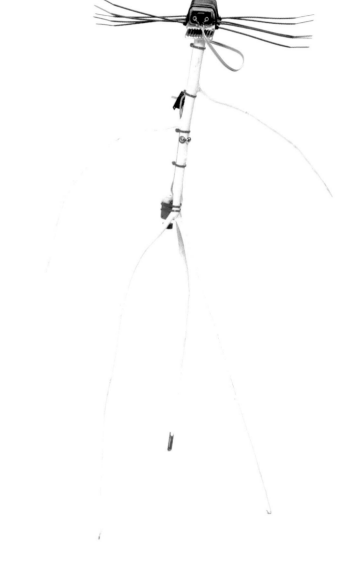

Even toys can help teach and spread the politics of eco-sustainability. Creatures, produced in a limited edition by Tobias Rockenfeld for Droog Design, are made of broken toys, components recovered from old household appliances and domestic waste. The results of this design took the forms of 18 unique models that move, fly, swim, light up and laugh. The designer wanted to share the hidden value in trash with kids. So he created toys that, unlike current trends, promote functionality and reuse over ultra-technological and colored forms, which often have a solely aesthetic value.

Auch Spielzeug kann zum Verständnis und zur Verbreitung von Nachhaltigkeit beitragen. Die von Tobias Rockenfeld für Droog Design als limitierte Edition hergestellten Creatures sind aus kaputten Spielsachen, wieder verwerteten Bauteilen alter Haushaltsgeräte und Haushaltsabfällen gemacht. Es entstanden 18 einzigartige Modelle, die sich auf dem Wasser oder auf dem Land fortbewegen, fliegen, blinken und lachen können. Ziel des Designers war es, Kindern den versteckten Wert von Abfallprodukten zu vermitteln. Bei der Herstellung dieser Spielsachen stehen Funktionalität und Wiederverwertung im Gegensatz zu Hightech und Farbenvielfalt im Vordergrund.

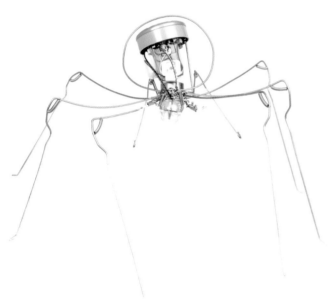

www.droog.com

Même les jouets peuvent éduquer à la compréhension et à la diffusion des politiques écologiques. Les Creatures, réalisées en édition limitée par Tobias Rockenfeld pour Droog Design, sont produites à partir de jouets cassés et de composants de récupération issus d'appareils électroménagers usés. La concrétisation de ce projet a pour résultat 18 modèles uniques, capables de bouger, voler, avancer sur l'eau, briller et rire. L'objectif du designer est de communiquer aux enfants la valeur cachée des déchets, en fabriquant des jouets qui, à l'opposé des tendances actuelles, privilégient la fonctionnalité et la réutilisation aux formes ultra technologiques et colorées, qui n'ont souvent qu'une valeur esthétique.

Tobias Rockenfeld for Droog (The Netherlands)
2008

Foldschool

Cardboard furniture
Möbel aus Pappkarton
Meubles en carton

While good design is generally associated with costly furniture and often extreme forms, this piece of furniture brings design back to its original dictates: aesthetics, functionality and low cost. Foldschool is a line of cardboard furniture for kids that can be assembled at home by simply using cardboard, a paper cutter and glue. Patterns for various objects can be downloaded easily from the Internet and kids can personalize their chosen models according to their wishes, for example by painting them. Foldschool's sustainability does not end with its material: the do-it-yourself aspect is in fact the great advantage since it avoids overproduction, transport and waste.

Üblicherweise wird anspruchsvolles Design mit kostspieligen Möbeln und extravaganten Formen verbunden. Das Ausstattungsobjekt Foldschool hingegen führt das Design wieder zu seinen Wurzeln zurück: Ästhetik, Funktionalität und geringe Kosten. Foldschool ist eine Kollektion von Kartonmöbeln für Kinder, die zu Hause zusammengesetzt werden können. Karton, Cutter und Leim genügen, um die Möbel anzufertigen. Das Schnittmuster für die verschiedenen Objekte kann bequem aus dem Internet heruntergeladen werden. Die Möbel können z. B. durch Bemalen individuell gestaltet werden. Die Zukunftsfähigkeit von Foldschool liegt aber nicht nur im Material: die Eigenproduktion ist der große Vorteil dieses Objekts, wodurch Überproduktion, Transport und Materialverschwendung vermieden werden.

www.foldschool.com

Nicola from Bern for Foldschool (Switzerland)
2007

Si le *furniture* design est généralement associé à des meubles coûteux aux formes souvent extravagantes, cet objet de décoration renvoie le design à ses préceptes initiaux : esthétique, fonctionnalité et coût réduit. Foldschool est une ligne de meubles pour enfants en carton, pouvant être assemblés facilement chez soi à l'aide de carton, d'un cutter et de colle. Le tracé destiné aux différents objets peut être facilement téléchargé sur Internet et les enfants peuvent ainsi personnaliser à l'envie le modèle choisi, par exemple en le coloriant. Foldschool respecte l'environnement en utilisant ce matériau mais aussi grâce à l'autoproduction : en réalité, ces objets ont pour grand avantage d'éviter les surproductions, le transport et les pertes de matériaux.

H-RACER FCJJ-18

Alternative-energy toy car
Spielzeugauto mit Wasserstoffantrieb
Petite voiture à énergie alternative

The H-RACER FCJJ-18 is the smallest clean-energy car in the world. Imitating the hybrid models of famous auto makers like Toyota, Honda and Daimler-Chrysler, this toy uses a full two sources of alternative energy: hydrogen and solar energy. Hydrogen fuel is created by simply adding water to the tank of the little refueling station included with the car. The station then converts the water into hydrogen using solar energy—no batteries required. A blue light signals when the car needs a "refill," making the H-RACER even more beguiling. Horizon Fuel Cell Technologies has been trying to introduce hydrogen into a wide variety of fields since 2003. With this project, the company wanted to use a fun way to emphasize the advantages of this technology, which is renewable, widely available, non-toxic and has zero emissions, even when just used for a toy.

H-RACER FCJJ-18 ist das kleinste Auto, das mit sauberen Energie betrieben wird. Es ahmt die Hybrid-Modelle angesehener Autohersteller wie Toyota, Honda und Daimler-Chrysler nach und benutzt gleich zwei alternative Energiequellen, nämlich Wasserstoff und Sonnenenergie. Die Wasserstoffzufuhr erfolgt über die mitgelieferte „Tankstelle", eine Brennstoffzelle, die mit Wasser gefüllt wird. Batterien sind nicht nötig. Das Wasser wird mit Hilfe von Sonnenenergie in Wasserstoff umgewandelt. Wenn das Auto „nachtanken" muss, leuchtet eine blaue Lampe auf, die dem H-RACER zudem ein ansprechendes Design verleiht. Horizon Fuel Cell Technologies versucht seit 2003 Wasserstoff in verschiedenen Bereichen einzuführen. Mit diesem Projekt hebt das Unternehmen auf amüsante Weise die Vorteile dieser Technologie auf, die erneuerbar, leicht anwendbar, nicht schädlich und zudem emissionsfrei ist, auch wenn es sich dabei nur um ein Spielzeugauto handelt.

H-RACER FCJJ-18 est la plus petite automobile au monde à exploiter une énergie propre. Imitant les modèles des plus grands constructeurs automobiles comme Toyota, Honda et Daimler-Chrysler, ce jouet utilise au moins deux sources d'énergies alternatives : l'hydrogène et l'énergie solaire. Son fonctionnement ne nécessite pas de piles et est rendu possible par la simple présence d'eau, à ajouter dans la petite cellule du réservoir. La micro-centrale convertit l'eau en hydrogène, grâce à l'énergie solaire. Lorsque la « recharge » est nécessaire, une lumière bleue s'allume et rend le H-RACER encore plus amusant. Avec ce projet, Fuel Cell Technologies, qui cherche depuis 2003 à introduire l'hydrogène dans les secteurs les plus variés, a tenu à souligner de manière amusante les avantages de cette technologie (même à l'échelle d'un simple jouet), renouvelable, facilement disponible, non toxique et ne dégageant aucune émission.

www.horizonfuelcell.com

Taras Wankewycz for Horizon Fuel Cell Technologies Pte. Ltd. (Singapore)
2006

PlayMais®

Building blocks
Natürliche Bausteine
Jeu de construction

In this game, creativity takes its cue from a completely natural material, one that is even seasonally "renewable." It may seem surprising, but PlayMais® shows that it is possible to construct battleships, farms and animals with the sole use of corn. This also means the creations can be dyed with natural food coloring and therefore remain 100% biodegradable and non-toxic. Rather than using a system of joints, the blocks are attached to one another by being dampened and lightly pressed together. PlayMais® places no limits on the imagination: each block can be re-cut to create the figures and forms needed for the game of the moment.

Mais ist der Grundstoff für dieses Spielzeug, das aus diesem 100% natürlichen und zudem jahreszeitlich erneuerbaren Material besteht. Es mag noch so erstaunlich erscheinen, aber mit PlayMais® können Piratenschiffe, Bauernhäuser und Tiere gebaut werden. Der bunte Spielspaß wird auf Basis von Mais, Wasser und Lebensmittelfarbe hergestellt. Die Bausteine sind 100% biologisch abbaubar und völlig unbedenklich. Auch wenn jegliche Verbindungsstücke fehlen, ist der Maisbaustein nicht ungeeignet, um etwas damit bauen zu können. Einfaches Anfeuchten mit Wasser und ein leichter Druck auf die Teilchen genügt, um sie aneinander zu heften. PlayMais® setzt der Phantasie keine Grenzen: jeder Baustein kann zugeschnitten oder geformt werden, um so Figuren und Formen zu erfinden.

www.playmais.com

Cornpack GmbH & Co. KG (Germany)
2000

Dans ce jeu, la créativité nait d'un matériau très naturel, qui plus est « renouvelable » périodiquement. Aussi surprenant que cela puisse paraître, PlayMais® démontre en réalité qu'il est possible de construire galions, bâtiments et animaux en n'utilisant que du maïs. Celui-ci permet de teinter les pièces du jeu avec des colorants naturels alimentaires, biodégradables à 100% et non toxiques. La forme des blocs, privés de connexions, rend leur assemblage en apparence impossible; il suffit pourtant de les humidifier et de les écraser légèrement l'un sur l'autre pour les faire tenir. PlayMais® ouvre la porte à toutes les fantaisies: chaque bloc peut être modelé pour créer les personnages et les formes nécessaires au scénario imaginé.

Play Rethink

Board game
Brettspiel
Jeu de société

The Rethink Games company offers a board game that gives free rein to imagination and creativity in order to foster ecological consciousness. The goal of Play Rethink is to re-conceive everyday objects in a new way based on the principles of ecodesign. The rules are simple and intuitive. First, players select the design category, distinguished by color, by spinning the cardboard game wheel—for example recycling, renewable energy, multifunctional, easy assembly. Once the category is established, players begin redesigning the object in question, making sketches and drawings of, say, how to create a dustpan by reusing a shoe sole, or how to replace coat buttons with forks. One can also "play" with ideas and suggestions on the Play Rethink website and develop an area of cultural exchange, a precious resource for the development of a sustainable society.

Das Unternehmen Rethink Games stellt ein Gesellschaftsspiel vor, das die Phantasie und Kreativität zur Entwicklung eines eigenen Umweltbewusstseins fördert. Ziel bei Play Rethink ist es, Alltagsgegenstände aus Sicht des Ökodesigns neu zu bedenken. Die Regeln sind einfach und intuitiv: zuerst werden die Planungsbereiche ausgewählt, indem man das Rad auf der Spieltafel dreht. Jeder Bereich ist mit einer Farbe gekennzeichnet. Nachdem der Bereich ausgewählt worden ist – zum Beispiel Recycling, erneuerbare Energien, Multifunktionalität, leichte Zusammensetzbarkeit – beginnen die Mitspieler den jeweiligen Gegenstand neu zu planen. So entstehen Skizzen und Zeichnungen, wie man z. B. eine Schuhsohle als Kehrichtschaufel wiederverwenden oder wie man die Knöpfe an einem Mantel durch Gabeln ersetzen kann. Auch auf der Homepage von Play Rethink kann man mit zahlreichen Ideen und Tipps „spielen". Es ist eine Plattform für den kulturellen Austausch entstanden, die einen wichtigen Beitrag für die Entstehung einer nachhaltigen Gesellschaft leistet.

www.playrethink.com

La société Rethink Games propose un jeu de société laissant la place à la fantaisie et à la créativité, et participant au développement d'une conscience écologique. Le but de Play Rethink est de repenser les objets quotidiens selon les principes de l'écodesign. Les règles sont simples et intuitives : il faut avant tout délimiter son secteur de projet, distingué par une couleur, en faisant tourner la roue sur le plateau de jeu. Une fois le secteur défini (par exemple recyclage, énergies renouvelables, multifonctionnalité ou facilité d'assemblage) les joueurs doivent repenser l'objet en question. On dessine et esquisse pour créer une pelle à poussière à partir d'une semelle de chaussure ou pour remplacer les boutons d'un manteau par des fourchettes. Il est aussi possible de « jouer » sur le site Internet de Play Rethink en apportant vos idées et suggestions et en créant ainsi un espace d'échange culturel, ressource précieuse au développement d'une société durable.

Lili Larratea for Rethink Games (UK)
2007

Puppy
Toy and furnishing object
Spielzeug und Ausstattungsobjekt
Jouet et objet déco

Puppy is an example of how an apparently unsustainable product can unexpectedly follow the dictates of ecodesign. Not only is this stylized polypropylene dog made of just one material, but it is also multifunctional. It was in fact created as a kid's toy but quickly increased in value as a piece of furniture and even a collector's item. If needed, Puppy can be used as a chair, proving the assertion made by well-known Finnish designer Eero Aarnio that various objects can double as seating, while a chair remains that alone. By becoming an object of affection with, moreover, an artistic value, Puppy is not easily discarded—another reason to laud it as an example of ecodesign.

Puppy ist auf den ersten Blick nicht nachhaltig, aber es steht dennoch für die Philosophie von Ökodesign. Der stilisierte Welpe aus Polypropylen besteht aus einem einzigen Material und ist multifunktional. Ursprünglich als Kinderspielzeug konzipiert, wurde er in der Folgezeit nicht nur zu einem Sitzmöbel sondern vor allem zu einem begehrten Sammlerobjekt. Auch sein berühmter Designer Eero Aarnio war der Auffassung, dass die Funktion eines Sitzplatzes durch verschiedene Objekte ausgeübt werden kann, während ein Stuhl immer nur ein Stuhl bleibt. Puppy wächst seinem Besitzer nicht nur ans Herz, sondern hat zudem einen künstlerischen Wert. Ganz im Sinne des Ökodesigns trennt man sich nicht leichtfertig von ihm.

www.magisdesign.com

Puppy est l'exemple type du produit en apparence non durable mais suivant en réalité à la lettre les principes de l'écodesign. Ce chien en polypropylène aux formes stylisées est avant tout mono-matériau. Il est de plus multifonctionnel : d'abord jouet pour enfant, il a ensuite gagné en valeur en devenant également objet de décoration et même pièce de collection. En l'occurence, Puppy peut aussi devenir siège, ce qui prouve ainsi que, comme l'indique le fameux designer finlandais Eero Aarnio, la fonction d'assise peut être endossée par de nombreux objets, tandis qu'un fauteuil reste toujours ce qu'il est. En devenant objet d'affection, doté en plus d'une valeur artistique, il sera difficilement jeté sur un coup de tête, respectant ainsi une fois encore les codes de l'écodesign.

Eero Aarnio for Magis (Italy)
2005

283

Sedici Animali

Wooden puzzle
Holzpuzzle
Puzzle en bois

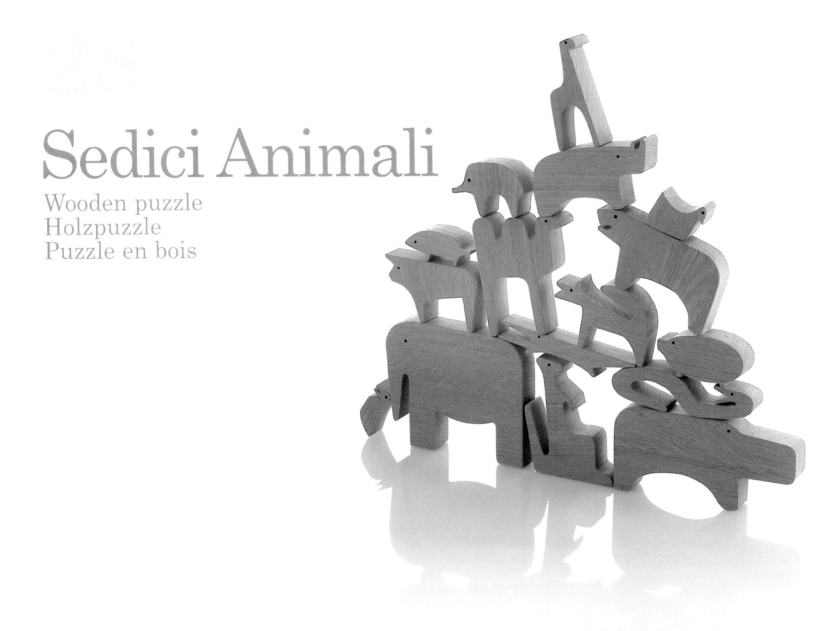

In the 1950s, as plastic was becoming the most popular material used in industrial production, Enzo Mari drew on tradition and designed a product for kids that, in those days, went against the trends. Sedici Animali (Sixteen Animals), a puzzle and a game in one, is made of unfinished oak wood and therefore lacks the harmful chemical substances of a surface finish. Today the sustainable approach followed by the Italian designer is increasingly widespread in the world of toy production. Meanwhile, Sixteen Animals has become a collector's item and each year is re-released in a limited edition.

In den 1950er Jahren, als Plastik zum meist verwendeten Material in der Industrieproduktion aufstieg, entwarf Enzo Mari ein Spielzeug, das, obwohl es sich an die Tradition anlehnte, zu jener Zeit eher eine Gegentendenz darstellte: Sedici Animali (sechzehn Tiere). Das Puzzle, das zugleich auch ein Spiel ist, wurde aus unbehandeltem Eichenholz hergestellt, ohne schädliche chemische Stoffe für die Oberflächenbehandlung zu verwenden. Die nachhaltige Linie, die der italienische Designer schon damals verfolgte, verbreitet sich heute in der Spielzeugherstellung immer weiter. Sedici Animali ist zu einem begehrten Sammlerobjekt geworden und wird jedes Jahr in einer limitierten Auflage angeboten.

Dans les années 1950, alors que le plastique envahissait la production industrielle, Enzo Mari réalisa un produit destiné aux enfants qui, tout en revisitant la tradition, restait marginal à cette époque. Sedici Animali (seize animaux), puzzle et jouet, était réalisé en bois de rouvre brut et sa surface était polie sans utiliser de substances chimiques nocives. La ligne durable développée par le créateur italien trouve aujourd'hui une diffusion grandissante dans la production de jouets et entre temps, Sedici Animali est carrément devenu un objet collector : une série limitée est éditée chaque année.

Enzo Mari for Danese (Italy)
1957

285

Packaging

Packaging

Verpackung
Packaging

Introduction

Einleitung
Introduction

Have you ever thought about how many packages we consume every day? Packaging makes up around 80% of the waste that ends up in our landfills. Considering the fact that every purchase comes with a package, the enormous amount is plain to see.

Though packaging has its own life cycle with respect to the product it contains and protects, it should also be designed to function better. Possibilities and solutions would multiply this way, producing not just environmental but also economic benefits.

Ecodesign proposes various solutions to the problem. For one thing, packaging can have a longer life when its reuse is taken into account during the design phase. Materials can be chosen more wisely, with a designer opting to use just one material or those deriving from renewable sources in the short-term, like non-oil plastics (PlantLove's PLA). When this is impossible, a good designer should think ahead to the eventual separation of the various materials (GreenBottle). Packaging can also be produced directly from natural materials (EcoWay's banana leaves) or can even be edible (Cookie Cup). Such solutions offer valid and sustainable alternatives without limiting the communicative value of the packaging, which is an important tool for enhancing the product it contains in the first place.

The different types of packaging were divided based on the industry their products belong to: food, body care and giftware/souvenirs.

Haben Sie jemals daran gedacht, wie viel Verpackung wir jeden Tag wegwerfen? Etwa 80% der Abfälle, die in Abfalldeponien landen, bestehen aus Verpackungen. Diese enorme Menge ist leicht nachzuvollziehen, wenn wir nur an die Verpackung aller Gegenstände denken, die wir kaufen.

Die Verpackung hat im Vergleich zum darin enthaltenen Produkt einen eigenen Lebenszyklus. Für eine optimierte Nutzung muss sie zusammen mit dem Produkt entwickelt werden. So können vielfältige Verpackungslösungen mit positiven Auswirkungen auf die Umwelt und die Wirtschaftlichkeit entstehen.

Gemäß den Grundsätzen von Ökodesign gibt es verschiedene Lösungsansätze. Die Lebensdauer einer Verpackung kann verlängert werden, indem bereits während der Planungsphase die spätere Wiederverwendung berücksichtigt wird. Eine weitere Möglichkeit ist eine intelligente Materialauswahl. Die Verwendung von nur einem Material oder kurzfristig erneuerbarer Energien, wie z. B. No-Oil-Kunststoffe (PLA von PlantLove) wäre ein Beispiel hierfür. Sollte dies nicht möglich sein, muss während der Entwicklungsphase überlegt werden, wie die verschiedenen Materialien voneinander getrennt werden können (GreenBottle). Verpackungen können direkt aus Naturprodukten hergestellt werden (EcoWay) oder sogar essbar sein (Cookie Cup). Diese Lösungen bieten wertvolle Alternativen, ohne den kommunikativen Wert der Verpackung zu beeinträchtigen.

Die vorgestellten Verpackungen sind nach ihrem Inhalt gegliedert: Lebensmittel, Körperpflege und verschiedene Alltagsgegenstände.

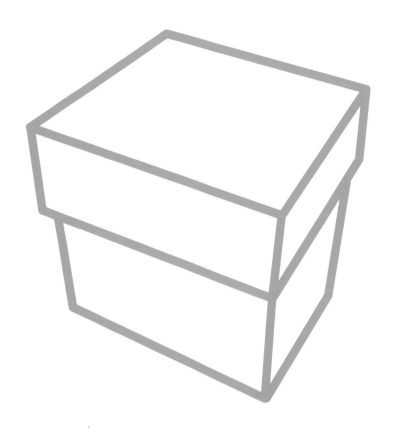

Avez-vous déjà pensé à la quantité d'emballages consommés quotidiennement ? Environ 80% des déchets versés en décharges sont constitués d'emballages. Si l'on pense qu'à chaque objet acheté correspond un emballage qui sera jeté, cette quantité démesurée nous semble plus concrète.

L'emballage a une durée de vie propre par rapport au produit qu'il contient et protège, mais il doit être pensé en même temps que ce dernier, pour un meilleur rendement.

L'écodesign propose différentes solutions au problème : la vie de l'emballage peut être prolongée en prévoyant par exemple sa réutilisation dès la phase de projetation; le choix des matériaux gagne en pertinence si l'on opte pour le monomatériau ou pour des sources renouvelables à court terme, comme le plastique sans pétrole (le PLA de PlantLove) ; dans les cas où ce n'est pas possible, un bon créateur devra penser au moyen de séparer les différents matériaux en fin de vie (GreenBottle); les emballages peuvent être produits directement avec des éléments naturels (les feuilles de bananier d'EcoWay) ou être comestibles (Cookie Cup). Ces solutions offrent des alternatives valides et durables, sans limiter la valeur de communication de l'emballage, qui reste avant tout un instrument important de valorisation du produit.

Les emballages présentés ici ont été divisés, selon le secteur d'appartenance du produit contenu : alimentaire, soins du corps et gadgets.

Cookie Cup

Edible espresso cup
Essbare Espressotasse
Tasse à café comestible

The Cookie Cup is a fun synthesis of Italian culinary habits: an espresso cup that can be eaten and thereby replaces the ever-present cookies. It turns grabbing a cup of coffee into a completely new experience. The team at the Lavazza Training Centre responsible for the design, also known for its collaboration with the famous Spanish cook Ferran Adrià, invented a recipe for the pastry that is covered on the inside by a special icing sugar and heat-resistant gum arabic. Lavazza's famous blue logo is printed on the outside. Designed by Enrique Luis Sardi, the cup won the Lavazza prize at the Turin Food Design competition in 2003. The Cookie Cup is an example of sustainable design that responds to everyday traditions in an original way.

Als witzige Synthese der italienischen Essgewohnheiten ersetzt Cookie Cup als essbare Kaffeetasse den üblicherweise beim Frühstück obligatorischen Keks und verwandelt somit die Espressopause in eine ungewöhnliche Erfahrung. Das Team vom Training Centre Lavazza, bekannt auch durch seine Zusammen-arbeit mit dem spanischen Chefkoch Ferran Adrià, entwickelte das besondere Rezept für den Mürbeteig. Dieser Teig ist mit einer Zuckerglasur überzogen, die hohen Temperaturen standhalten kann und auf der auch das Lavazza-Logo angebracht ist. Doch der größte Vorteil ist, dass die Tasse die Umwelt nicht belastet, da sie nicht weggeworfen wird, ja nicht einmal gewaschen werden muss. Die Tasse, die nach einem Design von Enrique Luis Sardi hergestellt wurde, gewann 2003 den „Lavazza-Preis" beim Wettbewerb „Food Design Torino". Cookie Cup ist ein Beispiel für nachhaltiges Design, das für tägliche Gewohnheiten neue Lösungen liefert.

www.lavazza.com

Cookie Cup est une synthèse amusante des habitudes culinaires italiennes : la tasse à café est en réalité comestible et prend ainsi la place de l'indétrônable petit gâteau. Avec ce produit, le premier repas de la journée ne pollue en rien l'environnement car il n'est pas jeté et n'a pas besoin d'être lavé. Connue également pour avoir collaboré avec le fameux chef espagnol Ferran Adrià, l'équipe qui en est à l'origine, le Training Centre Lavazza, a inventé une recette de pâte feuilletée, recouverte d'un glaçage spécial au sucre, capable de résister à des températures élevées. Le fameux logo bleu de Lavazza est imprimé sur une feuille d'hostie. Cette tasse, réalisée sur des plans d'Enrique Luis Sardi a remporté le prix Lavazza lors du concours Food Design Torino en 2003. Cookie Cup est un exemple de design durable, répondant de manière originale aux habitudes quotidiennes.

Enrique Luis Sardi for Lavazza (Italy)
2003
prototype

EcoWay

Natural take-away packaging
Natürliche Take-away-Verpackung
Emballage naturel à emporter

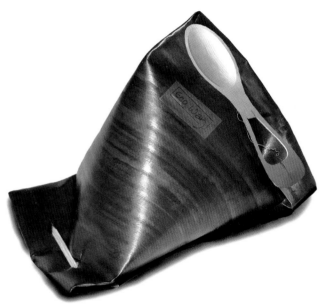

Eco Way is take-away food packaging made of banana leaves. The patina covering them has a consistency similar to wax, making them perfect for holding even hot or greasy food. Since they maintain their robust features long after being removed from the plant, cutting is all that is required to transform them into packaging. The package is closed by folding the leaf and securing it with small wooden clasps if needed—i.e. no glue is used. It is opened by tearing the leaf along its natural lines. The realization of this design, which was presented at the Dining 2015 competition organized by Designboom in 2008, could lead to a drastic reduction in the packaging waste that takes up so much space in our dump sites.

Eco Way ist eine Verpackung aus Bananenbaumblättern für Take-away-Mahlzeiten. Die obere Schicht der Blätter hat eine wachsähnliche Konsistenz. Daher eignen sie sich ideal als Verpackung für feuchte oder fettige Nahrungsmittel. Außerdem behalten die Bananenbaumblätter auch lange Zeit nachdem sie vom Baum abgeschnitten wurden ihre Eigenschaften. Die Verpackung wird durch einfaches Biegen der Blätter oder auch mit kleinen Holznadeln verschlossen, d. h. ohne den Einsatz von Klebstoff. Zum Öffnen genügt hingegen das Abreißen des Blattes entlang der natürlichen Blattfaser. Das Projekt, das zu einer drastischen Reduzierung der riesigen Mengen von Verpackungsabfällen führen könnte, wurde 2008 beim Design-Wettbewerb Dining 2015 von Designboom vorgestellt.

Réalisé avec des feuilles de bananier, Eco Way est un emballage destiné aux aliments à emporter. La pellicule qui les recouvre, dont la consistance est semblable à celle de la cire, les rend parfaits pour contenir des aliments gras ou humides. Conservant leurs propriétés longtemps après avoir été récoltées, le travail nécessaire pour transformer ces feuilles en emballage se limite à leur découpe. La fermeture s'effectue ensuite en pliant les feuilles, parfois retenues par un petit fermoir en bois, mais sans utilisation de colle. Pour l'ouvrir, il suffit de déchirer la feuille le long de ses filaments naturels. La réalisation de ce projet, présenté au concours Dining 2015 organisé par Designboom en 2008, pourrait engendrer une réduction phénoménale des déchets d'emballage qui envahissent les décharges en quantités importantes.

www.designboom.com

Tal Marco for designboom (Israel)
2007

Pandora Card

Disposable cutlery
Wegwerfbesteck
Couverts jetables

It has been widely noted that the production of disposable goods leads to excess garbage in our dumps and a waste of resources. Pandora Card cutlery, however, is the exception that proves the rule. Made from a starch derivative (polylactic acid or PLA), it is completely biodegradable. Particular attention was also paid at the research phase to decreasing production waste and facilitating packaging and transport: its linear design and small size mean that few materials are needed to make it. Pandora Card cutlery is not meant to be a substitute for the everyday version. Rather, it was conceived for use in hospitals or special situations like excursions.

Einweggegenstände produzieren nicht nur übermäßige Abfallmengen, sondern sind auch eine Verschwendung von Energiequellen. Das Besteck Pandora Card ist eine beachtenswerte Ausnahme: es besteht aus einem Polylactide-Kunststoff (PLA) und ist vollständig biologisch abbaubar. Besondere Aufmerksamkeit galt zudem der Senkung von Emissionen während der Produktion und des Transports. Das lineare Design und die geringen Abmessungen tragen zur optimalen Nutzung der Materialmengen bei und vermindern gleichzeitig die Produktionsabfälle. Das Besteck Pandora Card ist nicht für den täglichen Privatgebrauch gedacht, sondern vielmehr zur Verwendung in Krankenhäusern oder bei Ausflügen.

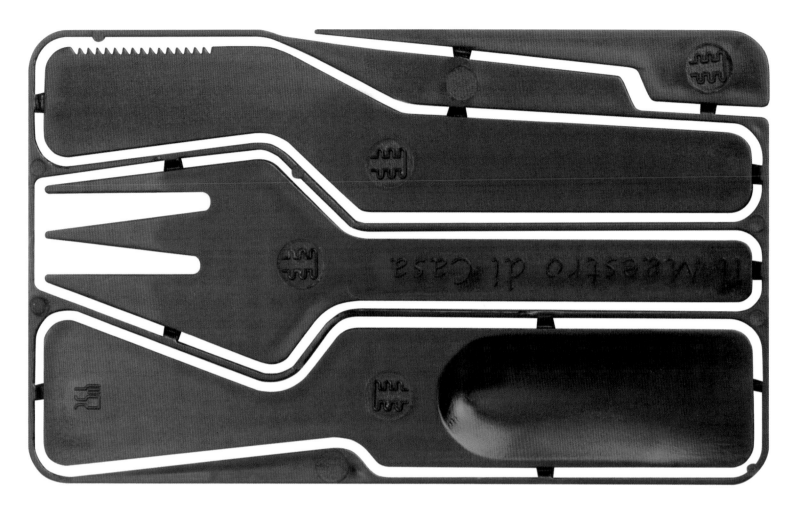

www.pandoradesign.it

Il est de notoriété publique que la production de couverts jetables entraîne une quantité importante de déchets dans les décharges et s'avère un gâchis des ressources. Les couverts Pandora Card sont l'exception qui confirme la règle : composés d'un dérivé de l'amidon (le PLA, acide polylactique), ils sont totalement biodégradables. De plus, leurs créateurs ont étudié avec attention les moyens de diminuer les pertes de production et de faciliter l'emballage et le transport : leur design linéaire et leurs dimensions réduites permettent une optimisation réelle des quantités de matériau employées. Les couverts Pandora Card n'entendent pas se substituer aux couverts de cuisine mais visent plutôt une utilisation dans les hôpitaux ou dans des situations particulières comme la randonnée.

Giulio Iacchetti for Pandora design (Italy)
2004

301

GreenBottle

Packaging for liquids
Verpackung für Flüssigkeiten
Emballage pour denrées liquides

The outer layer of this packaging for liquid food items is made of recycled white paper, with an inside layer of recyclable PLA (polylactic acid). The design was tested by an English supermarket chain and it showed that this material releases no harmful elements into the liquids contained therein. Furthermore, its environmental impact is less than 48% compared to tetra packs or HDPE (high-density polyethylene) packaging. When discarded, GreenBottle's two parts are recycled separately and the paper, in particular, is reused to produce food cartons.

Diese Trinkmilchverpackung besteht außen aus Recycling-Papier und innen aus einer dünnen, recycelbaren Schicht aus PLA (Polylactide). Das Material, das von einer englischen Super-marktkette getestet wurde, gibt keine schädlichen Stoffe an die enthaltenen Flüssigkeiten ab. Zudem ist die Umweltbelastung um 48% geringer als bei Tetrapack oder anderen Polyethylen-Verpackungen. Bei der Entsorgung werden die beiden Elemente, aus denen GreenBottle besteht, getrennt wieder verwertet, das Papier wird beispielsweise zur Herstellung von Lebensmittel-kartons eingesetzt.

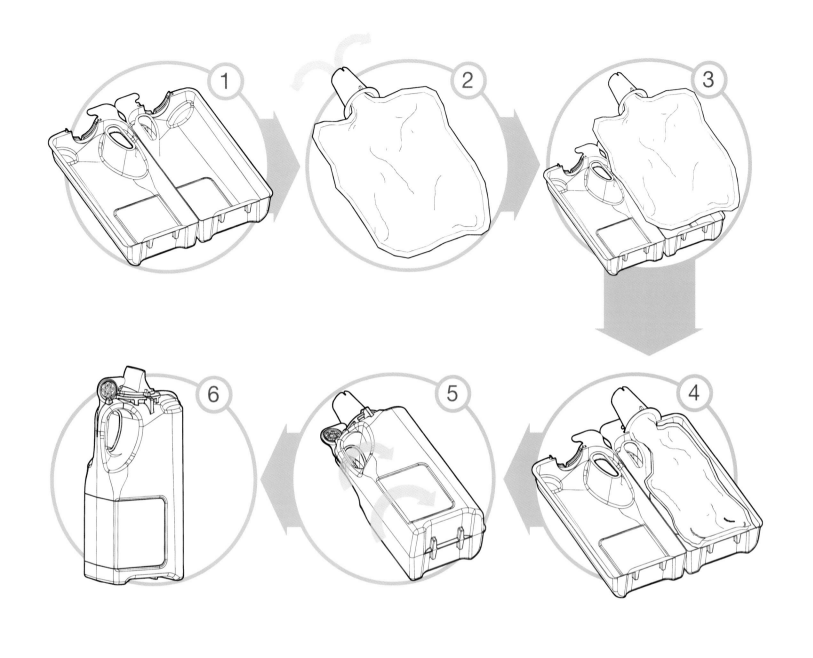

Cet emballage pour aliments liquides est constitué, à l'extérieur, de papier blanc recyclé et à l'intérieur, de PLA (acide polylactique) recyclable. Le projet, testé par une chaîne de supermarchés anglais, a démontré que ce matériau n'est aucunement nocif pour les liquides qu'il contient et son impact environnemental est inférieur de 48% à celui du Tetrapack ou des emballages en HDPE (polyéthylène à haute densité). Au moment du désassemblage, les deux éléments composant la GreenBottle sont recyclés séparément : le carton est notamment réutilisé dans la production de cartons alimentaires.

Martin Myerscough for GreenBottle Limited (UK)
2007

360° Paper Water Bottle

Biodegradable water bottle
Papierflasche
Bouteille en papier

More and more people around the world drink water from plastic bottles. The environmental impact this causes is increasing out of all proportion, in terms of both the exploitation of water resources and the mass production of plastic packaging. The data speaks for itself: in the United States alone, 2.7 million tons of PET plastic bottles were produced in 2006, four-fifths of which were thrown away. Brandimage tackled the problem by proposing a bottle made from paper. The multipack that holds it is made of bamboo fiber and palm leaves, pressed together with a thin PLA (polylactic acid) film, which makes it waterproof. 360° Paper Water Bottle is 100% sustainable because it minimizes environmental impact not only after it is discarded, but also during production. For one thing, no ink is used for the labeling, which is created with pressure alone.

Weltweit trinken immer mehr Menschen Wasser aus Plastikflaschen. Die Belastung der Umwelt wächst stetig, sowohl was den Verbrauch der Wasserressourcen, als auch die Produktion von Plastikflaschen betrifft. 2006 wurden allein in Amerika 2,7 Millionen Tonnen PET-Flaschen hergestellt. Davon landeten vier Fünftel in den Abfall-deponien. Das Produktdesign-Unternehmen Brandimage entwickelte eine Flasche, die vollkommen aus Papier besteht und zu 100% abbaubar ist. Der Multipack, in dem die Flasche eingebettet ist, besteht aus Bambusfasern und Palmenblättern, die mit einem dünnen PLA-Blatt, das die Flasche wasserdicht macht, zusammengepresst wurden. 360° Paper Water Bottle ist ein 100%ig nachhaltiges Produkt, weil es die Umweltauswirkungen nicht erst nach der Entsorgung, sondern bereits während der Herstellung minimiert: die Etikettierung erfolgt z. B. nur durch Pressen und ohne die Verwendung von Farben.

Les consommateurs d'eau en bouteille sont de plus en plus nombreux. Leur impact environnemental augmente démesurément, que ce soit en termes d'exploitation des ressources hydriques ou de production massive d'emballages en plastique. Les chiffres parlent d'eux-mêmes : en 2006, 2,7 millions de tonnes de bouteilles en PET ont été produites pour l'Amérique, dont les quatre cinquièmes ont fini à la décharge. Brandimage a affronté le problème en proposant une bouteille entièrement en papier. Dans leur pack de transport, les bouteilles sont rassemblées par des fibres de bambou et des feuilles de palmier, pressées contre une fine feuille de PLA, qui les rend imperméables. 360° Paper Water Bottle est un produit entièrement durable car il minimise son impact environnemental après usage mais aussi durant sa production : l'étiquette, par exemple, est appliquée par simple impression, sans utilisation d'encre.

Jim Warner for Brandimage - Desgrippes & Laga (USA)
2008
prototype

PlantLove

Cosmetics packaging
Verpackung für Kosmetik
Emballage pour cosmétiques

The PlantLove line shows how extremely common, high-impact objects like cosmetics can be re-designed in sustainable ways. The lipstick applicators and containers are made entirely of PLA (polylactic acid), while the packaging is made of recycled paperboard. Special care was also taken during the manufacturing process to eliminate greenhouse gases. In fact, the Canadian company responsible for the product stands out for its desire to make its customers aware of environmental issues. The name PlantLove comes from the fact that the lipsticks' packaging contains sunflower seeds and can be directly planted as such, without having to extract the seeds. At one time, even virtual flowers could be planted at their website and for each flower a donation was made to Conservation International. In 2008, the company received an honorable mention at the DuPont Awards for Packaging Innovation.

Die Produktreihe PlantLove ist ein Beispiel dafür, dass ein bekanntes Produkt mit hoher Umweltauswirkung, wie z. B. Kosmetikartikel, nach umweltfreundlichen Aspekten neu entwickelt werden kann. Die Lippenstiftapplikatoren und Behälter dieser Kosmetikserie bestehen ausschließlich aus PLA, die Verpackung aus recyceltem Karton. Während des Herstellungsprozesses wurde besonders auf die Vermeidung von Treibhausgasen geachtet. Die kanadische Herstellerfirma hat das ehrgeizige Vorhaben, ihre Kunden für den Umweltschutz zu sensibilisieren. Der Name der Produktreihe, PlantLove, geht darauf zurück, dass die Verpackung der Lippenstifte, die Sonnenblumensamen enthält, direkt nach dem Gebrauch in die Erde eingepflanzt werden kann, ohne dass die Kerne entnommen werden müssen. Außerdem können auf der Homepage virtuelle Blumen gepflanzt werden, für die eine Spende zu Gunsten von Conservation International abgegeben wird. 2008 wurden die Innovationen von Cargo Cosmetics im Rahmen des DuPont Awards for Packaging Innovation hervorgehoben.

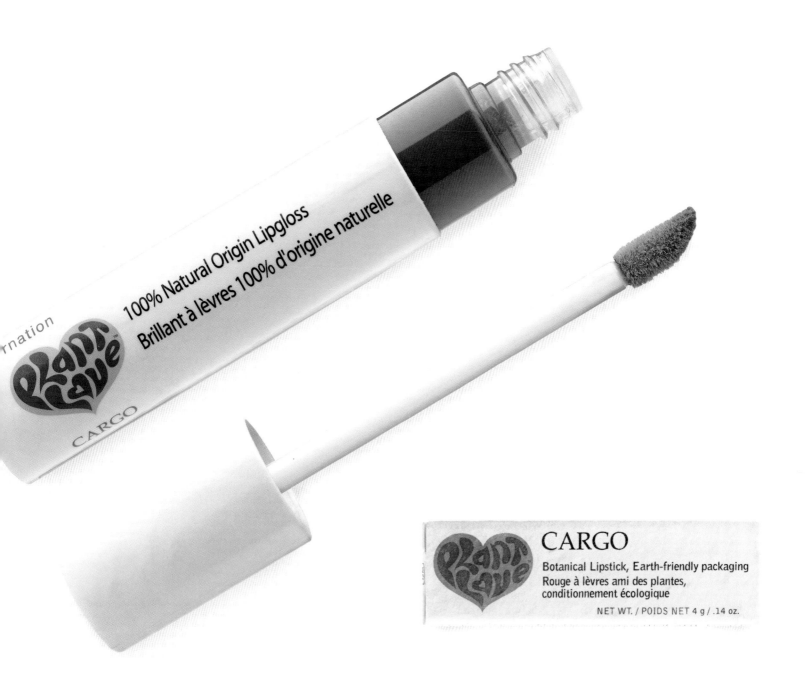

100% Natural Origin Lipgloss
Brillant à lèvres 100% d'origine naturelle

CARGO

Botanical Lipstick, Earth-friendly packaging
Rouge à lèvres ami des plantes,
conditionnement écologique

NET WT. / POIDS NET 4 g / .14 oz.

www.cargocosmetics.com

La ligne PlantLove prouve qu'il est possible de repenser en termes durables des produits largement diffusés comme les cosmétiques. Les applicateurs de rouge à lèvres et les contenants de la ligne sont entièrement réalisés en PLA, tandis que l'emballage est en carton recyclé. Durant le processus de production, une attention particulière est portée à l'élimination du gaz à effet de serre. La société productrice canadienne se distingue également par sa volonté de sensibiliser ses propres clients aux thématiques environnementales : le nom de la ligne PlantLove dérive du fait que les emballages des rouges à lèvres contiennent des graines de tournesol et peuvent être plantés directement, sans devoir en extraire la graine. Il est aussi possible de planter des fleurs virtuelles sur le site internet : chaque fleur plantée correspond à une donation au Conservation International. En 2008, la société a reçu une mention spéciale au DuPont Awards dans la catégorie Emballage Innovant.

Hana Zalzal for Cargo Cosmetics (Canada)
2007

C.OVER

Organizer
Terminplaner
Organiseur

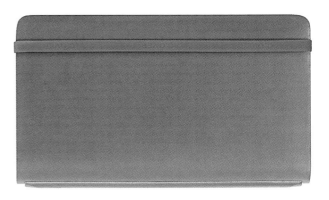

C.OVER brings together aesthetics and functionality, eliminating all that is superfluous and additional. Optimized in both its functions and dimensions, this organizer is characterized by a hi-tech spirit. The organizer is put together with a series of elastics and metal spheres, according to need. The thickness is a quarter of that of traditional block notes and ring-bound organizers. C.OVER's design, which is covered by an international patent, is therefore eco-compatible for both its flexibility and its compact size.

C.OVER vereint Ästhetik und Funktionalität und vermeidet alles, was überflüssig und nebensächlich ist. Der Organizer wurde in seinen Funktionen und seiner Größe optimiert. Gummibänder, die mit Metallkugeln befestigt werden, passen die Agenda den jeweiligen Bedürfnisse an. Dank eines innovativen Ringsystems wurde der Umfang auf ein Viertel der herkömmlichen Notizhefte und Terminkalender reduziert. Flexibilität und Kompaktheit sind somit die Faktoren, die das Design von C.OVER öko-verträglich machen. Dieses System ist durch ein internationales Patent geschützt.

www.greenwitch.it

C.OVER allie esthétique et fonctionnalité en éliminant le superflu et l'accessoire. Optimisé tant dans ses fonctions que ses dimensions, cet organiseur se caractérise par un esprit hi-tech : une série d'élastiques et de sphères métalliques permet de composer l'agenda selon ses besoins. L'épaisseur est réduite à un quart de celle des blocs-notes et organiseurs à spirales. Flexible et compact, C.OVER devient éco-compatible grâce aux qualités de son design. Ce système est couvert par un brevet international.

Aldo Petillo for Greenwitch (Italy)
2006

EcoStapler

Staple-less stapler
Heftzange ohne Heftklammern
Agrafeuse sans agrafes

The EcoStapler is an example of the perfect union between functionality and sustainability. This pocket-size object is lightweight and can staple up to three sheets at a time, without the use of metal staples. The mechanism is simple: the interior blade cuts a thin strip of the paper, which then gets folded in so that the pages are joined firmly together. The pages can be read and turned without undoing the joint. Considering the fact that at least one staple is used in every office each day, Wasteonline estimated that with the EcoStapler, the equivalent of 72 tons of metallic waste a year would be saved in England alone. The stapler is sold in recyclable PET and recycled cardboard packaging.

EcoStapler ist ein gelungenes Beispiel für die Verbindung von Funktionalität und Nachhaltigkeit. Dieser kleine und leichte Gegenstand kann bis zu drei Seiten Papier heften, ohne das Metallklammern benötigt werden. Die Funktionsweise ist einfach: Im Inneren befindet sich eine Klinge, die einen kleinen Schlitz in das Papier schneidet. Dann werden die Seiten nach innen gefaltet, wodurch sie fest zusammenhaften. Die gehefteten Blätter können gelesen und geblättert werden, ohne die Haftung zu beeinträchtigen. Wenn man davon ausgeht, dass in jedem Büro mindestens einmal pro Tag eine Heftklammer verwendet wird, so könnten mit EcoStapler gemäß einer Schätzung von Wasteonline allein in England etwa 72 Tonnen an Metallabfällen pro Jahr vermieden werden. Das Heftgerät wird in einer Verpackung aus recyceltem PET und recyceltem Karton verkauft.

www.ecozone.com

L'EcoStapler est l'union parfaite de la fonctionnalité et du respect de l'environnement : cet objet léger et compact peut accrocher jusqu'à trois feuilles à la fois, sans utiliser d'agrafes métalliques. Le mécanisme est simple : la lame intérieure coupe une fine lame de feuille, repliée ensuite à l'intérieur de manière à ce que les feuilles se retrouvent solidement réunies. Il est ainsi possible de lire et de tourner les pages sans craindre qu'elles ne se détachent. Si chaque bureau utilise au moins une barre d'agrafes par jour, EcoStapler permettrait d'économiser, selon Wasteonline, une quantité de déchets métalliques équivalente à 72 tonnes par an, rien qu'en Angleterre. La pinceuse est vendue dans un emballage en PET recyclable et carton recyclé.

INFORM DESIGNS for Ecozone (UK)
2007

Graphic design

Grafikdesign
Design graphique

Introduction

Einleitung
Introduction

On the broad stage of visual communication, graphic design guarantees the immediacy and clarity of the message to be delivered. When it comes to complex themes like ecology and sustainability, graphics make it easy to inform in a simple, direct way by provoking impact and interest. This conveys the importance of conscious behavior towards the environment, often more effectively than by using other informative means.

The selections in this chapter communicate environmental sustainability on various levels, from the global care of the planet proposed by PlanetEarth to raise awareness about deforestation in South America to the cleaning of California's beaches. Communicating also means raising consciousness, providing a tool with which to "read" what is offered on the market in the right way. Valcucine, for example, promotes the sustainability of its products, while the WWF's Tree Ring Magnet is an instrument of denunciation, indicating products that are not eco-friendly. Finally, the section includes graphic designs that are themselves produced in a sustainable way. The advertising poster by Adidas, for instance, communicates with color even though it only uses black and white ink.

Every case involves industrial products with their own specific life cycle, which make environmental awareness the strength of a company and an instrument for expression. The various designs were divided according to the themes they involve: water, paper, waste and mobility.

Im Falle von komplexen Themen wie z. B. Ökologie oder Nachhaltigkeit ermöglicht die Grafik eine klare und eindeutige Informationsübermittlung dank der visuellen Wirkung und dem daraus entstehenden Interesse. Auf diese Weise schafft sie es, oft mehr als andere Informationsmedien, die Wichtigkeit eines umweltbewussten Handelns zu verdeutlichen.

Die hier vorgestellten Produkte stehen für verschiedene Lösungen des Umweltschutzes. Sei es die durch PlanetEarth empfohlene globale Pflege des Planeten, die Sensibilisierung für die Zerstörung des Regenwalds in Südamerika oder die Aufräumaktionen an der kalifornischen Küste. Kommunikation bedeutet auch, anderen etwas bewusst machen, ihnen ein Mittel anbieten, um das, was auf dem Markt angeboten wird, auf richtige Weise zu „lesen". Valcucine betont z. B. die Nachhaltigkeit der eigenen Produkte, während Tree Ring Magnet vom World Wildlife Fund auf jene Produkte hinweist, die keine Rücksicht auf die Umwelt nehmen. Das Kapitel zeigt schließlich auch einige grafische Beispiele, die ausschließlich auf umweltfreundliche Weise hergestellt wurden, wie das Adidas-Werbeplakat.

In allen Fällen wird bei diesen Erzeugnissen die Rücksichtnahme auf die Umwelt als besonderer Vorzug ausgewiesen und als direktes Ausdrucksmittel verwendet. Die Projekte wurden nach folgenden Themen unterteilt: Wasser, Papier, Abfälle und Mobilität.

Dans l'immense contexte de la communication visuelle, le projet graphique garantit l'immédiateté et la clarté du message à transmettre. Dans le cas de thématiques complexes comme celles de l'écologie ou du développement durable, l'image informe de manière simple et directe, grâce à l'impact qu'elle suscite. De cette manière, elle réussit souvent mieux que les autres moyens d'information à faire comprendre l'importance d'un comportement conscient, dans le cadre de l'environnement.

La sélection proposée ici montre des produits communiquant sur le développement durable à différents niveaux : de la protection globale de la planète suggérée par PlanetEarth, à la sensibilisation à la déforestation en Amérique du Sud ou à la propreté des plages californiennes. Communiquer signifie aussi faire prendre conscience, offrir un instrument aidant à « décrypter » de manière correcte ce qu'offre le marché : Valcucine, par exemple, promeut la durabilité de ses produits, tandis que le Tree Ring Magnet du WWF est un instrument de dénonciation, permettant d'identifier les produits non respectueux de l'environnement. Le chapitre montre enfin quelques projets graphiques réalisés de manière écologique, comme la campagne d'affichage d'Adidas, qui communique par l'intermédiaire de la couleur, tout en n'utilisant que de l'encre noire.

Dans tous les cas, on parle ici de produits industriels ayant leur propre cycle de vie, qui font de leur intérêt pour l'environnement un point fort et un instrument d'expression. Les différents projets ont été divisés selon les thématiques qu'ils impliquent : eau, papier, déchets et mobilité.

drinkable watercard

Container-card for water
Postkarte und Wasserbehälter
Carte postale réserve d'eau

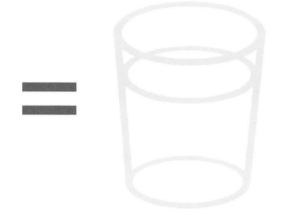

These "drinkable" postcards, produced in a limited edition for the exhibition "Acqua dello Spazio Opos" (Opos Space Water) held in Milan in 2003 contains the equivalent of a glass of water and can be mailed like any other postal product. With this concept, Italian designer Paolo Ulian wanted to emphasize the lack of water resources in many countries where living conditions are difficult. In addition to the obviously symbolic gesture of using drinkable watercard to supply water to those in need, ethical value is to be found in its attempt to raise awareness among those who take it for granted that they can turn on a tap and quench their thirst whenever they want.

Diese „trinkbaren" Postkarten wurden in limitierter Stückzahl für die Ausstellung „Acqua dello Spazio Opos", die 2003 in Mailand stattfand, entwickelt. Sie enthalten so viel Trinkwasser wie in ein Glas passen würde und können wie jedes andere Postprodukt verschickt werden. Das Projekt des Italieners Paolo Ulian soll an die Wasserknappheit in zahlreichen Ländern und die damit verbundenen schwierigen Lebensbedingungen erinnern. Neben der symbolischen Geste, Wasser an jemanden zu liefern, der es braucht, liegt der ethische Wert der drinkable watercard darin, diejenigen, die das Öffnen des Wasserhahns für etwas Selbstverständliches halten, auf dieses Problem aufmerksam zu machen.

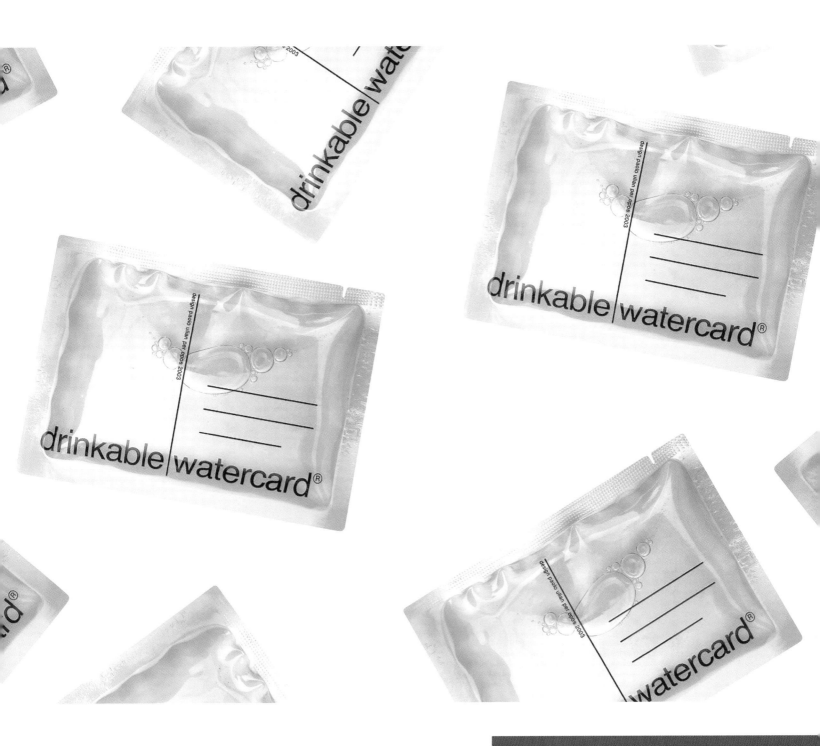

www.paoloulian.it

Ces cartes postales « buvables », produites en édition limitée pour l'exposition « Acqua dello Spazio Opos » de Milan en 2003, contiennent l'équivalent d'un verre d'eau et peuvent être envoyées comme n'importe qu'elle carte postale. Le projet de l'italien Paolo Ulian entend mettre l'accent sur le manque de ressources hydriques dans de nombreux pays vivant dans des conditions difficiles. La valeur éthique de la drinkable watercard, au-delà du geste ouvertement symbolique de fournir de l'eau à qui en a besoin, réside dans la tentative de sensibiliser ceux qui considèrent désormais comme acquis le simple fait d'ouvrir un robinet pour pouvoir se désaltérer.

Paolo Ulian for Opos (Italy)
2003

Use only what you need

Water consumption
Wasserkonsum
Consommation d'eau

The challenge posed by the Denver Water Board in Colorado may have been demanding, but it was also indispensable: to decrease water consumption by 22% by the year 2015. With the slogan "Use only what you need," the awareness campaign inspired by this objective used a "minimalist" graphic to emphasize the intelligent consumption of water. Of the advertising surfaces available, the slogan itself only occupied the space that was strictly necessary. The people of Denver contributed to the costs of creating and spreading this message by participating in an internet forum, community outreach programs and face-to-face meetings, thereby demonstrating the success of the initiative. Whoever has since applied the message to their daily practice will have noted its direct benefits, since consuming only what is strictly necessary also means paying lower bills.

Das Ziel ist ehrgeizig: Reduziering des Wasserkonsums bis 2015 um 22%. Dies haben sich 2005 die Wasserbetriebe der Stadt Denver in Colorado vorgenommen. Die zu diesem Zweck entwickelte Kampagne mit dem Slogan „Use only what you need" rief mit einer reduzierten Bildsprache zum intelligenten Konsum von Wasser auf. Der Slogan nahm nur den nötigsten Raum auf der zur Verfügung stehenden Werbefläche ein. Die Bewohner von Denver trugen nicht nur aktiv zu den Kosten und zur Verbreitung der Botschaft in Online-Foren und in Face-to-face Treffen bei, sondern auch zum Erfolg der Initiative. Wer den Slogan in seinem Alltag umsetzte, konnte unmittelbar davon profitieren, denn der sparsame Wasserverbrauch senkt die Wasserrechnung.

Le défi est difficile à relever mais indispensable : diminuer la consommation d'eau de 22 % d'ici à 2015. Voici l'objectif que s'est fixé en 2005 le Board of Water de Denver, dans le Colorado. Avec le slogan « Use only what you need » (N'utilisez que le strict nécessaire), la campagne de sensibilisation à la surconsommation d'eau met l'accent sur une consommation intelligente de cette denrée rare par une affiche « minimaliste » : le slogan n'occupe sur le panneau que l'espace qui lui est nécessaire. La population de Denver a contribué aux coûts de réalisation et de diffusion du message en participant à des forums sur le Web, des réunions de quartier et des entretiens individuels, démontrant ainsi le succès de l'initiative. Ceux qui ont appliqué le message dans leur pratique quotidienne en auront constaté les bénéfices directs : ne consommer que le strict nécessaire diminue le montant des factures.

www.useonlywhatyouneed.org

Sukle Advertising + Design (USA)
2006-2009

319

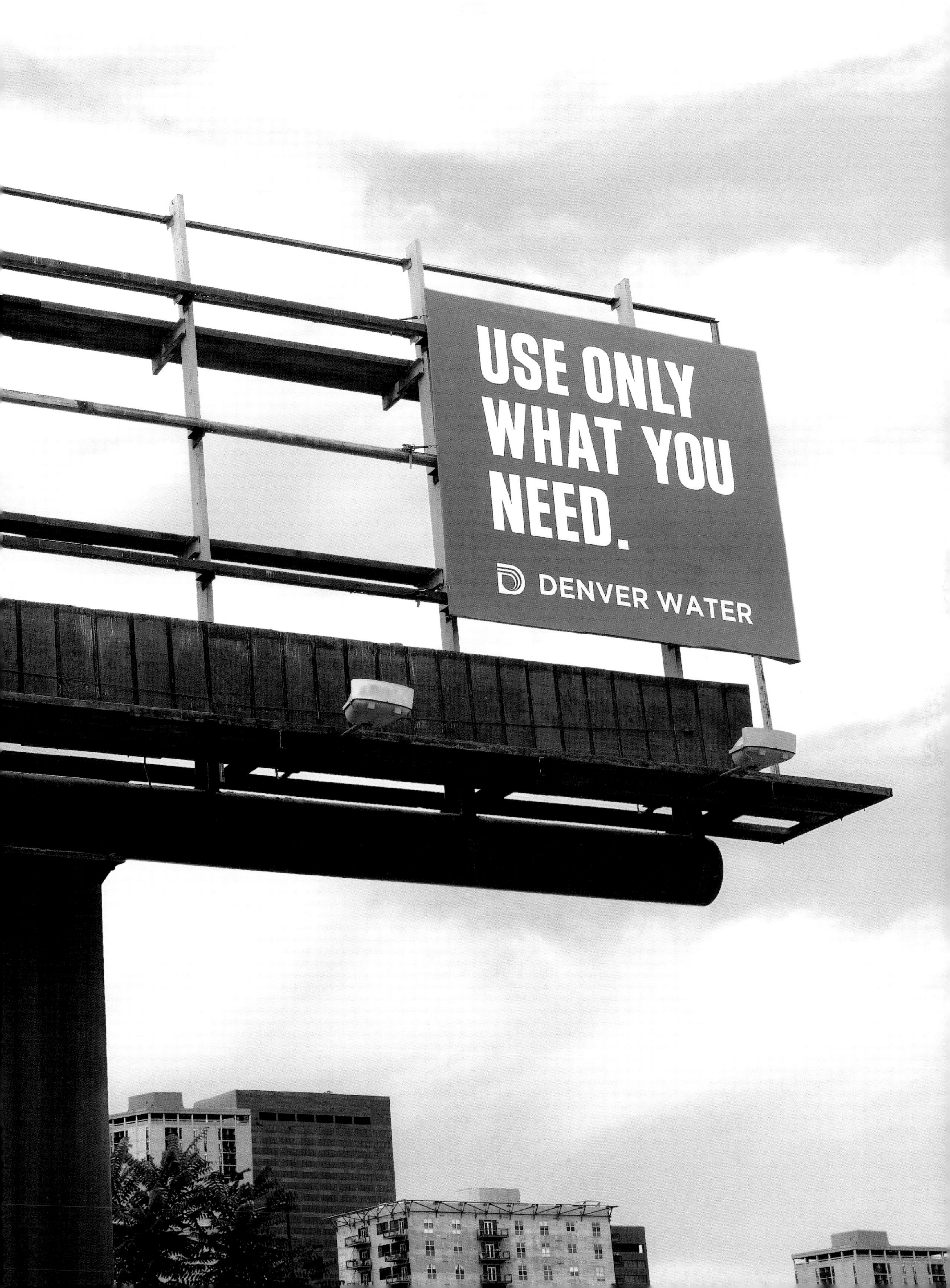
USE ONLY
WHAT YOU
NEED.
DENVER WATER

Express Yourself

Advertising poster
Werbeplakat
Panneau publicitaire

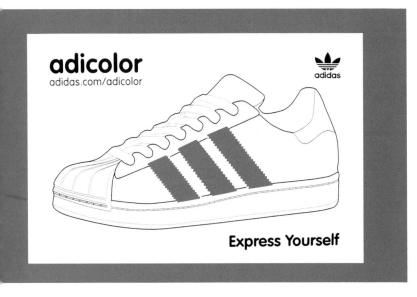

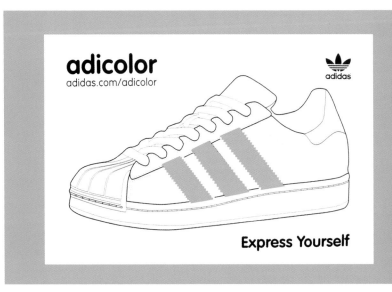

For its 2007 Australian ad campaign, Adidas proposed a simple but clever concept. The sober advertising poster presented four elements in black: the outline of a shoe, the logo, the campaign name and its slogan. The special feature was the brand's trademark three stripes, which were cut out so that the color, which gives the campaign its name, was simply the wall behind the poster. What makes this design eco-friendly is the color itself. Or rather, its lack thereof, since black and white printing reduces the waste of natural resources, and using color that already exists in the environment makes room for the tones that surround us in an unusual way.

Für eine australische Werbekampagne hat Adidas 2007 ein einfaches wie geniales Konzept umgesetzt. Das schlichte Werbeplakat zeigte vier schwarze Elemente: die Form eines Adidas-Schuhs, das Logo, den Namen und den Werbeslogan. Die Besonderheit bestand in den drei Streifen, dem Markenzeichen von Adidas. An diesen Stellen war das Plakat ausgespart, so dass die dort zu sehenden Muster oder Farben nichts anderes als die Wand hinter dem Plakat war. Umweltfreundlich waren bei diesem Konzept daher die Farben selbst. Der Schwarz-Weiß-Druck bedeutete einen geringeren Verbrauch von Umweltressourcen und durch die Verwendung der bereits bestehenden Farben war es zudem möglich, Kosten einzusparen.

save paper · save the planet

www.saatchi.com

Il n'est pas facile de transmettre un message de manière immédiate sur un objet du quotidien. Le distributeur de serviettes proposé par WWF a réussi : à l'avant, une carte de l'Amérique du Sud a simplement été découpée au laser. Rempli de serviettes en papier, rigoureusement issues du recyclage, il laisse apparaître au fur et à mesure de son utilisation les graves conséquences d'une action aussi simple que de se sécher les mains sur le poumon vert de la planète : la carte reste finalement noire et vide. Ce distributeur vise également un objectif plus concret. En plus d'informer les citoyens d'une utilisation parcimonieuse du papier, les recettes engendrées par le distributeur contribuent à récolter des fonds pour le projet de sauvegarde des forêts sud-américaines.

**Cliff Kagawa Holm and Silas Jansson
for Saatchi & Saatchi Cph (Denmark)
2007**

327

Cleanup Day

Ecological day
Umweltschutztag
Journée écologique

www.coastal.ca.gov

**Paul Foulkes, Tyler Hampton and Jeffrey Goodby
for Goodby Silversten & Partners
and California Coastal Commission (USA)
2005**

Sometimes a grotesque irony can help stir the conscience. This is what characterized the 2005 publicity campaign inspired by the government of California to raise awareness about safeguarding the coastal environment. For the postcards inviting people to a day of collective cleaning, a powerful graphic design was chosen in which the boundary between the natural and the artificial is confused: garbage forms such an integral part of the environment that it even traps an animal, to the point of substituting part of its body, conveying a fitting sense of unease. The universality of the message is such that anyone can feel called to the cause.

Um auf die Situation der Küstengebiete aufmerksam zu machen, startete die kalifornische Regierung 2005 eine Werbekampagne, die zum Nachdenken anregen sollte und in der die Bewohner aufgefordert wurden, an einem bestimmten Tag bei der Beseitigung der Abfälle zu helfen. Die surrealen Motive der Kampagne sollten schockieren und einen bleibenden Eindruck beim Betrachter hinterlassen. Bei den Plakaten ist die Grenze zwischen natürlichen und künstlichen Objekten aufgehoben. Die Müllberge werden Teil der Natur, ergreifen Besitz von den Tieren und verwachsen mit ihnen. Die Botschaft ist simpel und plakativ, so dass jeder sich angesprochen fühlt.

Une ironie grotesque peut parfois ouvrir les yeux. La campagne publicitaire de 2005 du gouvernement californien en a justement fait l'emploi pour sensibiliser à la sauvegarde de l'environnement côtier. Les invitations conviant à la journée collective de nettoyage proposaient un design graphique choc, où la limite entre naturel et artificiel est ténue : les déchets font partie de l'environnement et emprisonnent les animaux jusqu'à se substituer à certaines parties de leur corps. Ceci transmet un véritable sentiment de gêne. L'universalité de ce message vise à inciter tout un chacun à se joindre à la cause.

Non-Native Species of the California Coast

The
Radial
Turtle

CALIFORNIA COASTAL CLEANUP DAY
September 16th · 9am-noon

Fight for Nature

The car and the environment
Auto und Umwelt
Automobile et environnement

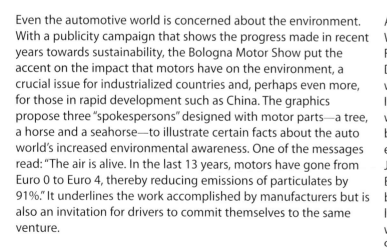

Even the automotive world is concerned about the environment. With a publicity campaign that shows the progress made in recent years towards sustainability, the Bologna Motor Show put the accent on the impact that motors have on the environment, a crucial issue for industrialized countries and, perhaps even more, for those in rapid development such as China. The graphics propose three "spokespersons" designed with motor parts—a tree, a horse and a seahorse—to illustrate certain facts about the auto world's increased environmental awareness. One of the messages read: "The air is alive. In the last 13 years, motors have gone from Euro 0 to Euro 4, thereby reducing emissions of particulates by 91%." It underlines the work accomplished by manufacturers but is also an invitation for drivers to commit themselves to the same venture.

Auch die Autowelt denkt an die Umwelt. 2007 zeigte eine Werbekampagne im Rahmen der Motor Show in Bologna die Fortschritte der Automobilbranche in Richtung Nachhaltigkeit. Die negativen Auswirkungen von Fahrzeugen auf die Umwelt wurden dabei nicht außer Acht gelassen. Vor allem für Industrieländer und für jene Länder, die sich rasant entwickeln, wie zum Beispiel China, ist dies eine zentrale Frage. Die Kampagne benutzt eine Metapher aus der Tier- und Pflanzenwelt: ein Baum, ein Pferd und ein Seepferdchen, die aus Motorteilen bestehen. Jedes dieser Motive erläutert anhand von Daten die zunehmende Beachtung der Umwelt durch die Autoindustrie. So erfährt man beim Baum-Bild mit dem Motto „Die Luft lebt", dass sich in den letzten 13 Jahren die Motoren von der Abgasnorm Euro 0 bis Euro 4 weiterentwickelten. Dadurch konnten Feinstaubemissionen um 91% vermindert werden. Die Botschaft unterstreicht nicht nur die durch die Autohersteller erbrachte Leistung, sondern soll gleichzeitig eine Aufforderung an alle Autofahrer sein, einen Beitrag zum Umweltschutz zu leisten.

L'ARIA E'VIVA.
IN 13 ANNI I MOTORI SONO PASSATI
DA EURO ZERO A EURO QUATTRO
RIDUCENDO LE EMISSIONI
DI PARTICOLATO DEL 91%.*

Le secteur automobile pense aussi à l'environnement : par sa campagne publicitaire présentant les progrès des dernières années en matière d'écologie, le Motor Show de Bologne a mis en avant l'impact des moteurs sur l'environnement, question cruciale pour les pays industrialisés et peut-être plus pour les pays à fort développement, comme la Chine. Le graphisme propose trois « porte-voix », un arbre, un cheval et un hippocampe, constitués de pièces de moteur illustrant l'attention croissante portée par le secteur automobile sur l'environnement. On peut notamment y lire : « L'air vit. Ces 13 dernières années, les moteurs sont passés de la norme euro 0 à euro 4, réduisant les émissions de particules de 91% ». Le message souligne le travail fourni par les constructeurs mais invite également les automobilistes à s'efforcer de suivre cette ligne de conduite.

Raffaele Balducci, Lorenzo Tommasi,
Nicola Rinaldo, Marco Filos and Edwin Herrera
for Armando Testa Advertising Agency
and Promotor/UNRAE (Italy)
2007

Planet Earth

The health of the planet
Gebrauchsanweisung für den Planeten Erde
La santé de la planète

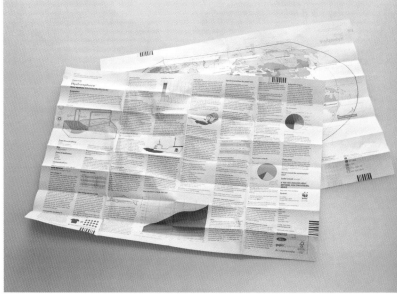

Austrian designer Angie Rattay seems to have found the cure for the precarious health of the planet, and she explains it all in the project "Planet Earth—Directions for Use". At first glance, the cardboard box looks like the package for a common medicine. Inside, however, are four drug-information leaflets showing the planet's various health problems and explaining the responsibility and ecological behavior required to save it. Explanatory texts, graphic illustrations and maps make it clear that only by following these behavioral directives will it be possible to succeed in this intent. So the only real medicine is the reader or the intended recipient of the campaign. Winner of the jury prize at the EDAwards 2008, Planet Earth was created out of recycled paper, printed with sustainable processes and distributed throughout Austria by public entities.

Die österreichische Designerin Angie Rattay hat scheinbar die Behandlung für den „kranken" Planeten Erde gefunden und erklärt diese in ihrem Projekt „Planet Earth – Gebrauchsinformation". In einer Schachtel, die wie eine gewöhnliche Medikamentenpackung aussieht, befinden sich vier Beipackzettel, die über die verschiedenen Umweltprobleme informieren und die jeweiligen Ursachen erläutern sowie ein umweltbewusstes Verhalten zur Rettung des Planeten aufzeigen. Texterklärungen, grafische Darstellungen und Landkarten betonen, dass nur durch Einhaltung von bestimmten Verhaltensregeln dieses Ziel erreicht werden kann. Aber das eigentliche und wirksamste Medikament ist der Leser, bzw. der Empfänger dieser Kampagne. Planet Earth besteht aus Recyclingpapier, wird mit nachhaltigen Prozessen gedruckt und von öffentlichen Einrichtungen verteilt. Das Projekt hat den Jury-Preis bei den EDAwards 2008 gewonnen.

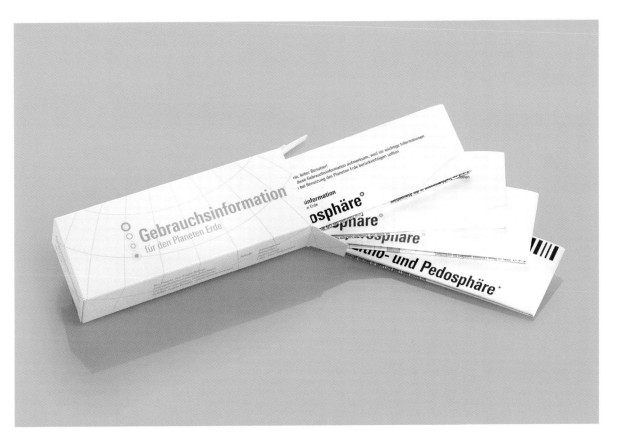

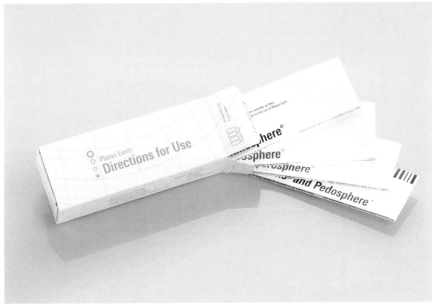

www.angierattay.net

La designer autrichienne Angie Rattay semble avoir trouvé le remède à la santé précaire de notre planète et l'expose dans le projet « Planet Earth – Directions for Use ». Une petite boite en carton, semblable à une boite de médicaments, contient quatre notices illustrant les différents problèmes de la planète et expliquant les comportements et responsabilités écologiques permettant de la sauver. Des textes explicatifs, illustrations graphiques et cartes indiquent clairement les comportements à adopter pour espérer atteindre ce but. L'unique pharmacien est alors celui qui lit, c'est à dire le destinataire même de la campagne. Gagnant du prix du jury aux EDAwards 2008, Planet Earth est réalisé en papier recyclé, imprimé par des procédés écocompatibles et distribué en Autriche par les services publics.

Angie Rattay and Ulrich Einweg for Angie Rattay Design (Austria)
2007

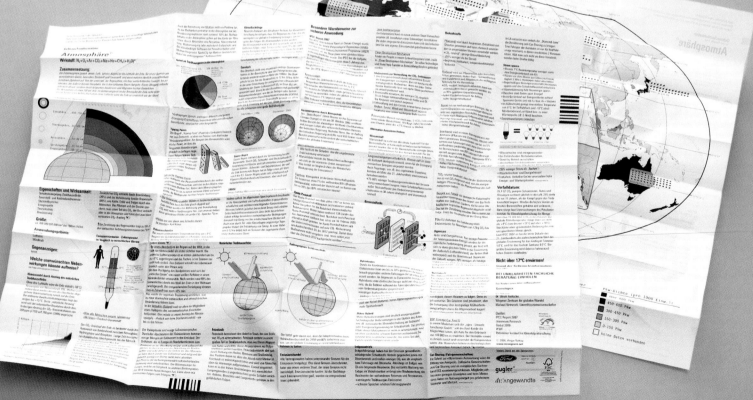
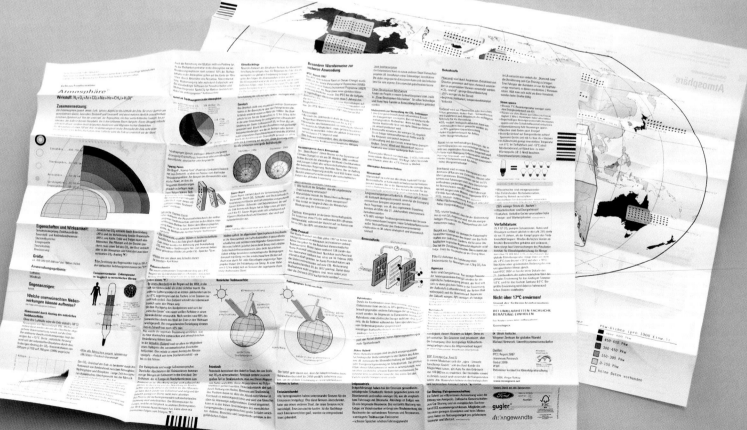

Dear Users!
Please read these instructions carefully, as they
contain important information for the use of Planet Earth.

Planet Earth
Directions for Use

Atmosphere°

Dear Users!
Please read these instructions carefully, as they
contain important information for the use of Planet Earth.

Planet Earth
Directions for Use

Biosphere°

Dear Users!
Please read t...
important inf...

Planet Earth
Directions for Use

Hydrosphere◎

Dear Users!
Please read these instructions carefully, as they contain
important information for the use of Planet Earth.

Planet Earth
Directions for Use

Litho- and Pedosphe

How much does it weigh?
Sustainability campaign
Nachhaltigkeitskampagne
Campagne pour le développement durable

Did you know that for every cold, about 1lb of tissue paper is used, whose manufacturing produces 6.5 oz of carbon dioxide, and that in one year each person consumes about 6.5 lbs in total? Clearly, the issue of sustainability involves both the production and the consumption of objects. Starting from this premise, the Italian company Valcucine spread a promotional campaign throughout Milan that poses questions about the consequences of daily activities like shopping, answering a cell phone or looking for parking. The answers quoted on the posters quantify the resources used in terms of weight, clearly conveying the environmental impact of these activities. It is an example of an effective and informative campaign with the goal of making everyone aware of their responsibilities.

Wussten Sie, dass bei jedem Schnupfen durchschnittlich 0,5 kg Papiertaschentücher verbraucht werden, deren Herstellung 188 g Kohlendioxid verursachen, und dass jedes Jahr jeder Mensch etwa 3 kg davon benutzt? Nachhaltigkeit ist eine Verhaltensweise, die nicht nur die Produktion, sondern auch den Verbrauch berücksichtigt. Ausgehend von diesen Überlegungen hat das italienische Unternehmen Valcucine in Mailand eine Kommunikationskampagne gestartet, die die Folgen alltäglicher Handlungen, wie z. B. Einkaufen, einen Handyanruf entgegennehmen oder einen Parkplatz suchen, veranschaulicht. Die Plakate beantworten bestimmte Fragen, indem der Verbrauch der Ressourcen in Kilogramm angegeben wird. Sie zeigen so deutlich die Auswirkungen auf unsere Umwelt. Ziel ist es, mit einer durchaus wirksamen Kampagne das Umweltbewusstsein der Menschen zu stärken.

www.valcucine.it

Saviez-vous que chaque rhume consomme en moyenne 0,5 kg de mouchoirs en papier, dont la production dégage 188 g d'anhydride carbonique et qu'en un an, chaque personne en consomme facilement 3 kg ? Il est évident que le développement durable est un comportement qui ne concerne pas seulement la production des objets, mais aussi leur consommation. En partant de cette idée, l'entreprise italienne Valcucine a lancé à Milan une campagne de communication mettant en avant les conséquences de nos activités quotidiennes, comme faire les courses, répondre à son téléphone portable ou trouver une place de parking. Les réponses renseignées sur les panneaux quantifient les ressources utilisées en termes de masse et rendent plus clair l'impact de ces activités sur l'environnement. Le but de cette campagne d'information très efficace est évidemment de nous responsabiliser.

**Daniele Prosdocimo, Gianluca Gruarin
for Valcucine and Ismaele De Pas for Zonatortona
(Italy)
2007**

Roma Fountains Map

Map/flask
Trinklasche/Stadtplan
Carte/gourde

The life of a city map for tourists tends to last about as long as a vacation. With this in mind, young designer Emanuele Pizzolorusso came up with the idea of printing a map of Rome on a soft, multi-layer package so it can double as a water flask. The map would be distributed empty, and therefore two-dimensional, at various information hubs throughout the city. By indicating all the public fountains in the center, it also promotes the use of public drinking water over plastic bottles, thereby avoiding the grave environmental impact that goes with them. In addition to being informative and educational, Roma Fountains Map becomes a practical, re-usable souvenir.

Die Lebenszeit von Stadtplänen ist meistens auf die Länge eines Urlaubs begrenzt. Das Projekt des jungen Designers Emanuele Pizzolorusso besteht in einem Rom-Stadtplan mit doppelter Funktion: der Plan ist auf einem weichen, mehrschichtigen Beutel gedruckt, der als Trinkflasche benutzt werden kann. Der Beutel wird den Touristen in den verschiedenen Informationsstellen leer übergeben. Auf dem abgebildeten Plan sind alle Brunnen des historischen Stadtzentrums verzeichnet, so dass der Tourist das öffentliche Trinkwasser statt der üblichen Plastikflaschen nutzen kann. Die gravierenden Umweltauswirkungen, die durch die Herstellung der unzähligen PET-Fläschchen verursacht werden, könnten so reduziert werden. Abgesehen von der informativen und lehrreichen Funktion der Roma Fountains Map ist dieser Plan gleichzeitig auch ein nützliches Souvenir, das man immer wieder verwenden kann.

Les cartes des villes destinées aux touristes ont généralement une durée de vie limitée à quelques jours de vacances. Le projet du jeune designer Emanuele Pizzolorusso propose une carte de Rome à double-emploi : la carte est imprimée sur un emballage souple et résistant, utilisable comme gourde pour transporter de l'eau. Distribuée vide, donc plate, dans les différents points d'information touristique, la carte indique toutes les fontaines publiques présentes dans le centre-ville et permet ainsi d'utiliser l'eau potable publique en lieu et place des bouteilles d'eau : le projet permet ainsi d'en limiter l'impact environnemental notable. En plus d'être informative et éducative, Roma Fountains Map est aussi un souvenir utile, car réutilisable.

www.pizzolorusso.com

Emanuele Pizzolorusso
for Mini Design Award (Italy)
2008
prototype

Appendix

Anhang
Annexes

Alternative energy
The use of sources other than oil for the production of energy, including renewable, natural elements (biomass) or inexhaustible fuels (wind, sun, hydrogen and water) that can be found anywhere. Alternative energy, also called "green" or "clean," can be obtained through the controlled combustion of biomass and the use of wind vanes, photovoltaic cells or combustion cells (fuel cells) to transform hydrogen (the simplest application of which are PEM cells).

Biodegradability
This term was first used in the 20th century to indicate the ability of a compound to separate into simple elements and re-enter the cycle of nature. It takes on more specific meanings according to the scientific environment (geology, physics, chemistry or biochemistry).

Community outreach
This expression covers the involvement of components that are not directly tied to a given community and therefore refers to the wider community. In the world of communications and multimedia, it indicates reaching new sectors of the community, with the objective of acquiring more credibility and opportunities by branching out from one specific target.

Eco-compatibility
This defines how compatible an industrial system and its product and processes are with the environment. A product is defined as eco-compatible when it has a well-established relationship with its context. Such a relationship ensures functionality and well-being with reduced consumption of resources and a low level of pollution. In this sense, an eco-compatible product promotes sustainable development in environmental, economic and social terms.

Environmental impact
The set of effects on the environment caused by an event, action or behavior. Also understood broadly to relate to social and economic contexts.

Environmental Product Declaration (EPD)
Associated with the European ISO 14000 regulation, it informs consumers of the characteristics and environmental performance of a product in an objective, comparable and credible way. To that end, an analysis of the environmental aspects and the potential impact for the entire life cycle of the product is carried out (LCA - Life Cycle Assessment). The EPD is voluntary and can be certified by the company internally or by external bodies.

Ergonomics
A scientific discipline that studies the interaction between human beings and the elements of a given system. Its purpose is to optimize human well-being and product performance.

Ethylene Vinyl Acetate (EVA)
A copolymer derived from ethylene and vinyl acetate. It is used, for example, in plastic food wrap, toys and for various products in the electrical, medical and footwear fields.

Expanded polypropylene (EPP)
A very hard, elastic polymer resistant to repeated bending. It has greater structural stability when subjected to heat than other common polymers and is impermeable to most chemical substances. EPP is used widely in everything from furniture and toys to shock absorbers in the automotive world.

Guerrilla marketing
A low-budget advertising campaign aimed at provoking surprise. The definition was

Alternative Energien
Energiequellen, die eine Alternative zum Erdöl bilden und die durch die Nutzung von natürlichen erneuerbaren Elementen (Biomasse) oder unerschöpflichen Elementen (Wind, Sonne, Wasserstoff, Wasser), die überall vorhanden sind, entstehen. Diese „grünen" oder „sauberen" Energien können aus verschiedenen Quellen stammen: aus der kontrollierten Verbrennung von Biomasse, der Verwendung von Windenergieanlagen, Solarzellen oder Brennstoffzellen (fuel cell) zur Wandlung von chemischer in elektrischer Energie (die einfachste Anwendung hierbei ist die Protonen-Austausch-Membran).

Biologisch abbaubar
Dieser Begriff entstand im 20. Jahrhundert und beschreibt die Fähigkeit einer chemischen Verbindung, sich in einfache Elemente zu teilen, die wieder in den natürlichen Zyklus eintreten können. Je nach Fachbereich (Geologie, Physik, Chemie, Biochemie) erhält der Begriff eine spezifischere Bedeutung.

Community outreach
Ist die Einbeziehung von Mitgliedern, die nicht direkt mit einer bestimmten Gemeinschaft (community) verbunden sind. In diesem Sinne ist von einer „erweiterten Gemeinschaft" die Rede. In der Kommunikations- und Multimediabranche bezeichnet dieser Begriff die Einbindung neuer Sektoren in eine Gemeinschaft mit dem Ziel, dadurch mehr Glaubwürdigkeit zu erwerben und durch das Austreten aus einer spezifischen Zielgruppe mehr Möglichkeiten zu haben.

Environmental Product Declaration (EPD)
Die Umweltproduktdeklaration entstand auf Basis der europäischen Norm ISO 14000 und hat zum Ziel, den Endverbraucher auf objektive, vergleichbare und glaubwürdige Weise über die umweltfreundlichen Eigen-

schaften und Leistungen eines Produktes zu informieren. Zu diesem Zweck werden Analysen zum Lebenszyklus des Produktes (LCA - Life Cycle Assessment) durchgeführt, sowie die Umweltaspekte und potentiellen Auswirkungen während des gesamten Lebenszyklus des Produktes untersucht. Die EPD ist freiwillig und kann firmenintern oder durch außenstehende Organe zertifiziert werden.

Ergonomie

Ist eine Wissenschaft, die die Interaktion zwischen Mensch und den Elementen eines gegebenen Systems untersucht. Ziel der Ergonomie ist die Vereinbarung eines besseren menschlichen Befindens mit höheren Produktleistungen.

Ethylenvinylacetat (EVA)

Ist ein Copolymer, das aus Ethylen und Vinylacetat gewonnen wird. Es findet Anwendung bei Frischhaltefolien für Nahrungsmittel, bei Spielsachen, bei elektrischen und medizinischen Anwendungen und bei der Schuhherstellung.

Expandiertes Polypropylen (EPP)

Ist ein sehr beständiges und elastisches Polymer, das wiederholten Biegungen standhält. Im Vergleich zu anderen Polymeren ist es temperaturbeständiger. Es weist zudem eine gute Beständigkeit gegen den Großteil der chemischen Stoffe auf, sofern es nicht übermäßig hohen Temperaturen ausgesetzt wird. EPP wird in vielen verschiedenen Marktbereichen eingesetzt, von Ausstattungsgegenständen über Spiele bis hin zu Autoteilen.

Guerilla-Marketing

Der Begriff wurde 1984 vom amerikanischen Werbefachmann Jay Conrad Levinson geprägt. Er bezeichnet eine Werbeaktion, die mit geringem wirtschaftlichem Aufwand einen Überraschungseffekt bezweckt. Die eingesetzten Mittel sind unkonventionell

Acide Polylactique (PLA)

Polymère dérivé de l'amidon. Ses caractéristiques sont à mi-chemin entre le PET et le polyester ; sa valeur ajoutée consiste en sa capacité d'hydrolyse (scission d'une substance en deux ou plusieurs composants, sous action de l'eau) à une température supérieure à 60°C et une humidité supérieure de 20% ; il est biodégradable.

Biodégradabilité

Terme né au XXe siècle indiquant la capacité d'un compost à se séparer en éléments simples et à réintégrer le cycle naturel. Il assume des acceptions plus spécifiques selon le domaine scientifique (géologie, physique, chimie, biochimie).

Cell Polymer Electrolyte Membrane (PEM – membrane électrolyte polymère)

Voir ÉNERGIES ALTERNATIVES.

Cycle de vie

Arc complet de l'existence du produit, partant de l'extraction de la matière première (dont ses différentes transformations et transports), il comprend les opérations d'assemblage et de finition aboutissant au produit fini, prêt à intégrer le marché et se poursuit avec la phase d'utilisation. Il se termine par la phase de désassemblage, durant laquelle le produit est destiné à différents traitements : démolition ou désassemblage, selon les possibilités de recyclage, de récupération ou de réemploi des matériaux ou de ses composants.

Community outreach (approche communautaire)

Renvoie à l'implication d'éléments qui ne sont pas directement liés à une communauté donnée. On parle en ce sens de communauté élargie. Dans les secteurs de la communication et du multimédia, ce terme indique l'atteinte de nouveaux

secteurs de la communauté, avec pour objectif d'acquérir davantage de crédibilité et d'élargir les opportunités en sortant d'une cible spécifique.

Déclaration écologique du produit (DEP)

Cette déclaration née de la réglementation européenne ISO 14000 a pour but d'informer les acheteurs sur les caractéristiques et les prestations environnementales d'un produit, de manière objective, comparable et crédible. On analyse à cette fin le cycle de vie (LCA – Life Cycle Assestment), les aspects environnementaux et les impacts potentiels durant le cycle de vie du produit. La DEP (ou Déclaration écologique du produit) est volontaire et peut être certifiée en interne par l'entreprise ou par des organes externes.

Développement durable

En 1987, la Commission Mondiale sur l'Environnement et Développement de l'ONU (CMED) établit dans le document appelé « rapport Brundtland » une définition du développement durable, aujourd'hui mondialement reconnue : « Par développement durable, on entend un développement qui répond aux besoins du présent sans compromettre la capacité des générations futures de répondre aux leurs. » Le développement durable est envisagé aujourd'hui en termes environnementaux, sociaux, économiques et culturels. Tandis que la durabilité environnementale est un concept quantifiable puisqu'il indique un maintien dans le temps de l'équilibre physique des géosphère et biosphère, la durabilité sociale se réfère au concept abstrait et qualitatif du bien-être. Les sociétés durables privilégient les produits respectant les nécessités environnementales par une consommation minime des ressources. Le développement durable au niveau culturel concerne les aspects qualitatifs de la vie de l'homme et vise une

coined in 1984 by U.S. adman Jay Conrad Levinson. The means used are unconventional, often aggressive and appeal to the psychological mechanisms of the intended user.

Hydroponic plants
Plants that grow in water. The general definition extends however to all plants that can live outside soil with their roots submerged in a nutritious solution. In hydroponic cultures the nutritional elements are dissolved in water and easily absorbed, which causes the plants to grow faster.

Life cycle
The entire life span of a product: from the extraction of its raw materials (with their various transformations and attendant transport); to all assembly and finishing operations that make the final product ready for the market; through the entire period of its use; and finally to the disposal phase when the product is destined for various methods of demolition or disassembly, depending on whether its materials or some of its parts can be recycled, recovered or reused.

Macrophyte purification system
Natural water purification that takes place through so-called macrophytes. These aquatic plants absorb oxygen and conduct it to the roots. Within a few months, they are covered in a film of bacteria, which facilitates the purification. The system includes water sediment basins, a filtration section with plants and a final purification process.

Non-renewable sources
Energy and material resources that tend to run out over the long-term and are therefore expensive and contaminate the environment. They include combustible fossil fuels like coal, oil, natural gas and uranium (for nuclear fission). In general, such resources are concentrated in a few areas of the planet and often in the hands of a small number of multinational corporations.

Mono-material
Adjective for a product created with just one material.

No-oil plastics
Polymers that derive from organic substances.

Oil plastics
Polymers that derive from oil.

Open-source
This term is normally used to indicate software that can be accessed freely, at no cost, and downloaded online, for example. Those who hold the rights to this software promote the improvement of the product by allowing users to make changes.

Polyethylene (PE)
The most common, simple polymer. It is easily workable since it becomes malleable and elastic when subjected to heat. It is used in telephone and television cables because of its excellent insulating properties. Like many other polymers, polyethylene can be expanded; that is, it can assume a porous structure that guarantees increased thermal and acoustic insulation. It is also often used to make packaging, containers, protective surfaces, back pads for knapsacks, gadgets, etc.

Polyethylene terephthalate (PET)
A polymer used for the production of liquid and food containers, photographic equipment, and audio and video cassette tapes. Its compatibility with food is sanctioned by the regulations of several countries.

Polylactic Acid (PLA)
A polymer derived from starch. Its characteristics fall somewhere between those of PET and polyester. It is unique for its biodegradability in the presence of hydrolysis (the split of a substance into two or more components upon contact with water) at a temperature higher than 60°C and a humidity greater than 20%.

Polymer
Plastic material.

Polymer Electrolyte Membrane (PEM) Cell
See ALTERNATIVE ENERGY.

Polystyrene (PS)
A thermoplastic polymer, which means that it is malleable and elastic when subjected to heat. It is colorless, transparent and very rigid and is used in many sectors (e.g. food, domestic and industrial). In fact, it is used in the production of transparent and colored containers, kitchenware, automobiles and electrical appliances like washing machines, dishwashers and fridges.

und oft aggressiv und zielen auf die Auslösung psychologischer Mechanismen bei den Konsumenten ab.

Hydrokultur
Form der Pflanzenhaltung, bei der die Pflanzen nicht im Boden, sondern in einer nährenden Lösung wurzeln. Bei Hydrokulturen werden die Nährstoffe in Wasser aufgelöst und sind so einfach absorbierbar. Einige Pflanzen gedeihen dadurch schneller.

Lebenszyklus
Gesamte Lebensdauer eines Produktes. Diese beginnt bei der Gewinnung der Rohstoffe (mit den entsprechenden Transformationen und Transporten). Sie beinhaltet auch alle Vorgänge zur Zusammensetzung oder Nacharbeit, die zum fertigen Endprodukt, das auf den Markt gebracht wird, führen und die anschließende Nutzungsdauer. Sie schließt sich zum Zeitpunkt der Entsorgung ab, wenn das Produkt den verschiedenen Prozessen zur Verschrottung oder Zerlegung unterzogen wird. Je nach Möglichkeit wird das Produkt recycelt, wieder verwertet oder die Materialien aus denen es besteht bzw. seine Bauteile werden wieder verwendet.

Monomaterial
Ein Produkt wurde mit einem einzigen Material hergestellt.

Nachhaltigkeit
1987 legte die Weltkommission für Umwelt und Entwicklung der UNO (WCED) in dem so genannten „Brundtland-Bericht" eine Definition von Nachhaltigkeit bzw. nachhaltiger Entwicklung fest, die heute universell anerkannt ist: „Nachhaltige Entwicklung *ist Entwicklung, die die Bedürfnisse der Gegenwart befriedigt, ohne zu riskieren, dass künftige Generationen ihre eigenen Bedürfnisse nicht befriedigen können".* Heute wird Nachhaltigkeit auch im Hinblick auf Umwelt, Gesellschaft, Wirtschaft und Kultur betrachtet. Während Nachhaltigkeit im Bezug auf die Umwelt klar quantifizierbar ist, da sie die dauerhafte Erhaltung des physischen Gleichgewichts der Geo- und Biosphäre impliziert, bezieht sich gesellschaftliche Nachhaltigkeit auf das abstrakte und qualitative Konzept des Wohlstandes. Nachhaltige Gesellschaften bevorzugen zudem Produkte, die die Umweltbedürfnisse durch einen minimalen Verbrauch an Ressourcen berücksichtigen. Kulturelle Nachhaltigkeit bezieht sich auf die qualita-

tiven Aspekte des menschlichen Lebens und betrifft die Kontinuität zwischen den Generationen. Wirtschaftliche Nachhaltigkeit stellt schließlich sicher, dass Impulse unternehmerischen Handelns und die damit einhergehenden Entwicklungen das jeweilige Gebiet und die darin vorkommenden Ressourcen nicht gefährden.

Nicht erneuerbare Energiequellen
Sind Energie- und Materialquellen, die sich langfristig aufbrauchen und aus Sicht der Umwelt zu kostspielig und verschmutzend sind. Sie umfassen fossile Brennstoffe wie Kohle, Erdöl, Erdgas und Uran (für die Kernspaltung). Im Allgemeinen sind diese Rohstoffquellen nur in bestimmten Gebieten zu finden und stehen oft unter der Kontrolle weniger multinationaler Konzerne.

„No-oil-Kunststoffe"
Polymere, die aus organischen Stoffen gewonnen werden.

„Oil-Kunststoffe"
Polymere, die aus Erdöl gewonnen werden.

Open Source
Dieser Begriff meint „quelloffen" und bezeichnet normalerweise eine Software, die frei zugänglich ist und kostenlos im Internet heruntergeladen werden kann. Die Lizenzinhaber dieser Software erlauben den Benutzern, Änderungen vorzunehmen und fördern somit die Verbesserung und Weiterentwicklung des Produktes.

Polyethylen (PE)
Polyethylen ist das weit verbreiteste und einfachste Polymer. Es ist leicht zu verarbeiten, da es durch den Einfluss von Wärme verformbar ist. Auf Grund seiner ausgezeichneten Isolierfähigkeit wird es für die Herstellung von Telefon- und Fernsehkabeln verwendet. Wie viele andere Polymere kann auch Polyethylen in der expandierten Form verwendet werden, d.h. es kann eine poröse Struktur annehmen, die eine hohe thermische und akustische Isolierung gewährleistet. Häufig wird Polyethylen bei der Herstellung von Verpackungsmaterial, Behältern, Schutzteilen, Rucksackrücken, Gadgets etc. verwendet.

Polyethylenterephthalat (PET)
Ist ein Polymer, das für die Herstellung von Flüssigkeits- und Nahrungsmittelbehältern sowie für Fotoausrüstungen, Audiobändern oder Videokassetten verwendet wird. Die Nahrungsmittelverträglichkeit wird in vielen

certaine continuité intergénérationnelle. La durabilité au niveau économique, enfin, contrôle que les créations d'entreprise et le développement qui leur est lié ne mettent pas en péril le territoire et les ressources.

Éco-compatibilité
Ce terme définit la compatibilité des systèmes industriels et de leurs produits et processus, avec l'environnement. Un produit est appelé éco-compatible lorsque le rapport entretenu avec son contexte est bien établi : ce rapport garantit fonctionnalité et bien-être par une consommation réduite des ressources et un niveau faible de pollution. Un produit éco-compatible promeut en ce sens le développement durable en termes environnemental, économique et social.

Énergies alternatives
Exploitation de sources alternatives au pétrole pour la production d'énergie, par l'utilisation d'éléments naturels renouvelables (biomasse) ou inépuisables (vent, soleil, hydrogène, eau) et présents partout. On peut obtenir une énergie alternative, aussi appelée « verte » ou « propre » par combustion contrôlée de la biomasse, l'emploi de pales éoliennes, de cellules photovoltaïques ou de cellules à combustion (*fuell cell*) pour la transformation de l'hydrogène (son application la plus simple est celle employée par les cellules PEM).

Ergonomie
Discipline scientifique étudiant l'interaction entre l'être humain et les éléments d'un système donné. Sa finalité est d'optimiser le bien-être humain et les prestations des produits.

Éthylène-Vinyle Acétate (EVA)
Copolymère dérivé de l'éthylène et de l'acétate de vinyle. Il est par exemple employé dans la production de film alimentaire, de jouets, dans le domaine électrique, médical et dans l'industrie de la chaussure.

« *Guerrilla Marketing* »
Sa définition a été créée en 1984 par le publicitaire américain Jay Conrad Levinson. C'est un type de promotion publicitaire à faible budget misant sur la surprise et la provocation. Les moyens utilisés sont peu conventionnels et souvent agressifs ; ils s'appuient sur les mécanismes psychologiques des utilisateurs finaux.

Impact environnemental
Ensemble des effets causés par un

évènement, une action ou un comportement sur l'environnement, y compris au sens large, sur le contexte social et économique.

Mono-matériau
Indique qu'un produit n'a été réalisé qu'avec un seul type de matériau.

Open-source
La traduction littérale serait « Source ouverte ». Terme normalement employé pour indiquer qu'un logiciel est libre de droits, gratuit, téléchargeable par exemple en ligne. Les détenteurs des droits de ces logiciels permettent aux utilisateurs d'apporter des modifications et favorisent ainsi l'amélioration du produit.

Phytodépuration
Système de dépuration naturelle des eaux, effectué par des plantes dites macrophytes. Elles ont la capacité d'absorber l'oxygène extérieur pour le conduire vers leurs racines : en quelques mois, elles se recouvrent d'une pellicule de bactéries, permettant la dépuration. Le système comprend des bassins de sédimentation de l'eau, une section filtrante contenant les plantes et un système de dépuration finale.

Plantes hydroponiques
Plantes poussant dans l'eau ; la définition s'étend cependant généralement à toutes les plantes capables de vivre hors-sol mais dont les racines sont immergées dans une solution nutritive. Dans les cultures hydroponiques, les nutriments sont dissous dans l'eau et donc facilement absorbables. Les plantes croissent ainsi plus rapidement.

Plastiques « no-oil »
Polymères dérivés de matières organiques.

Plastiques « oil »
Polymères dérivés du pétrole.

Polyéthylène (PE)
Le polyéthylène est le polymère le plus répandu et le plus simple. On le travaille facilement car il devient malléable et élastique sous l'effet de la chaleur. Grâce à d'excellentes propriétés isolantes, on l'utilise dans la production de câbles téléphoniques et audiovisuels. Comme de nombreux autres polymères, le polyéthylène peut aussi être expansé, c'est à dire qu'il peut admettre une structure poreuse garantissant une isolation thermique et acoustique importante. Son emploi est fréquent dans la production

Prototype

The first element in a potential series. Since it is created before a product enters industrial production, it is useful for the evaluation of costs, time and market response. When non-functional, it is referred to as a model.

PVC

PVC (Polyvinyl chloride) is a polymer that can be produced in a flexible or a rigid form. Its main characteristics are resistance to deformation, breakage and dis-integration. It is usually used in the building, packaging and paper and cardboard industries.

Rapid prototyping

A recently-developed procedure in the production of prototypes. The object is designed on a computer through a description of its surfaces. The file thus defined is sent to the prototyping machine, which creates the prototype by combining layers of material. Forms that are very complex and difficult to create with traditional methods can be obtained in this way. Various materials can be used, including paper, thermoplastic polymers and metallic and silicone powders.

Re-conditioning or re-generation

When damaged or worn-out components of a product are replaced during the disposal phase and the product can thus be re-introduced to the market.

Sustainability

In 1987, in a document called "The Brundtland Report," the U.N. World Commission on Environment and Development (WCED) established a definition of sustainability, or sustainable development, that remains universally recognized: "development that meets the needs of the present without compromising the ability of future generations to meet their own needs." Today, sustainability is understood in environmental, social, economic and cultural terms. Environmental sustainability is a quantifiable concept regarding the maintenance of a physical equilibrium of geospheres and biospheres over time. Social sustainability, on the other hand, refers to the abstract concept of wellbeing. Sustainable societies favor products that respect environmental needs with a minimal consumption of resources. Cultural sustainability refers to qualitative aspects of human life with inter-generational continuity as its objective. Economic sustainability, finally, ensures that entrepreneurial work and development do not put land and resources at risk.

Ländern durch gesetzliche Vorschriften geregelt.

Polylactide (PLA)

Auch „Polymilchsäure" genannt, ist ein aus Stärke gewonnenes Polymer. Seine Eigenschaften liegen zwischen denen von PET und Polyester. Sein Mehrwert besteht darin, dass es bei einer Hydrolyse (Spaltung eines chemischen Stoffes in ein oder mehrere Bestandteile durch Reaktion mit Wasser) bei einer Temperatur über 60 °C und einer Feuchtigkeit über 20% biologisch abbaubar ist.

Polymer

Kunststoff.

Polymer Electrolyte Membrane Cell (PEM)

Siehe ALTERNATIVE ENERGIEN.

Polystyrol (PS)

Ist ein Thermoplast, d.h. ein farbloser, durchsichtiger und sehr fester, in einem bestimmten Temperaturbereich einfach verformbarer und elastischer Kunststoff. Er wird in vielen verschiedenen Bereichen eingesetzt (Nahrungsmittel, Haushalt, Industrie), u.a. für durchsichtige und farbige Behälter, Geschirr oder bei der Herstellung von Haushaltsgeräten wie Geschirrspüler, Kühlschränke oder auch Autos.

Polyvinylchlorid (PVC)

PVC ist ein Polymer (= chemische Verbindung), das sowohl in flexibler als auch in fester Form hergestellt werden kann. Seine wichtigsten Eigenschaften sind die Beständigkeit gegenüber Verformungen, Brüchen oder Verfall. Üblicherweise wird dieses Material im Bauwesen, bei Verpackungen und bei der Papiererzeugung verwendet.

Prototyp

Ein Vorabexemplar einer späteren möglichen Serienfertigung. Es wird hergestellt, bevor ein Produkt einer industriellen Produktion unterzogen wird. Es dient der Überprüfung der Kosten, der Lebenszeit und der Rezeption auf dem Markt. Wenn der Prototyp nicht funktionsfähig ist, wird er als Modell bezeichnet.

Rapid Prototyping

Auch Schneller Prototypenbau genannt, bezeichnet ein neues Verfahren zur schnellen Herstellung von Musterbauteilen. Das Objekt wird aufgrund der Beschreibung seiner Oberflächen am Computer nachgezeichnet. Die so entstandene Datei wird an die Maschine für den Prototypenbau übertragen, die den Prototypen durch

Addierung der verschiedenen Material-schichten erstellt. So können sehr komplexe und schwierige Formen, die mit herkömmlichen Methoden nur schwer realisierbar wären, gestaltet werden. Es können dabei auch verschiedene Materialien verwendet werden wie Papier, Thermoplaste, Metall- und Siliziumstaub.

Refurbishing
Bezeichnet die Ersetzung von beschädigten oder abgenutzten Bauteilen eines Gegenstandes, wodurch das Produkt nicht entsorgt, sondern erneut auf den Markt gebracht werden kann.

Umweltauswirkungen
Gesamtheit der Auswirkungen auf die Umwelt, die durch ein Ereignis, eine Handlung oder ein Verhalten herbeigeführt werden. Neben den primären Umweltauswirkungen können auch Folgewirkungen auf die Gesellschaft und Wirtschaft auftreten.

Umweltverträglichkeit
Beschreibt die Verträglichkeit industrieller Systeme und ihrer Produkte und Prozesse mit der Umwelt. Ein Produkt wird als umweltverträglich bezeichnet, wenn es verschiedene Kriterien erfüllt. Dabei sollten Funktionalität und Wohlbefinden bei einem reduzierten Verbrauch von Ressourcen und einem niedrigen Umweltverschmutzungsgrad gewährleistet werden. In diesem Sinne fördert ein umweltverträgliches Produkt die nachhaltige Entwicklung mit Rücksicht auf die Umwelt, die Wirtschaft und die Gesellschaft.

Wasseraufbereitung durch Pflanzen („Phytoreinigung")
Es ist ein natürliches Wasseraufbereitungssystem, das durch so genannte Makrophyten erfolgt. Diese Wasserpflanzen können Sauerstoff von außen aufnehmen und ihn zu ihren Wurzeln leiten. Innerhalb von wenigen Monaten werden diese mit einer Bakterienschicht bedeckt, die die Wasseraufbereitung übernimmt. Das Wasseraufbereitungssystem besteht aus Wannen, einer Filteranlage mit Pflanzen und einer Endaufbereitungsanlage.

d'emballages, récipients, protections, éléments de sacs à dos, gadgets, etc.

Polyéthylène téréphtalate (PET)
Polymère utilisé dans la production d'emballages alimentaires (liquides et solides), de matériel photographique et de bandes audio et vidéo. Sa compatibilité avec les aliments est sanctionnée par les réglementations de nombreux pays.

Polymère
Matière plastique.

Polypropylène expansé (EPP)
Polymère très dur et élastique pouvant résister à des pliures répétées. Par rapport aux autres polymères d'usage commun, il est doté d'une stabilité structurelle aux hautes températures plus importante. Il est inattaquable par une grande partie des substances chimiques, tant que la température n'est pas trop élevée. L'EPP est largement employé dans les articles de décoration et jouets, jusqu'aux amortisseurs, dans le domaine automobile.

Polystyrène (PS)
Polymère thermoplastique, c'est-à-dire malléable et élastique sous l'action de la chaleur, incolore, transparent et très rigide. Il est employé dans de nombreux secteurs (alimentaire, domestique et industriel) et est en fait utilisé dans la production de récipients transparents et colorés, de vaisselle, pour la réalisation d'électroménager de type lave-linge, lave-vaisselle, réfrigérateurs et d'automobiles.

Prototypation rapide
Procédé récemment développé pour la réalisation de prototypes. L'objet est virtualisé par ordinateur grâce à la description de sa surface. Le fichier ainsi créé est envoyé à la machine de prototypation, qui en réalise un prototype par ajout de couches de matériau. On peut ainsi obtenir des formes très complexes et difficiles à réaliser par les méthodes traditionnelles. Il est possible d'employer plusieurs matériaux : papier, polymères

thermoplastiques, poudres métalliques et silices.

Prototype
Premier élément d'une série potentielle. Réalisé avant qu'un produit n'entre dans la production industrielle, il est utile à l'évaluation des coûts, des temps de cycle et de la réponse du marché. On parlera de modèle s'il est inanimé.

PVC (polychlorure de vinyle)
Le PVC est un polymère pouvant être flexible ou rigide. Ses principales caractéristiques sont la résistance aux déformations, à la rupture et au désagrégement. Il est habituellement employé dans le bâtiment, les emballages et en papeterie.

Reconditionnement ou régénération
On parle de reconditionnement ou de régénération lorsque les composants endommagés ou usés d'un produit sont remplacés durant la phase de désassemblage. Le produit peut ensuite réapparaître sur le marché.

Sources non renouvelables
Ressources énergétiques et matérielles qui tendent à s'épuiser à long terme et sont ainsi trop coûteuses et contaminantes sur le plan environnemental. Elles comprennent les combustibles fossiles comme le charbon, le pétrole, le gaz naturel et l'uranium (pour la fission nucléaire). Ces ressources sont généralement concentrées dans certaines régions de la planète et souvent entre les mains de multinationales.

Air Car Eureka: courtesy of INGEENIUM Creative Mobility

Aquaduct: courtesy of IDEO

Atlantic Zero Emission: courtesy of Alberto Cervetti

Bel-Air: courtesy of © Veronique Huyghe

Bendant Lamp: courtesy of Robert Hakalski

BH-701: p. 165: courtesy of Nokia; pp. 164, 166, 167: Laura Giordano for BackLight

Bikedispenser: courtesy of Herman van Ommen

BioLogic: courtesy of Photo Studio: Superstudio 13, Milan; Photography: Santi Caleca

BOOTLEG: courtesy of Gruppo S.p.a.

BUCCIA: courtesy of Makio Hasuike & Co.

Cabbage Chair: Masayuki Hayashi

Catifa: courtesy of arper

CityCruiser: p. 186: courtesy of Trixi.com; p. 187: courtesy of Veloform GmbH, Rodney Prynne; pp. 188-189: courtesy of Veloform GmbH, Michael Richter

Cleanup Day: courtesy of Claude Shade

Coffee Table: courtesy of Studio BoCa

Cookie Cup: courtesy of Lavazza; Fabrizio Esposito for BackLight

CORON: courtesy of Nahoko Koyama and MIXKO

C.OVER: courtesy of Greenwitch

Creatures: courtesy of Gerard van Hees

Crocs: courtesy of Crocs

Czeers: courtesy of Czeers Solarboats

Dopie: courtesy of Dopie

drinkable watercard: courtesy of Paolo Ulian

Dyson Airblade™: courtesy of Dyson

easyglider X6: courtesy of Easy-Glider AG

Eco-chic: courtesy of Gattinoni

EcoStapler: Laura Giordano for BackLight

EcoWay: courtesy of Shahar Aharoni

Energy Bucket: courtesy of Curzio Castellan

ENV: courtesy of Intelligent Energy

EVA: courtesy of adriano design

Express Yourself: courtesy of SMART

Fight for Nature: courtesy of Armando Testa Advertising Agency

FLAKE: courtesy of Woodnotes

FLUIDA.IT: courtesy of Carlo Coppitz

Foldschool: courtesy of www.kuengfu.ch

Fontanella: courtesy of Massimo Gattel

F50 Tunit: courtesy of adidas AG

GreenBottle: www.blink2.co.uk

Greenkitchen: courtesy of Claudio Sdorza, Milka Eskola

GROW.2: courtesy of Teresita Cochran

Handpresso: courtesy of Nielsen Innovation

How much does it weigh?: courtesy of Valcucine

H-RACER FCJJ-18: courtesy of Horizon Fuel Cell Technologies

ic! berlin: courtesy of ic! berlin

I'm NOT A Plastic Bag: p. 236: courtesy of Anya Hindmarch; p. 237: courtesy of Steven Emberton

iSave: courtesy of Being Object Design

Kada: courtesy of Miro Zagnoli

Kitchenette: courtesy of Petra Dijkstra

Lanikai: courtesy of Akemi Hayami

Light Wind: courtesy of Ingmar Cramers

Local River: p. 48 (left), p. 49: courtesy of Gaetan Robillard; p. 48 (right), pp. 50 and 51: courtesy of Mathieu Lehanneur

Loco: courtesy of LIFE PESARO

MARBELLA: courtesy of Juan Antonio Monsalve

Mix: p. 136: courtesy of Ivan Sarfatti; p. 137: courtesy of Leo Torri

Modular Bird House: courtesy of RESOLUTION: 4 ARCHITECTURE

naturevsfuture®: p. 254: courtesy of Fiona Aboud; pp. 255, 256, 257: courtesy of Simon Gerzina

Net Chair: courtesy of Alessandro Paderni

One: courtesy of Thomas J. Owen

Ori.Tami: courtesy of Ezio Prandini, Campeggi

ornj bags: courtesy of Rachel Angelini

Pandora Card: courtesy of Pandora design

Paper Basket: courtesy of Miro Zagnoli

Parans SP2: courtesy of Parans

Phylla: courtesy of Centro Ricerche Fiat

Planet Earth: courtesy of © Jansenberger

PlanetSolar: courtesy of PlanetSolar

PlantLove: courtesy of Cargo Cosmetics

PlayMais®: courtesy of Cornpack GmbH & Co. KG

Play Rethink: p. 280 (top): courtesy of Rethink Games: p. 280 (bottom) courtesy of Jaime Robb; p. 281: courtesy of Yolanda Burgos Maturana

Postaphone: courtesy of Priestmangoode

Puppy: Me Too Collection by Magis: courtesy of Magis

Remade: p. 170: courtesy of Nokia; pp. 171, 172, 173: courtesy of Photo © Nokia 2007

River Glow: courtesy of The Living

Roma Fountains Map: courtesy of Emanuele Pizzolorusso

Sac à faire: courtesy of Marlene Liska

Sedici animali: courtesy of Gio Pini

Segway i2: courtesy of Segway Inc., copyright © 2009

Sky: pp. 140, 141, 142: courtesy of Tom Vack; p. 143: courtesy of Ivan Sarfatti

SoftBowl: courtesy of Robert Hakalski

soft collection: courtesy of Todd MacAllen

Solar Beach Tote: courtesy of Reware

Solar Impulse: pp. 214, 215 (top), 216-217: courtesy of © Solar Impulse/EPFL Claudio Leonardi; p. 215 (bottom): courtesy of © Solar Impulse/Stéphane Gros

SolarStore: pp. 154, 155 (bottom): Laura Giordano for BackLight; p. 155 (top): courtesy of Industrial Design Consultancy Ltd.

Solar Street Lamp: courtesy of Nikola Knezevic

Solio Classic: courtesy of Better Energy Systems

Split Bamboo: courtesy of Jinhong Lin

Starch Chair: courtesy of Max Lamb

Sugar & Spice: courtesy of ©2008 WOLVERINE WORLD WIDE INC.

Sushehat: courtesy of Peter De Vries

systemX: courtesy of N/A

Tavolo Infinito: courtesy of Studio H2O

Tile Kitchen: Function tiles for Droog (Dry Bathing project) by Arnout Visser, Erik Jan Kwakkel and Peter van der Jagt. Photo: courtesy of E. Moritz

Tree Ring Magnet: courtesy of Dave Brown

Upon Floor: courtesy of Ingmar Kurth

USBCELL: courtesy of Axel Michel

Use only what you need: courtesy of Denver Water, 2009

Viking: courtesy of Poltrona Frau

WWF Paper Dispenser: Laura Giordano for BackLight

XO: courtesy of fuseproject

Zeno: courtesy of Leo Torri

360° Paper Water Bottle: courtesy of Brandimage